FOCUS ON

THE BIRTH
OF A NATION

❖❖

edited by
FRED SILVA

A SPECTRUM BOOK

Prentice-Hall, Inc.
Englewood Cliffs, N.J.

FILM FOCUS

Ronald Gottesman and Harry M. Geduld
General Editors

THE FILM FOCUS SERIES PRESENTS THE BEST THAT HAS BEEN WRITTEN ABOUT THE ART OF FILM AND THE MEN WHO CREATED IT. COMBINING CRITICISM WITH HISTORY, BIOGRAPHY, AND ANALYSIS OF TECHNQUE, THE VOLUMES IN THE SERIES EXPLORE THE MANY DIMENSIONS OF THE FILM MEDIUM AND ITS IMPACT ON MODERN SOCIETY.

FRED SILVA, *Associate Professor of English at the State University of New York at Albany, teaches American Literature and Film. In addition to writing articles on film and film study, he is a film consultant to the New York State Council for the Arts.*

© 1971 by PRENTICE-HALL, INC.
Englewood Cliffs, New Jersey

A SPECTRUM BOOK

ISBN: C 0-13-077230-5
      P 0-13-077222-4

Library of Congress Catalog Card Number 71-163859

10 9 8 7 6 5 4 3 2 1

PRENTICE-HALL INTERNATIONAL, INC. (*London*)
PRENTICE-HALL OF AUSTRALIA, PTY. LTD. (*Sydney*)
PRENTICE-HALL OF CANADA, LTD. (*Toronto*)
PRENTICE-HALL OF INDIA PRIVATE LIMITED (*New Delhi*)
PRENTICE-HALL OF JAPAN, INC. (*Tokyo*)

CONTENTS

ESSAYS

ACKNOWLEDGMENTS

Preparing this volume taught me much about D. W. Griffith, *The Birth of a Nation,* and the convolutions of American cultural history 1915–70. I also learned how much this volume depended on the aid of many institutions and people whom I acknowledge with pleasure. The State University of New York Research Foundation provided an initial grant-in-aid for travel and materials. The Museum of Modern Art generously allowed me to consult *The Birth of a Nation* Scrapbooks of the D. W. Griffith Collection, in which I found many of the contemporary reviews, essays, and letters contained in this volume. While at the Museum of Modern Art I was graciously assisted by The Film Study Center staff: Mrs. Eileen Bowser, Regina Cornwall, Charles Silver, and Mrs. Mary Corliss, and the Library staff: Bernard Karpel, Mrs. Inga Forslund, and Joel Zuker. Miss Elizabeth Salzer of the Interlibrary Loan Office of The State University of New York (Albany) Library was especially helpful in procuring rare materials. Diane Hack cheerfully typed much of the manuscript. Richard Goldman read the manuscript perceptively and offered invaluable advice. Claudia Wilson guided the project from manuscript to book with genuine insight and wonderful good humor. My wife, Joan, provided as always the special framework within which all this could happen.

THE BIRTH OF A NATION

Epoch Producing Corporation, 1915

EXECUTIVE PRODUCER	D. W. Griffith
DIRECTOR	D. W. Griffith
ASSISTANT DIRECTOR	George Siegmann
SCRIPT	D. W. Griffith and Frank E. Woods, from Rev. Thomas Dixon's *The Clansman* and *The Leopard's Spots*
DIRECTOR OF PHOTOGRAPHY	G. W. ("Billy") Bitzer
ASSISTANT CAMERAMAN	Karl Brown
MUSIC COMPILER	Joseph Carl Breil, assisted by D. W. Griffith

TIME: ORIGINAL LENGTH 13,058 FEET, OR 13 REELS; LATER CUT TO THE CURRENT LENGTH OF 12,000 FEET, OR 12 REELS

Filmed at the Reliance-Majestic studio, Sunset Boulevard, Los Angeles, California, and various outdoor locations in the area. First shown at Clune's Auditorium, Los Angeles, February 8, 1915, under the title *The Clansman*; world premiere at the Liberty Theater, New York City, March 3, 1915.

CAST

Ben Cameron, *"The Little Colonel"*	HENRY B. WALTHALL
Flora	MAE MARSH
Flora as a child	VIOLET WILKEY
Margaret, the older sister	MIRIAM COOPER
Mrs. Cameron	JOSEPHINE CROWELL
Dr. Cameron	SPOTTISWOODE AITKEN
Wade Cameron	ANDRE BERANGER
Duke Cameron	MAXFIELD STANLEY
Mammy	JENNIE LEE
Jake	WILLIAM DE VAULL
Elsie Stoneman	LILLIAN GISH
The Hon. Austin Stoneman	RALPH LEWIS
Phil Stoneman	ELMER CLIFTON
Ted Stoneman	ROBERT HARRON
Lydia Brown, Stoneman's housekeeper	MARY ALDEN
Stoneman's Negro servant	TOM WILSON
Senator Sumner	SAM DE GRASSE
Silas Lynch	GEORGE SIEGMANN
Gus	WALTER LONG

White Arm Joe	ELMO LINCOLN
Jeff, the blacksmith	WALLACE REID
Abraham Lincoln	JOSEPH HENABERRY
Mrs. Lincoln	ALBERTA LEE
Gen. Ulysses S. Grant	DONALD CRISP
Gen. Robert E. Lee	HOWARD GAYE
The Sentry	WILLIAM FREEMAN
Laura Keene	OLGA GREY
John Wilkes Booth	RAOUL WALSH
Union soldier	EUGENE PALETTE
Piedmont girl	BESSIE LOVE
Volunteer	CHARLES STEVENS
Man who falls from roof	ERICH VON STROHEIM

Introduction

by FRED SILVA

D. W. Griffith's *The Birth of a Nation* exploded into American culture at the Liberty Theater in New York City on a bitterly cold night March 3, 1915. The critical dust has yet to settle. From the beginning so much contradictory legend, half-truth, rancor, and praise have swirled around the film that only now have film scholars and critics begun to assemble the pieces of history, sociology, aesthetic, and biography which will enable future viewers to see Griffith's masterwork not only as an outmoded, biased account of Reconstruction, filled with unquestionably racist attitudes, but as a genuine cinematic achievement.

Tracing the recorded impact of *The Birth of a Nation* through newspapers, magazines, and film books from 1915 to the present raises many questions about the complicated movement of mass culture in America during these years. The film trade papers in New York and Chicago immediately awarded *The Birth of a Nation* the highest possible marks for its considerable accomplishment and designated D. W. Griffith the undisputed reigning genius of American film. Whatever Griffith's reputation later became, *The Birth of a Nation* in 1915 elevated him to the pinnacle of his fame. Popular newspapers across America covered thousands of pages with enthusiastic references to the film, even though much of the information came from publicity releases and emphasized the size and sweep of *The Birth of a Nation*. These often exaggerated accounts of the size of the cast, the beauty of the stars, and the complexity of assembling the production obviously crept into later film histories and personal reminiscences. The newspapers naturally also recorded the outrage of Negroes who, with their white sympathizers, campaigned energetically first for the film's suppression and then for censorship laws to prevent future presentation of such films. Reactions in the Northeast and South reflected the regional interests and inclinations one would expect.

In most of the years since, *The Birth of a Nation* has been an uneasy

1

presence in American film history. No one could disregard it, but the problems of its content always intruded upon and often precluded calm discussion. The number of times the film has created a local uproar must now number close to 500. References to or articles about *The Birth of a Nation* have tended to be either atacks on Griffith's racial position or apologia explaining that Reconstruction really *was* that bad. More recently, as film has received recognition as one of the most powerful cultural and aesthetic forces in the twentieth century, such people as Everett Carter and Seymour Stern have devoted serious attention to *The Birth of a Nation*'s unique place in American culture and its indisputable contribution to film art. Although isolated studies have started to appear, much still needs to be done: cultural studies of the period, a scholarly Griffith biography, and extended critical treatments of his extraordinary film output, including *The Birth of a Nation*.

A reading of the responses to *The Birth of a Nation* since 1915 indicates the nature of its embarrassment to American film criticism. How does one comment on a work so clearly derogatory to millions of people within the country? If the work were shoddy, ineffectual claptrap, perhaps it could be dismissed. But what if the work also happened to be the first realization of the ultimate possibilities of a new art form? The critical question intensifies: Can a work of art be judged successful apart from its content? To what extent does an artist's world vision enter into the evaluation of a work of art? Although factuality and bias usually arise as criteria for evaluating other more specific and ephemeral forms—reportage and propaganda—is *The Birth of a Nation* an instance where these matters must be considered in a work of art? When does the information in a fictive work have to be accurate? The most important area for future exploration may involve the peculiar responsibility of the artist to his society on certain issues critical to its survival. A clearer definition of the relationship between the artist and his world may turn out to be the furthest social ramification of *The Birth of a Nation*.

The standard, if incomplete, histories of film indicate that the film that is the subject of all this attention came into being because events had produced the necessary conditions: The industry had made moves toward genuine feature-length films; the Aitken Brothers had formed the Reliance-Majestic Company and had given Griffith considerable production freedom and money; Griffith had spent five remarkable years (1908–13) learning and shaping the basic syntax of film, along with the uniquely talented cameraman, G. W. "Billy" Bitzer. Curiously, the basic material for *The Birth of a Nation* had appeared during this period of Griffith's early development. Thomas Dixon, Jr.'s dramatized version of his sensational *The Clansman* (1905) had toured so extensively throughout America that the ill-fated Kinemacolor Company spent $25,000 shooting footage of the play, which printed so poorly it could not be used. Linda Arvidson Griffith relates how Frank E. Woods, who had written the continuity for Kinemacolor's abortive screen version of *The Clansman,* became Griffith's scenario writer at Mutual-Reliance.[1] When Griffith began to search for a truly big subject to film, Woods presented him with *The Clansman.* To this basic material, Griffith added elements from another Dixon novel, *The Leopard's Spots,* and from the stage version of *The Clansman.* Lillian Gish indicates that Griffith, not content with purely literary material, consulted Woodrow Wilson's *A History of the American People* and a number of other scholarly sources to provide the film's remarkable authenticity.[2]

To all of this D. W. Griffith brought a sense of Southern history, which he had carried since his birth in Kentucky as the son of a Confederate colonel.[3] Speaking in an introduction filmed for the 1930 sound version of *The Birth of a Nation,* Griffith stated:

> I suppose it began when I was a child. I used to get under the table and listen to my father and his friends talk about the battles and what they'd been through and their struggles. Those things impress you deeply—and I suppose that got into *The Birth.*[4]

The result of all these conditions became the first masterwork in film history. Nothing like it had existed before; nothing quite like it will appear again. It was the first genuine feature film, the first two-dollar admission movie, the first gold-mine money-making movie, the first film to be shown complete with ushers and related theater trappings, the first film to generate reviews and advertising in many nontrade papers. *The Birth of a Nation* also remains the most controversial American film ever made.

Even before *The Birth of a Nation* opened in New York City, the NAACP had tried to prevent its screening in Los Angeles. Four days after the New York opening, the NAACP announced its opposition to the screening. This kind of protest did eventually affect the final form

---

[1] Linda Arvidson (Mrs. D. W. Griffith), *When the Movies Were Young* (1925; reprint ed., New York: Dover Publications, 1969), pp. 249–51.

[2] Lillian Gish with Ann Pinchot, *Lillian Gish: The Movies, Mr. Griffith, and Me* (Englewood Cliffs, N. J.: Prentice-Hall, Inc., 1969), p. 136.

[3] The filmography included in this volume lists the eleven Civil War pictures Griffith directed during his Biograph years, 1908–13.

[4] Transcribed from the 1930 sound version of *The Birth of a Nation.* A preshooting script version of these remarks exists in the Griffith papers deposited in the Museum of Modern Art Film Study Center.

of *The Birth of a Nation*. When the film, still titled *The Clansman,* opened in Los Angeles at Clune's Auditorium on February 15, 1915, it consisted of 1,544 individual shots, or 13,058 feet, totalling thirteen reels or three hours. This version, now permanently titled *The Birth of a Nation,* opened at the Liberty Theater in New York on March 3, 1915. After five weeks of pressure from pro-Negro sources in New York City, Griffith agreed to cut a number of the more offensive shots (such as flashes of white girls being attacked by wild Negroes) and most of the original epilogue, including two major sequences: Lincoln's letter to Stanton affirming that he does not believe in racial equality and the deportation of Negroes to Africa as a solution to America's race problem. The approximately 558 feet removed have never been recovered. The remaining 1,375 shots, or 12,500 feet, became the complete or official print.[5] Various cuts were requested in other cities where *The Birth of a Nation* played. In addition, Griffith added a sequence shot at the Hampton Institute in Virginia, demonstrating Negro progress since Reconstruction.[6] This temporary epilogue apparently also no longer exists.

Controversy became a central element in screening *The Birth of a Nation.* On April 17, 1915, one week after its Boston premiere, 500 angry demonstrators massed outside the Tremont Theater. The following Monday, Governor Walsh, responding to a crowd reported to number four or five thousand, promised to seek legislation to prevent screening *The Birth of a Nation* and all other plays that created racial or religious prejudice. While Boston, the center of nineteenth-century abolitionist sentiment, witnessed the most intense and sustained instance of anti-*The Birth of a Nation* agitation, the film created dissension in almost every major American city and in countless smaller communities. Thomas Cripps's thorough analysis of the Boston reaction charts the intricacy of the situation. Letters of outrage or praise competed with extravagant advertisements, elaborate feature stories, and lovely pictures of the film's principals in newspapers and Sunday supplements all over America. Griffith and Dixon themselves wrote letters and issued statements, some of which appear in this volume, defending the film as well as their right to produce it. In the years since the initial screenings in 1915–17, the protest has always intensified at the film's various anniversaries—the twenty-fifth in 1940 and the fiftieth in 1965.

---

[5] An expanded discussion of the early exhibition and exploitation of *The Birth of a Nation* appears in Seymour Stern, "Griffith: I. *The Birth of a Nation,*" *Film Culture,* no. 36 (Spring–Summer 1965): 66–80.

[6] A columnist signing himself as "W.I.D." in "Films and Film Folk," *New York Mail,* July 13, 1915, commented: "I want to register an objection to one new addition to the great film . . . that being the tagging on at the end of some views of the Hampton Institute."

Many critics of *The Birth of a Nation* assailed the motives of Griffith and Dixon, who were accused of conspiring to degrade the Negro race. The film, according to Peter Noble and others, presented barren stereotypes from the hate-filled imagination of a Kentucky officer's son, a position supported by Dixon's opening-night statement that he would not have allowed anyone but the son of a Confederate soldier to film *The Clansman*. These attackers of Griffith, Dixon, and *The Birth of a Nation* included many social and political notables who declared almost unanimously that, regardless of the film's contribution to art, its racial prejudice destroyed its value. The film itself provides substantial evidence for this view.

The film's detractors pointed accurately to the simplistically black-and-white view of Negroes, who were shown as Old Faithful servants or Uncle Toms on the one hand and as uneducated boors or half-crazed savages on the other, incapable of common courtesy let alone self-government. The Negroes' lack of education provided some Amos 'n Andy comic misunderstandings, as well as one of the most outrageous sequences in *The Birth of a Nation*: shoeless Negro legislators eating joints of meat and drinking whiskey during a session of the South Carolina legislature.

The Birth of a Nation also excited the white fear of Negro violence, whether directed toward property or toward women. The climactic sequence unfolds in the final two reels, where an inflamed Negro militia pursue Dr. Cameron, who has been rescued from arrest. The Cameron party seeks shelter with two ex-Union soldiers and, as the title indicates, "The former enemies of North and South are united again in common defense of their Aryan birthright." While the Negro militia surround the cabin, other Negroes riot in Piedmont's streets. The situations look perilous until the Klan arrives.

The danger posed by Negro sexuality appears early in *The Birth of a Nation* when Griffith introduces Lydia Brown, Austin Stoneman's mulatto mistress, whom a title describes as: "The Great Leader's weakness that is to blight a nation." Somehow out of this sordid relationship spring Reconstruction excesses. The freed slaves express a great desire for interracial marriage, an aspiration with fatal consequences when Gus, the militia captain, crudely approaches little Flora Cameron and so badly frightens her that she leaps to her death. An ironic parallel develops when the mulatto Silas Lynch desires to marry Elsie Stoneman, his mentor's daughter. In the final reels, drunk with whiskey and power, he proposes to her. When she refuses his advances, he imprisons her in one of his rooms, from which the Klan rescues her.

The end of *The Birth of a Nation* intercuts four aspects of one abstract central action: the resolution of Negro-inspired chaos by the Klan, who rescue the cabin's defenders, restore order in the streets,

thwart Silas Lynch's forced marriage plans, and conduct white-dominated elections. Griffith's brilliant intercutting of these four strands in
the final two reels of the film builds the suspense and excitement of the
primal black-white struggle into truly epic proportions.

However, regardless of Griffith's magnificent editing, his handling of
historical truth created justifiable controversy. V. F. Calverton describes one example of the distortion:

> In *The Birth of a Nation* one is led to believe that Southern legisla-
> tures were dominated by Negroes. That is all part of the same
> legend. As a matter of fact, in only two states did the Negroes ever
> have a majority in the legislatures at any one time, and there only
> for a brief period. In Alabama, for instance, during 1868 and 1869,
> there were 106 whites and 27 Negroes in the legislature; in Arkansas
> at the same time there were 8 Negroes and 96 whites; in Georgia
> there were 186 whites and 33 Negroes; in Mississippi there were 106
> whites and 34 Negroes, and so on. In the main, the Negroes did not
> hold high offices but very inconspicuous ones. Only 2 Negroes ever
> served in the United States Senate, Hiram R. Revells and B. K.
> Bruce, and only 20 ever became members of the House. Of the Ne-
> groes who did serve in Congress, for instance, 10 were college men
> and most of the others were men of relatively high character.[7]

Nor does the literature regarding the rise of the Ku Klux Klan support
Griffith. According to *The Birth of a Nation,* Ben Cameron organized
the Klan in response to rambunctious Negroes, a theory which even
Griffith's simplistic source, Thomas Dixon, Jr.'s *The Clansman,* does
not dare to propose. The idea that the Klan rose solely to control
Negro excesses is untenable; repression of the freed slaves clearly
figured in the Klan's founding.[8]

But a thorough discussion of *The Birth of a Nation* will have to go
beyond the accuracy and emphasis of the subject matter into the
implications of the material and its connections to Griffith and his
world. Following the prerogatives of creative artists, who have always
shaped material according to their vision or biases, Griffith laced the
popular Southern view of Reconstruction history with a strong dose of
conscious or unconscious wish-fulfillment, for the Klan did not unite
the North and South as *The Birth of a Nation* implies. Presenting this

---

[7] V. F. Calverton, "Current History in the World of Fine Arts: Cultural Barom-
eter," *Current History* 49 (September 1938): 45.

[8] The most complete modern account of the complex origins and behavior of the
Klan is Allen W. Trelease, *The White Terror* (New York: Harper & Row, 1971).

popular version of Negro perfidy repressed by Klan action not only created immediate national uproar over the film but moreover so complicated Griffith's reputation and our current view of him that considerable unraveling will have to be done before we can see the man and his work clearly.

Unless he is considered in the context of his heritage and his later actions and comments, Griffith appears to be a seriously flawed genius. No one can deny either his creative powers or his administrative ability in producing *The Birth of a Nation*. His awesome marshaling of the enormous forces of cash, material, and people to create the first true feature film remains a monumental tribute to one man's commitment. If we are to believe the recollections of Lillian Gish, Roy Aitken, Joseph Henabery, and the contemporary accounts of various magazine reporters, everything connected with the film—the script, the set, the costumes, the casting—sprang from Griffith, making *The Birth of a Nation* one of the most completely authentic of all *auteur* films. Yet, paradoxically, the emotional energy needed for that sustained effort may be exactly the quality that clouded his judgment about racial matters. Always a man of emotion and sentiment, Griffith was never able to separate harsh realities from comfortable myths and see his heritage clearly.

Without excusing the obviously racist sentiments of *The Birth of a Nation*, the viewer must recognize that Griffith presented the values of a conquered people who viewed the rubble of what they had conceived as a civilized, moral way of life. The permanent values of the land, the humanistic possibilities of the aristocracy, the importance of place, the tragic impact of the Civil War, and the heightened sense of melodrama somewhat vaguely thought out in *The Birth of a Nation* achieve their fullest and most critical expression in the works of such men as William Faulkner, Allen Tate, and Robert Penn Warren, born a half-generation or so later than Griffith. He shares with many Southern writers and apologists a failure to confront the race issue honestly, a condition expressed later in the classic statement *I'll Take My Stand: The South and the Agrarian Tradition* (1930), including essays by John Crowe Ransom, Allen Tate, and Robert Penn Warren. One must note, however, that although Griffith was no better on racial matters than many of his fellow Southerners, he did modify the exaggerations of a foolish and incompetent writer, Thomas Dixon, Jr.

The reception of *The Birth of a Nation* genuinely shocked Griffith, who denied that he had presented the Negro unfairly and insisted that he intended no racist slurs. Truth was his sole objective, an assertion Thomas Dixon defended extensively in a number of letters and interviews, some of which appear in this volume. Soon after the film's

New York opening, Griffith apparently tried to soften its racial impact by adding an epilogue showing the Hampton Institute, a Negro industrial school in Virginia, as an indication of Negro progress.

Nearly thirty years after the first screening of *The Birth of a Nation,* Griffith apparently continued to think about the film and about the Negro in America. Barnet Bravermann, who died before finishing the director's biography, recorded a statement he said Griffith had made at the Robert Treat Hotel in Newark, New Jersey, in 1941:

> If *The Birth of a Nation* were done again, it would have to be made much clearer. Although the picture was made with no intention of embarrassing the Negro, as it stands today, it should not be shown to general audiences. It should be seen solely by film people and film students. The Negro race has had enough trouble, more than enough of its share of injustice, oppression, tragedy, suffering, and sorrow. And because of the social progress which Negroes have achieved in the face of these handicaps, it is best that *The Birth of a Nation* in its present form be withheld from public exhibition.[9]

The stress on achievement in spite of racial adversity, of course, does not acknowledge Griffith's own possible contribution to that underdog condition.

In 1943, writing to Bravermann, Griffith discussed his desire to film the life of George Washington Carver, whom he calls "a wonderful character," and about whom he had no doubt "that a most telling and beautiful picture could be made." Commenting on the small Negro movie audience and consequent financial risk, Griffith, ever the director, declares:

> However, if the proper financing, backing, etc., could be procured, I would certainly love to do the picture. It is a subject you could get your teeth into—in other words, it's a pip! A subject to pray to God over, to smile over, and to weep with[10]

Reading the letter, one senses that Griffith conceives of Carver as a hero who triumphs over great odds, his attraction to the figure characteristically emotional, nonanalytic, a subject "to smile over and to weep with." Perhaps this explains, as far as explanation is possible given the current sorry state of Griffith biography, why the director

[9] Collected papers of Barnet Bravermann, The Museum of Modern Art Film Study Center.

[10] Letter in the collected papers of Barnet Bravermann, The Museum of Modern Art Film Study Center.

presented the Negro as he did in *The Birth of a Nation*. He simply never achieved a detached view of himself and his heritage. Although no excuse can be made for the man's simplistic views of the Negro's role in Reconstruction, future critics and scholars will have to exercise the balance he did not and conclude sadly that the impoverished attitudes were unquestionably his sincere view of the truth, from which, paradoxically, he produced the first authentic American film masterpiece. Griffith may have given the definitive insight in the 1930 foreword to *The Birth of a Nation*, replying to Walter Huston's question if the Civil War stories Griffith heard as a child were true:

> You can't hear your father tell of fighting day after day, night after night with nothing to eat but parched corn . . . and your mother staying up night after night sewing robes for the Klan and not feel it is true. The Klan at that time was needed. Yes, I think it's true, but as Pontius Pilate asked: "Truth . . . what is Truth?"

The ironic truth may be that only a man motivated by this melodramatic emotion could create both the upsetting images and the permanent beauties of *The Birth of a Nation*. Unquestionably much more needs to be said about Griffith the man, but that must wait the appearance of an exhaustive scholarly biography.

Surely the most necessary critical task will be to examine the film itself more carefully than has been done so far. Such close analysis will reveal that *The Birth of a Nation* functioned in two ways: It exploited more fully than had been done before the intrinsic characteristics of cinema—inclinations toward such matters as realism, detail, movement, and emotion; and it demonstrated how a feature film, particularly a spectacular one, might be edited, developed, and structured. In short, *The Birth of a Nation* announced the presence of an artist who had finally discovered the true nature of his medium and the full extent of his talent.

The aura of authenticity that dominates *The Birth of a Nation* springs from two sources: audience expectations and Griffith himself. Because from the start motion-picture audiences have demanded photographic reality, much energy has been expended in creating the "real." Even the pure fantasy of *2001: A Space Odyssey* needed Stanley Kubrick's incredibly detailed sets to convince viewers of its reality. Griffith's personal vision of film's potential worked to satisfy this audience desire. In a 1915 interview, explaining film's growing popularity, Griffith speaks of "the good old American faculty of wanting to be 'shown' things," which leads to his conclusion that it "is the ever-present, realistic, actual now that 'gets' the great American public, and nothing ever devised by the mind of man can show it like motion pictures." On the basis of this, Griffith foresees a remarkable possibility:

> The time will come, and in less than ten years, . . . when the children in the public schools will be taught practically everything by moving pictures. Certainly they will never be obliged to read history again.
>
> Imagine a public library of the near future, for instance. There will be long rows of boxes or pillars, properly classified and indexed, of course. At each box a push button and before each box a seat. Suppose you wish to "read up" on a certain episode in Napoleon's life. Instead of consulting all the authorities, wading laboriously through a host of books, and ending bewildered, without a clear idea of exactly what did happen, you will merely seat yourself at a properly adjusted window, in a scientifically prepared room, press the button, and actually see what happened.
>
> There will be no opinions expressed. You will merely be present at the making of history. All the work of writing, revising, collating, and reproducing will have been carefully attended to by a corps of recognized experts, and you will have received a vivid and complete expression.[11]

Aware of the power of historical authenticity, Griffith took great care in *The Birth of a Nation* to develop the framework events—slavery, abolition, and the Civil War—and to connect them to the narrative events—the Stoneman-Cameron relationships. Lillian Gish, Seymour Stern, Billy Bitzer, and others record Griffith's research in history books, in Matthew Brady photographs, and among history professors to develop a very elaborately documented context for the Stoneman-Cameron interaction. Griffith included a series of historical set pieces at appropriate places in the film: the arrival of the slaves, Lincoln signing a call for volunteers, the Appomattox surrender, Lincoln's assassination, and the newly elected South Carolina House of Representatives. In addition, the second portion of *The Birth of a Nation* opens with quotes from Woodrow Wilson's *A History of the American People,* connecting Reconstruction excesses to the rise of the Ku Klux Klan, and closes with a quote from Daniel Webster: "Liberty and Union, one and inseparable, now and forever." This authenticity naturally extends as well to the nonhistoric sequences in *The Birth of a Nation* that come either from Dixon's *The Clansman* or *The Leopard's Spots* or from Griffith's own vision of the South during the years 1860 to 1875.

---

[11] Richard Barry, "Five-Dollar Movies Prophesied," *Editor* 40 (April 24, 1915): 409.

This desire for authenticity and realism, found also in the theater of melodrama to which the young Griffith had been attracted first as actor and then as playwright, created a need for acres of detail. As it turned out, one of the key discoveries of early filmmakers was the value of a detail not only as a narrative, attention-getting device, but also as a means of suggesting poetic significance. The ability of the camera to exclude all distracting material extends the poetic possibilities of detail. Whatever hovers within the frame becomes literally a kind of synechdoche. The shot of Mrs. Cameron's and Flora's hands pulling Ben back into the house and the family after the war depends for its powerful effect on just this appreciation of the impact of details to express the whole. What would have been simply another homecoming if Mrs. Cameron had come out on the porch became instead the poetic touch of genius.

Griffith's attention to detail contributes much to the reality of the film. Not many years before *The Birth of a Nation,* film directors, including Griffith at first, frequently used painted flats for their films. But in the military hospital sequence of *The Birth of a Nation,* for example, although the chief interest naturally centers on Ben Cameron, ministered to by his mother and Elsie Stoneman, Griffith composes a background of activity and detail which ties into and supports the foreground narrative action. Nurses, doctors, and patients move unobtrusively in the background and thus add considerable density to the shots. At the moment when Mrs. Cameron discovers her own son, wounded but alive, another mother in the background receives the condolences of an army doctor. The creation of a dense net of reality, always central to Griffith's imagination, reached a peak in the still more opulent detail of the Babylonian sequences of *Intolerance.*

The necessity for movement, so central to the whole idea of film that some theorists have posited the chase as the essential cinematic action, presented particular problems in *The Birth of a Nation* because of its extraordinary three-hour length, at least twice as long as most films of that time. Griffith facilitates the movement of *The Birth of a Nation* by transforming the quest motif into the action of pursuit, which operates both as idea and as physical reality in the film. Ideas, when translated into physical reality, create unforeseen conflicts. Many of the film's characters come to envision goals that conflict with their previously existing aims or that create new counterresponses in other people whose aims differ from their own. The clashes created by these cross-purposes provide the central energy for much of the film's narrative. Austin Stoneman's political desire to punish the South by raising the blacks over the whites aggravates the new Negro aspiration to intermarry. Consequently, Gus pursues Flora Cameron to her suicidal leap and Silas Lynch imprisons Elsie Stoneman in his sitting room. These actions lead to pursuit and retribution by Ben Cameron's Ku Klux Klan. The Klan embodies an idea that likewise creates complications: The budding romance between Ben and Elsie halts temporarily when her father requests that she stop seeing a Klan leader. A shot of Ben's Klan robe on the ground between the two potential lovers underlines the situation with a powerful cinematic image. Griffith's irony, of course, emerges when Elsie escapes Lynch through the intercession of Ben, the man she had rejected. Elsie's ultimate good is as much a goal of the spectacular Klan rides as is the restoration of the antebellum Southern way of life. Physical chase and thematic chase combine at the film's end.

The theme of conflicting pursuits also appears on the most general and encompassing of the film's levels. Lincoln, seeking to preserve the Union, employs Sherman, the conqueror who marches to the sea—the move toward peace results in the move toward war. Then Lincoln's trajectory intersects Booth's insane arc to create the symbolic center of the film. Ford's Theater becomes the metaphor for Griffith's historical vision: Elsie and Phil Stoneman, present at the assassination, witness the collision of national and personal aims so that one man's goal crushes another man's and at the same moment precipitates the rise of Austin Stoneman and the oppression of the South during Reconstruction.

Griffith's most general statement—eternal peace and love for all mankind—emerges in the now standard epilogue sequence of *The Birth of a Nation,* where the marriages of the Stoneman and the Cameron children occur on the river banks and the god of war dissolves into the Prince of Peace.[12] Although this strikes some viewers as cloying sentimentality, the overall movement of Griffith's vision in the film, which opened with the slaves arriving in the new world and now closes with Christ's appearance at *The Birth of a Nation,* has been toward this point. The Civil War and Reconstruction have been only digressions from the general movement of the world and of America toward an apotheosis of peace. Griffith thus places marches and chases before his apparently rapt audience as forms of the cycles of history working in the lives of men. A correlative of the need for movement is the need for a controlling structure. Griffith solved this problem through the use of several devices: prologue and epilogue statements, careful cause-and-effect narrative sequences, and recurrent thematic patterns. To an extraordinary extent, movement itself became part of *The Birth of a Nation*'s structure.

---

[12] This analysis describes the movement of the now accepted version of the film. The original epilogue, showing Negroes being transported back to Africa, can be viewed as Griffith's detailed plan for American peace.

Griffith explored another of film's central strengths, its emotional power, in both delicate and raging moments. No scene suggests more completely the genteel beauty of Southern life than the lovely moment when the camera pans to the kitten and puppies playing at Dr. Cameron's feet. Equally unforgettable is Flora Cameron displaying her "Southern ermine," unprocessed cotton. The "Little Colonel's" return home to the outreached hands of his mother and sister conveys the same kind of understated, yet powerful emotion. These quiet moments are more than matched by violent, generally overstated, scenes of Negro vulgarity and animalism. The energy of the lynching and the gathering of the Klan at *The Birth of a Nation*'s end completes the film's emotional range.

None of these scenes or sections communicate any particular intellectuality or reasoned inquiry, yet their power cannot be denied. They remind us that film generally, and *The Birth of a Nation* specifically, is particularly effective as a presentation of emotion and not as an analysis of ideas.

Ironically, Griffith's researched scenes frequently lack the impact of some of the more spontaneous scenes. The number of viewers who recall the Appomattox surrender must be only a fraction of those who remember the Union sentry mooning over Elsie Stoneman. The charm and delight of that scene reveal something about both Griffith the man, who retained the human touch, and Griffith the moviemaker, who understood completely the eternal attraction of feeling. The reviews, letters, and articles in Northern and Southern papers recorded a wide range of approval and disapproval, indicating that Griffith had mastered film's emotional possibility. Few of his major films depart from a characteristic formula: Griffith found very natural actors, constructed extremely realistic settings, and devised situations, often historical, for expressing highly emotional, often sentimental, stories.

Finally, careful consideration of *The Birth of a Nation* tells the student something about the construction of spectacle films. The director of epic films must balance grand historic, heroic forces against the ordinary individuals who give life to what otherwise would become empty operatic bombast. Griffith was able to maintain this balance because he understood completely the competing values of the mass and the individual. The memorable crowd scenes of *The Birth of a Nation* include the farewell ball at Piedmont and the departure of the young Confederate soldiers, battle scenes, Lincoln's assassination, the Reconstruction South Carolina legislative session, the riot-torn streets of Piedmont, and the Klan gatherings and rides, especially the Klan ride into Piedmont. Griffith circumscribes these potentially overwhelming scenes by quietly weaving into them suggestions of cause and effect relationships and overtones from previously communicated information. During the grand ball which precedes the Piedmont contingent's departure for war, Griffith cuts into the whirling crinolined ladies and handsome Confederate soldiers several times, interrupting the flow of the dance with shots showing "Little Colonel" Ben returning to Cameron House to watch over or tease his little sister Flora. The cutting relates the already established family feeling to the war preparation and implies that the men fight to preserve these genteel values. The shots also anticipate Ben's deep involvement in Klan activities to avenge his beloved Flora's suicide.

Later in *The Birth of a Nation,* Griffith alternates between a series of shots documenting Reconstruction scheming and upheaval and shots describing the budding Cameron-Stoneman romances, relationships that Griffith clearly believed embodied lasting reconstruction. The sequence, introduced with the title, "The love strain is still heard above the land's miserere" intercuts Ben's tentative approaches to Elsie with Phil Stoneman's hesitant overtures to Margaret Cameron. The outer frame of the story poignantly intrudes into a rose-filled garden when Margaret's mind flashes back to the shot of her dead soldier brother; she immediately rejects Phil Stoneman's advances. The present cannot easily be separated from the past, any more than history can be separated from the individual.

Griffith makes this same point with another subtle technique: Several scenes open with a fairly crowded frame, but quickly collapse to include only one isolated person. For example, when the Cameron boys leave for war, the entire Cameron family fills the front porch. But as soon as they leave, only the older sister Margaret remains wistfully looking after them. This sense of war-caused loneliness is echoed when Lincoln, surrounded by his advisors, signs the order calling for 75,000 Union volunteers. The advisors quickly withdraw, leaving Lincoln (like Margaret) alone, whereupon he weeps. Griffith always relates the larger situation to the individual, sometimes for emotional effect, sometimes to extend or intensify his meaning. This particular way of handling group movement, rooted perhaps in Griffith's early stage training, is analogous to the iris shot, which isolates a person or object in a more noticeable and mechanical way. Once again Griffith's meaning and technique coalesce into art.

All future explorations of and discoveries about Griffith—whether they deal with his cultural background, his personality, or his art— will not alter one incontrovertible idea: *The Birth of a Nation* came from a man who wanted passionately to tell a great story, using every trick he knew. Sensing that he had grasped the purpose of his art, he chose to lavish it on material close to the emotional core of his being. The first time he completely controlled the resources needed to execute his art, he struck his masterpiece. However imperfect his understanding of his own motives, Griffith's passion drives the film to its inevitable end, and all a spectator can do is watch the performance in awe.

The Birth of a Nation's all-inclusiveness anticipates a similar monumental quality in the other American landmark films: Orson Welles's *Citizen Kane* (1941) and Stanley Kubrick's *2001: A Space Odyssey* (1968). Each director, attempting to project his vision of an American reality, felt compelled to synthesize everything that earlier filmmakers had done; thus the result is both completely unoriginal and absolutely unique. Each film, a wondrous pulling together of cinematic accomplishment, describes a critical, unsettled area of American life: the elemental nature of racial strife, the intricate connections between capitalistic power and love, the emptiness of technology. These generalizations may pale, but the images continue to matter: the Klan rides, Rosebud burning, the bone becoming a spaceship. Each film thrives on enormous controversy, enlisting both cults and critics. Because each film sums up past endeavor, it also indicates the future of the form. *2001: A Space Odyssey,* the great American technological achievement; *Citizen Kane,* the great American sound film; *The Birth of a Nation,* the great American silent film—each states its case uniquely as it defines its era and creates its maker.

David Wark Griffith
by JAMES AGEE

He achieved what no other known man has ever achieved. To watch his work is like being witness to the beginning of melody, or the first conscious use of the lever or the wheel; the emergence, coordination, and first eloquence of language; the birth of an art: and to realize that this is all the work of one man.

We will never realize how good he really was until we have the chance to see his work as often as it deserves to be seen, to examine and enjoy it in detail as exact as his achievement. But even relying, as we mainly have to, on years-old memories, a good deal becomes clear.

One crude but unquestionable indication of his greatness was his power to create permanent images. All through his work there are images which are as impossible to forget, once you have seen them, as some of the grandest and simplest passages in music or poetry.

The most beautiful single shot I have seen in any movie is the battle charge in *The Birth of a Nation*. I have heard it praised for its realism, and that is deserved; but it is also far beyond realism. It seems to me to be a perfect realization of a collective dream of what the Civil War was like, as veterans might remember it fifty years later, or as children, fifty years later, might imagine it. I have had several clear mental images of that war, from almost as early as I can remember, and I didn't have the luck to see *The Birth of a Nation* until I was in my early twenties; but when I saw that charge, it was merely the clarification, and corroboration, of one of those visions, and took its place among them immediately without seeming to be of a different kind or order. It is the perfection that I know of, of the tragic glory that is possible, or used to be possible, in war; or in war as the best in the spirit imagines or remembers it.

From Agee on Film: Volume I by James Agee (New York: Grosset & Dunlap, Inc., 1958), pp. 313–18. Copyright 1948, © 1958 by James Agee Trust. Reprinted by permission of Grosset & Dunlap, Inc., and Peter Owen Ltd.

This is, I realize, mainly subjective; but it suggests to me the clearest and deepest aspect of Griffith's genius: he was a great primitive poet, a man capable, as only great and primitive artists can be, of intuitively perceiving and perfecting the tremendous magical images that underlie the memory and imagination of entire peoples. If he had achieved this only once, and only for me, I could not feel that he was what I believe he is; but he created many such images, and I suspect that many people besides me have recognized them, on that deepest level that art can draw on, reach, and serve. There are many others in that one film: the homecoming of the defeated hero; the ride of the Clansmen: the rapist and his victim among the dark leaves; a glimpse of a war hospital; dead young soldiers after battle; the dark, slow movement of the Union army away from the camera, along a valley which is quartered strongly between hill-shadow and sunlight; all these and still others have a dreamlike absoluteness which, indeed, cradles and suffuses the whole film.

This was the one time in movie history that a man of great ability worked freely, in an unspoiled medium, for an unspoiled audience, on a majestic theme which involved all that he was; and brought to it, besides his abilities as an inventor and artist, absolute passion, pity, courage, and honesty. *The Birth of a Nation* is equal with Brady's photographs, Lincoln's speeches, Whitman's war poems; for all its imperfections and absurdities it is equal, in fact, to the best work that has been done in this country. And among moving pictures it is alone, not necessarily as "the greatest"—whatever that means—but as the one great epic, tragic film.

(Today, *The Birth of a Nation* is boycotted or shown piecemeal; too many more or less well-meaning people still accuse Griffith of having made it an anti-Negro movie. At best, this is nonsense, and at worst, it is vicious nonsense. Even if it were an anti-Negro movie, a work of such quality should be shown, and shown whole. But the accusation is unjust. Griffith went to almost preposterous lengths to be fair to the Negroes as he understood them, and he understood them as a good type of Southerner does. I don't entirely agree with him; nor can I be sure that the film wouldn't cause trouble and misunderstanding, especially as advertised and exacerbated by contemporary abolitionists; but Griffith's absolute desire to be fair, and understandable, is written all over the picture; so are degrees of understanding, honesty, and compassion far beyond the capacity of his accusers. So, of course, are the salient facts of the so-called Reconstruction years.)

Griffith never managed to equal *The Birth of a Nation* again, nor was he ever to strike off, in any other film, so many of those final images. Nevertheless, he found many: the strikers in *Intolerance*—the

realism of those short scenes has never been surpassed, nor their shock
and restiveness as an image of near-revolution; the intercutting, at the
climax of that picture, between the climaxes of four parallel stories,
like the swinging together of tremendous gongs; the paralyzing excitement of the melodrama near the waterfall in *Way Down East*; Paul
Revere's ride and the battle of Bunker Hill in *America*; Danton's ride
in *Orphans of the Storm*; most subtle and remarkable of all, the early
morning scene in his German film, *Isn't Life Wonderful?*, in which the
apelike Dick Sutherland pursues Carol Dempster through a grove of
slender trees. All these images, and so many others of Griffith's, have a
sort of crude sublimity which nobody else in movies has managed to
achieve; this last one, like his images of our Civil War, seems to come
out of the deep subconscious: it is an absolute and prophetic image
of a nation and a people. I will always regret having missed *Abraham
Lincoln,* his last film to be released: a friend has told me of its wonderful opening in stormy midwinter night woods, the camera bearing along
toward the natal cabin; and that surely must have been one of Griffith's finest images.

Even in Griffith's best work there is enough that is poor, or foolish,
or merely old-fashioned, so that one has to understand, if by no means
forgive, those who laugh indiscriminately at his good work and his
bad. (With all that "understanding," I look forward to killing, some-
day, some specially happy giggler at the exquisite scene in which the
veteran comes home in *The Birth of a Nation*.) But even his poorest
work was never just bad. Whatever may be wrong with it, there is in
every instant, so well as I can remember, the unique purity and vitality
of birth or of a creature just born and first exerting its unprecedented,
incredible strength; and there are, besides, Griffith's overwhelming innocence and magnanimity of spirit; his moral and poetic earnestness;
his joy in his work; and his splendid intuitiveness, directness, common
sense, daring, and skill as an inventor and as an artist. Aside from his
talent or genius as an inventor and artist, he was all heart; and ruinous
as his excesses sometimes were in that respect, they were inseparable
from his virtues, and small beside them. He was remarkably good, as
a rule, in the whole middle range of feeling, but he was at his best just
short of his excesses, and he tended in general to work out toward the
dangerous edge. He was capable of realism that has never been beaten
and he might, if he had been able to appreciate his powers as a realist,
have found therein his growth and salvation. But he seems to have
been a realist only by accident, hit-and-run; essentially, he was a poet.
He doesn't appear ever to have realized one of the richest promises that
movies hold, as the perfect medium for realism raised to the level of
high poetry; nor, oddly enough, was he much of a dramatic poet. But
in epic and lyrical and narrative visual poetry, I can think of nobody

who has surpassed him, and of few to compare with him. And as a primitive tribal poet, combining something of the bard and the seer, he is beyond even Dovzhenko, and no others of their kind have worked in movies.

What he had above all, his ability as a craftsman and artist, would be hard enough—and quite unnecessary—to write of, if we had typical scenes before us, or within recent memory; since we have seen so little of his work in so many years, it is virtually impossible. I can remember very vividly his general spirit and manner—heroic, impetuous, tender, magniloquent, naive, beyond the endowment or daring of anybody since; just as vividly, I can remember the total impression of various major sequences. By my remembrance, his images were nearly always a little larger and wilder than life. The frame was always full, spontaneous, and lively. He knew wonderfully well how to contrast and combine different intensities throughout an immense range of emotion, movement, shadow, and light. Much of the liveliness was not intrinsic to the characters on the screen or their predicament, but was his own vitality and emotion; and much of it—notably in the amazing flickering and vivacity of his women—came of his almost maniacal realization of the importance of expressive movement.

It seems to me entirely reasonable to infer, from the extraordinary power and endurance in the memory of certain scenes in their total effect, that he was as brilliant a master of design and cutting and form as he was a composer of frames and a director of feeling and motion. But I cannot clearly remember one sequence or scene, shot-by-shot and rhythm-by-rhythm. I suspect, for instance, that analysis would show that the climactic sequence on the icy river in *Way Down East* is as finely constructed a piece of melodramatic storytelling as any in movies. But I can only venture to bet on this and to suggest that that sequence, like a hundred others of Griffith's, is eminently worth analysis.

My veneration for Griffith's achievements is all the deeper when I realize what handicaps he worked against, how limited a man he was. He had no remarkable power of intellect, or delicateness of soul; no subtlety; little restraint; little if any "taste," whether to help his work or harm it; Lord knows (and be thanked) no cleverness; no fundamental capacity, once he had achieved his first astonishing development, for change or growth. He wasn't particularly observant of people; nor do his movies suggest that he understood them at all deeply. He had noble powers of imagination, but little of the *intricacy* of imagination that most good poets also have. His sense of comedy was pathetically crude and numb. He had an exorbitant appetite for violence, for cruelty, and for the Siamese twin of cruelty, a kind of obsessive tenderness which at its worst was all but nauseating. Much as he invented,

his work was saturated in the style, the mannerisms, and the underlying assumptions and attitudes of the nineteenth-century provincial
theater; and although much of that was much better than most of us
realize, and any amount better than most of the styles and nonstyles
we accept and praise, much of it was cheap and false, and all of it,
good and bad, was dying when Griffith gave it a new lease on life,
and in spite of that new lease, died soon after, and took him down with
it. I doubt that Griffith ever clearly knew the good from the bad in this
theatricality; or, for that matter, clearly understood what was original in his work, and capable of almost unimaginably great development; and what was overderivative, essentially noncinematic, and dying. In any case, he did not manage to outgrow, or sufficiently to trans-
form, enough in his style that was bad, or merely obsolescent.

If what I hear is right about the opening scene in *Abraham Lincoln,*
this incapacity for radical change may have slowed him up but never
killed him as an artist; in his no longer fashionable way, he remained
capable, and inspired. He was merely unadaptable and unemployable,
like an old, sore, ardent individualist among contemporary progressives. Hollywood and, to a great extent, movies in general, grew down
from him rather than up past him; audiences, and the whole eye and
feeling of the world, have suffered the same degeneration; he didn't
have it in him to be amenable, even if he'd tried; and that was the end
of him. Or quite possibly he was finished, as smaller men are not, as
soon as he had reached the limit of his own powers of innovation, and
began to realize he was only repeating himself. Certainly, anyhow, he
was natural-born for the years of adventure and discovery, not for the
inevitable following era of safe-playing and of fat consolidation of
others' gains.

His last movie, which was never even released,[1] was made fourteen
or fifteen years ago [in 1931]; and for years before that, most people
had thought of him as a has-been. Nobody would hire him; he had
nothing to do. He lived too long, and that is one of few things that are
sadder than dying too soon.

There is not a man working in movies, or a man who cares for them,
who does not owe Griffith more than he owes anybody else.

---

[1] [Editor's note: Griffith's last film, *The Struggle,* opened at the Rivoli, New York
City, December 10, 1931, proved very unsuccessful, and was withdrawn soon thereafter.]

REVIEWS

MARK VANCE

◆◇◆

The Birth of a Nation is the main title David Wark Griffith, the director-in-chief of the Mutual Film Corporation, gave to his picturized version of Thomas Dixon's story of the South, *The Clansman*. It received its first New York public presentation in the Liberty Theatre, New York, March 3. The daily newspaper reviewers pronounced it as the last word in picturemaking. That its enormity and elaborateness made such an impression naturally resulted in the press comparing it with that Italian massive film production, *Cabiria* and saying without hesitancy that *The Birth of a Nation* overshadowed the foreign film spectacle. In the picturization of *The Clansman* Mr. Griffith has set such a pace it will take a long time before one will come along that can top it in point of production, acting, photography, and direction. Every bit of the film was laid, played, and made in America. One may find some flaws in the general running of the picture, but they are so small and insignificant that the bigness and greatness of the entire film production itself completely crowds out any little defects that might be singled out. The story of the Dixon novel, *The Clansman*, is pretty well known. The Camerons of the South and the Stonemans of the North and Silas Lynch, the mulatto lieutenant-governor, the Civil War, the opening and finish of the Civil War, the scenes attendant upon the assassination of Abraham Lincoln, the period of carpetbagging days and union Reconstruction following Lee's surrender, the terrorizing of the Southern whites by the newly freed blacks, and the rise of the Ku Klux Klan that later overpowers the Negroes and gives the white men the authority rightfully theirs, all these, including some wonderfully well-staged battle scenes taken at night, are realistically, graphically, and most superbly depicted by the camera. Griffith knows the value of striking, gripping, and melodramatic anticlimaxes and also is fully cognizant of the importance of having several big "punches" instead of one for camera visualization. Building up photoplay action and "posing" a picture which would look well reproduced in colors is a natural instinct with Griffith and he's one director who knows how

From Variety, *March 12, 1915.*

to get action typified intensely. In *The Birth of a Nation* Griffith took his time and thereby builded well. Thousands of feet of celluloid were used and some six months or so he and his codirectors worked day and night to shape the story into a thrilling, dramatic, wordless play that would not pass out overnight in the minds of the millions who are bound to see this picture before it has been laid away to rest. The battle scenes are wonderfully conceived and show two armies in such natural fighting array it is almost unbelievable that one is looking at a picture, staged by one whose only purpose was to make it get away from the usual stagey phoniness so apparent in numerous picture battle plays. And the departure of the soldiers was splendidly arranged. Then the death of the famous martyred president was so deftly and ably handled no one can find any fault. Of course there are many who will aver that Griffith should have shown the subsequent death of the assassin, John Wilkes Booth, but as he had an archvillain in the shape of the renegade, Gus, later to deal with severely it was best he stick closer to the story at hand. This same Gus, fiendish and with the lust of the beast in his eye, gives mad chase to the pet sister of "Little Colonel" Ben Cameron and she jumps to her death from a high cliff rather than permit herself be touched alive by that brute in human form. This was also nicely cameraed. Then comes the Reconstruction period following a camera scene of Grant and Lee ending the war at Appomatox. Harassing scenes showing the persecution of the whites with the Camerons more than getting their share and with Ben Cameron organizing the white-robed Ku Klux Klan, which later gives the picture one of the biggest moments of its entire version when it rides down the blacks and later saves a small band of whites about to be massacred alive. Here the renegade Gus is killed. Griffith picturized an allegorical conception at the end showing what universal peace meant to the nation. Some may not care for it, but in the church neighborhoods and where the staunchest of the peace advocates live it will go with a hurrah. There are something like 12,000 feet of film, but the program says it's all there in two acts. There is an intermission just preceding the stirring days of the carpetbaggery action. Griffith struck it right when he adapted the Dixon story for the film. He knew the South and he knew just what kind of a picture would please all white classes. Some places the censors are going to find fault. That's a persistent way some censors have. That scene of the lashing on the back of the old negro will undoubtedly come in for a full share of criticism. The scene of the "black congress" and the negro removing his shoe may be censured, but it's drawn from reported facts. But no matter what the censors censor there will be plenty of film action and interest left to make it the biggest-demanded film production of the present century. It's worth seeing anywhere. Many will see it twice, yea thrice and still obtain much satisfaction and entertainment. It's there with a multiple of thrills. Of the acting company, Henry Walthall made a manly, straightforward character of the "Little Colonel" and handled his big scenes most effectively. Mae Marsh as the pet sister did some remarkable work as the little girl who loved the South and loved her brother. In fact her work was little short of a revelation to many. Ralph Lewis was splendid as the leader of the House who helped Silas Lynch rise to power. George Siegmann got all there could be gotten out of this despicable character of Lynch. Walter Long made Gus, the renegade negro, a hated, much-despised type, his acting and makeup being complete. Mary Alden, Lillian Gish, Robert Harron, Jennie Lee, and Miriam Cooper deserve mention for their excellent work. The other minor characters were satisfactorily portrayed. Donald Crisp had a good makeup as Grant, while Joseph Henabery "posed" most acceptably as Lincoln. It may not be amiss to pass away from critical comment for the moment to say that as D. W. Griffith, the world's best film director, is and has been responsible for so many of the innovations in picturemaking, doing more to make filming an art than any one person, so D. W. Griffith has been the first to bring a "$2 picture" to the box office of a "$2 theater." When it was first reported about this "Griffith feature" would retail to the public at a $2 scale, the picture people shrugged their shoulders, said "50 cents at the most," and let it go at that. But as so many opinions of pictures and their possibilities have gone wrong, so, it appears, is the belief that there can not be a $2 picture as erroneous as many of the others. But it is fitting that Mr. Griffith should have so far progressed and advanced in the art he did so much to foster and improve until he became the first director of a successful film that can compete in $2 theaters with $2 stage productions. That is the concise picture record of a few years, within ten at the most, and for feature pictures, even less. *Cabiria* was an admittedly big film production, a spectacle or series of spectacles that held no general interest through the fault of the maker or director. It drew in certain territory and even then in a desultory manner. But *A Birth of a Nation* [sic] has universal appeal to America at least, and the superbness of this production will gain recognition anywhere, with the story carrying, though perhaps to lesser human-interest extent in foreign lands than at home, where the subject is more thoroughly understood. *A Birth of a Nation* [sic] is said to have cost $300,000. This is rather a high estimate, but other than the money the film represents, its returns are going to be certain. Not alone is this film playing at a $2 scale in a theater where an orchestra and operator besides the house staff are the principal necessary force, as against a stage production that might have a salary list of from $4,000 to $8,500 weekly, according to the piece, but *A Birth of a Nation* [sic] can give as many performances a week as the house wishes it to, and in this particular instance will not give less than fourteen, two shows daily. The stage production in a $2 theater would give eight performances as a rule, perhaps nine and, with a holiday intervening, ten. While the Liberty is advertising the Griffith film up to one dollar "with loge seats $2," the scale is practically a $2 one, made so by the demand for seats. *A Birth of a Nation* [*sic*] is a great epoch in picturemaking; it's great for pictures and it's great for the name and fame of David Wark Griffith. When a man like Griffith in a new field can do what he has done, he may as well be hailed while he is living.

W. STEPHEN BUSH

❖❖

The two outstanding features of Griffith's remarkable production, *The Birth of a Nation*, are its controversial spirit (especially obvious in the titles), and the splendor and magnificence of its spectacles. Based in the main on *The Clansman*, it breathes the spirit of that well-known book. *The Clansman* was a special plea for the South in the forum of history. The screen-adaptation has made the plea far more passionate and I might say partisan than the book or the play. It is impossible to give the reader a good idea of this production without sketching at least briefly the views and sentiments expressed and sharply emphasized and reiterated by the distinguished author. The very introduction tells us that the South never had a fair record made of its trials in the Reconstruction period. We are told both in pictures and in titles that African slaves were brought to this country by Northern traders who sold them to the South. Puritan divines blessed the traffic, but when slave trading was no longer profitable to the North the "traders of the seventeenth century became the abolitionists of the nineteenth century."

We next see a typical Northern congregation assembled to hear a sermon. About the platform from which the preacher addresses his audience stands a group of colored children. The preacher takes a

From The Moving Picture World *23 (March 13, 1915): 1586–87. Reprinted by permission of Quigley Publishing Company, Inc.*

young colored boy and passes with him through the congregation. A motherly looking old lady stretches out her arms in sympathy toward the child of the black race, but immediately repulses him with every manifestation of disgust caused by the odor which we must assume the boy carries around with him. Much is then said in titles about "state sovereignty" and we are reminded of what we read in school of Southern statesmen like Calhoun and Toombs and Northern statesmen like Vallandigham.

Mr. Griffith then unfolds a picture of conditions in the South before the Civil War, showing both in titles and pictures that the slaves had easy hours, plenty of time for recreation, comfortable quarters, and kind masters. Here a strange and puzzling character is introduced in the person of a man said "to have risen to great prominence in the House of Representatives in 1860." This man, who plays a very prominent part all through the production, is called "Austin Stoneman." The titles make it plain that this is a fictitious name. Stoneman has a daughter who is never allowed to enter his library. The reason for this must be found in the illicit relations between Stoneman and a mulatto woman. The latter is "insulted" by Charles Sumner. She works herself into a fury of passion. Stoneman enters to find her with part of her upper body exposed. The scene ends with Stoneman kissing the mulatto and with this title: "Thus the fatal weakness of one man blights the nation." [1] The man called Stoneman bears a striking facial and physical resemblance to the man who succeeded Lincoln in the presidential chair. The description of him in the titles forbids the belief that he is identical with President Andrew Johnson. He is an altogether mystical and apocryphal personage whose identity remains veiled until the very end. . . . The march of Sherman from Atlanta to the sea made the audience gasp with wonder and admiration. Nothing more impressive has ever been seen on the screen and I have to refer to *Cabiria* for a standard of comparison. Nor are the war spectacles the only impressive spectacular features. Two of the most wonderful pictures ever seen on the screen are Lincoln, signing the first call for volunteers, and the surrender of Lee to Grant at Appomattox. It may be said in passing that a finer impersonation of Lincoln has never been witnessed on any screen or on any stage. The audience was deeply stirred by the inspired portrayal of Lincoln and when it became known that the artist who had given the portrayal was present the audience gave him an impromptu ovation between the first and second parts. He lived up to the best of Lincoln traditions both in appearance and in action. The assassination of the martyred president is shown in full

---

[1] [Editor's note: Theodore Huff's *Shot Analysis of The Birth of a Nation* accurately records this title as "The great leader's weakness that is to blight a nation."]

detail on the screen. It was a task full of difficulties and one misstep might have proved fatal. The great tragedy is "acted o'er" in the most irreproachable and touching manner.

It must be mentioned too that Mr. Griffith has again shown himself a master in creating and prolonging suspense to the agonizing point. His favorite method of chasing pursued and pursuer through one room after another is still effective and always has the desired effect on the audience. When speaking of the spectacular features of *The Birth of a Nation*, I must not forget his treatment of the Ku Klux Klan. The weird and mystical garb of these defenders of "Aryan race supremacy" has given the director splendid opportunities which he utilized to fullest. When these "crusaders of the South" are seen mounted on superb horses, dashing furiously through field and forest and river to rescue innocent maidens from brutal assault or to punish "wicked Africans," the audience never fails to respond, but applauds while the spectacle lasts.

It is scarcely necessary to say that the photography is exceptionally fine in a production to which Griffith lends his name. He shows a good deal of his renowned skill in working "close-ups," creating many tense and thrilling situations.

The acting is such as might have been expected with a director of the type and power of Griffith. He has the art of bending his instruments to his uses. They work in strictest obedience to his orders and as a result the Griffith idea is always transferred to the screen with a negligible loss of power and directness. Mr. Walthall's performance was particularly fine. This gifted artist invariably succeeds in merging his personality into his part. He might at times have shown a little trace of the grime and the hardship of soldiering. It seemed somewhat improbable that a soldier could look so trim and spick-and-span after what the "Little Colonel" passed through. The parts of Stoneman and Silas Lynch were well taken care of, the old "southron" was a piece of very clever character acting. Not enough praise can be given to the settings, both exterior and interior. Mr. Griffith is justly famous for his ability in these things.

The audience which saw the play at the private exhibition in the Liberty Theater was a most friendly one. It was significant that on more than one occasion during the showing of the films there were hisses mingled with the applause. These hisses were not, of course, directed against the artistic quality of the film. They were evoked by the undisguised appeal to race prejudices. The tendency of the second part is to inflame race hatred. The negroes are shown as horrible brutes, given over to beastly excesses, defiant and criminal in their attitude toward the whites, and lusting after white women. Some of the details are plainly morbid and repulsive. The film having roused the disgust and hatred of the white against the black to the highest pitch, suggests as a remedy of the racial question the transportation of the negroes to Liberia, which Mr. Griffith assures us was Lincoln's idea.

Whatever fault might be found with the argumentative spirit found in both the titles and the pictures there can be no question that the appeal to the imagination will carry the picture a good way toward popular success. In the South of course, where memories of Reconstruction horrors are still vivid, the picture will have an immense vogue. It is altogether probable that its many fine points will outweigh its disadvantages in every other section of the country.

THE MOVING PICTURE WORLD

◆◆

D. W. Griffith's much-heralded *The Birth of a Nation,* founded on Thomas Dixon's story, *The Clansman,* had its initial public presentation in New York at the Liberty Theatre on March 3, before a capacity audience, including many listed in the *Who's Who* of filmdom and a large number of men and women prominent in literary and society circles. No picture presented in New York has been viewed by more exacting spectators and few, if any, have elicited such spontaneous and frequent applause.

At the close of the first of the two acts into which the production is divided, Mr. Dixon responded to calls for a speech. He said that he considered the picture superior to his book and likewise to his play, staged eight years ago. He declared that no one save the son of a soldier and a Southerner could have made such a picture, and introduced Mr. Griffith as the greatest director in the world.

Mr. Griffith stepped just far enough beyond the wings to be visible from all parts of the house. In a few concise sentences, delivered clearly and with dignity, he said that his aim was to place pictures on a par with the spoken word as a medium for artistic expression appealing to thinking people. He voiced the conviction that important ad-

From The Moving Picture World *23 (March 13, 1915): 1587. Reprinted by permission of Quigley Publishing Company, Inc.*

vances are being made in that direction and thanked the audience for
the reception being given *The Birth of a Nation*.

The first general showing of approval came early in the picture with
the depiction of thickly peopled street scenes in a Southern village previous to the war. Then, with the spectacles of towns burning at night,
and a succession of battles, some of which were fought by the light of
bonfires, the applause was nearly incessant for a full half-hour. In the
second act it was evident that the audience felt the grip of the story and
sympathized with the work of the Klu Klux Klan battling against
negro domination. The dramatic points of the story scored, as did a
number of comedy incidents. The audience was quickly moved from
suspense to laughter and back again to suspense.

In showing the film, the stage at the Liberty Theatre appeared
merely as a black background on which the screen was placed. Mr.
Griffith, it is said, refused all suggestions for scenic decorations, holding that attention should not be distracted from the picture. The
music on Wednesday evening, supplied by an orchestra, with the occasional singing of popular melodies by a chorus, was well in keeping
with the action of the screen and particularly inspiring in the battle
scenes. It was composed by Joseph Carl Briel. To lend an appropriate
touch to the surroundings as one entered the theater were men in the
uniforms of Union and Confederate soldiers, while the girl ushers were
costumed after the fashion of young ladies in the South of 1860.

The dramatic critics of all the New York daily papers attended the
premiere and in almost every instance the picture was reported at
length and in glowing terms. H. E. Aitken and Edwin Thanhouser
headed the delegation of Mutual officers, directors, and actors present,
and there was a liberal representation of men prominent in the artistic and business departments of other companies. The demand for seats
so far exceeded the supply that hundreds of people were turned away
at the box office and behind the loge chairs the line was three deep
throughout the evening. As a popular attraction, *The Birth of a Nation* looks like a sensational success.

WARD GREENE

❖❖

The story of the Creation was told in eight words, but should the pen of another Moses be raised today he would need ten times that number of pages to do credit to *The Birth of a Nation.*

There has been nothing to equal it—nothing. Not as a motion picture, nor a play, nor a book does it come to you; but as the soul and spirit and flesh of the heart of your country's history, ripped from the past and brought quivering with all human emotions before your eyes.

It swept the audience at the Atlanta Theater Monday night like a tidal wave. A youth in the gallery leaped to his feet and yelled and yelled. A little boy downstairs pounded the man's back in front of him and shrieked. The man did not know it. He was a middle-aged, hard-lipped citizen; but his face twitched and his throat gulped up and down. Here a young girl kept dabbing and dabbing at her eyes and there an old lady just sat and let the tears stream down her face unchecked.

AWAKENS MANY FEELINGS

For *The Birth of a Nation* is the awakener of every feeling. Your heart pulses with patriotism when those boys in grey march to battle with banners whipping and the band playing "Dixie"; you are wrung with compassion for the mother and her girls desolate at home; you are shocked by the clamor of mighty armies flung hell bent into conflict; your throat chokes for a boy who dies with a smile on his face beside the body of his chum, the enemy. Then "the South's best friend" crumples under the assassin's bullet and the land of the lost cause lies like a ragged wound under a black poison that pours out upon it. Loathing, disgust, hate envelope you, hot blood cries for vengeance. Until out of the night blazes the fiery cross that once burned high above old Scotland's hills and the legions of the Invisible Empire roar down to rescue, and that's when you are lifted by the hair and go crazy.

From The Atlanta Journal, *December 7, 1915. Reprinted by permission of the publisher.*

Race prejudice? Injustice? Suppression? You would not think of those things had you seen *The Birth of a Nation*. For none but a man with a spirit too picayunish and warped for words would pick such flaws in a spectacle so great and whole-hearted as this. In the first place, the picture does every credit to the negro race, lauds those faithful old black people whose fealty to their masters led them to dare the anger of mistaken fanatics, shows the true progress they have since made in industry and education. This picture is too big a thing to be bothered by such a gnat's sting of criticism.

TECHNICALLY PERFECT

Technically, *The Birth of a Nation* is perfect. Its stage settings, the acting of the principals, its faithfulness to historic fact, its every intimate detail, its photography, and its skillful blending of scenes laughable and pathetic—all are so well done that you don't even think about them during the picture.

Yet in retrospect they loom big. There is the scene which gives you the flash of a desolate family huddled on a hilltop and far below Sherman's invaders putting the city to the torch and raiding onward to where the sea laps the sand at Savannah.

There is the old Southern home in the very first part of the picture, when the orchestra plays "Sewanee Ribber." An old man sits there and by his side a cat and a puppy mawl each other. The cat claws viciously, you can almost hear the puppy whimper. And you laugh out loud at the joy of it.

THEY GO TO WAR

When they go to war, your breast swells at the sight of the flower of the Confederacy tripping away to the strains of "The Bonnie Blue Flag." But you smile sympathetically, too, at the darky buck-dancing on the corner and the little pickaninnies rolling funnily in the dust.

You marvel again at the rolling smoke and flash of shell and canister across a far-flung battle line, but you feel as much the pathos when the boy of the North pauses with uplifted bayonet above the body of his chum of the South, until he jerks back from the bullet and wavers down across that body and before he dies smiles that roguish lad's smile and steals his arm across the other's face before he, too, lets his curly head fall in the shadows of the other's shoulder blades.

There is the scene where the "Little Colonel" comes home after the war, wasted, wan, hopeless, pausing, uncertain outside the old mansion where the shattered gate hangs broken on the hinges. And his little sister comes to greet him. She flies out of the house and stops at the threshold and smiles at him. They do not fall into each other's arms, but stand there and try to joke a little to hide the pity in each other's eyes. He fingers the "Southern ermine" on her dress and it ravels away, just like the raw cotton she had bravely donned in honor of his homecoming. And then she cleaves to him with both arms around his neck. And when the picture fades away as he is drawn inside the door, the last thing you feel is the spasm of pain in his face, the last thing you see are twin hands clutched convulsively across his shoulders.

Wonderful Little Sister

That little sister—she is wonderful. Mae Marsh is the girl who plays the role, plays it with an abandon and sincerity that is not acting but living. There, at the last, when she goes to the dark spring for water, you see her smile gayly at a squirrel on a limb; you see the bright-eyed little animal swallow a nut. You follow her mad race through the woods from the black crazed by power. You are with her when she pauses on the precipice and when she plunges downward and rolls over and over at the bottom to writhe for a moment, crushed and broken, before her head snaps back.

She is but one of the stars. That gives you an idea of the lavishness of the picture. Wallace Reid, who is featured in other films as the whole show, is in this picture in but one scene. Yet he is worth it, for his battle with ten negroes in the ginshop of "White-armed Joe" thrills you to the core. He uppercuts one and hurls another across the room, brains a third with a chair, pitches a fourth out of the window, beats them back until a shot spurts grey smoke and he totters into the street and drops forward in a heap.

Ku Klux to Rescue

Then the Ku Klux Klan gathers. The scenes which follow defy description. In the little town of Piedmont the blacks are celebrating, far away across the hills the Klan assembles. Back and forth the scene changes—one moment a street in Piedmont swirling with mad negroes, the next a bugle blast from the orchestra and out of the distance the riders of the Klan sweeping on and on. Back to the street and a house where a white girl trembles in fear before the black horde without, back with the bugle blast to the onrush of the Klan. They are coming, they are coming!

Gallery Goes Wild

You know it and your spine prickles and in the gallery the yells cut loose with every bugle note. The negro mob grows wilder and wilder, the white-shrouded riders are tearing nearer and nearer. Then, with a last mighty blast from the bugle, they sweep into the town and with a shattering volley hammer into the crowd. They fire back, they break, they flee. The Klan beats on them and over them, here a rider knocked off his horse and there another whizzing clean out of the window to the back of his steed—on them and over them to rescue and retribution and final triumph.

And after it's all over, you are not raging nor shot with hatred, but mellowed into a deeper and purer understanding of the fires through which your forefathers battled to make this South of yours a nation reborn!

Don't Miss It

That's why they sold standing room only Monday night and why every matinee at 2:30 and every night performance at 8:30 this week will be packed.

"I wouldn't pay $2 to see any movie in the world," scoffed one man Monday.

A friend took him Monday night. Tuesday he spent $10 to take himself again, his wife, his two children, and his maiden aunt.

And if you haven't seen it, spend the money, borrow it, beg it, get it any old way. But see *The Birth of a Nation*.

NED McINTOSH

◆◆

Ancient Greece had her Homer. Modern America has her David W. Griffith. It was for Homer to show the glory and the grandeur and the

From The Atlanta Constitution, *December 7, 1915. Reprinted by permission of the publisher.*

heroics of war. It is for Griffith to show the horrors and hideousness and hell of it. So moves the world on apace!

Griffith's *The Birth of a Nation* opened at the Atlanta Theater last night and was seen by one of the largest audiences that ever crowded through the doors of the Atlanta Theater. Never before, perhaps, has an Atlanta audience so freely given vent to its emotions and appreciation as last night. Spasmodic at first, the plaudits of the great spectacle at length became altogether unrestrained. The clapping of hands was not sufficient, and cheer after cheer burst forth. He who gets standing room at *The Birth of a Nation* during the remainder of this week which the picture plays here will be lucky.

It makes you laugh and moves you to hot tears unashamed. It makes you love and hate. It makes you forget decorum and forces a cry into your throat. It thrills you with horror and moves you to marvel at vast spectacles. It makes you actually live through the greatest period of suffering and trial that this country has ever known.

To say that *The Birth of a Nation* is based on *The Clansman* is correct as far as it goes, but it doesn't go far enough. Griffith takes Dixon's teapot-tempest and builds a tornado.

The . . . conception of the man is wonderful.

With such scenes as a kitten and a puppy playing together, Griffith, in the beginning, relaxes the imagination and makes the mind forgetful of any preconceived idea or prejudice concerning the picture.

From this mental attitude, almost of dalliance, Griffith awakens the memories of childhood; warms the heart with romance; quickens the pulse with patriotism; forces the exultant cheer from the lips in the midst of great battles; turns the heart sick with scenes of bloodshed; dims the eyes with tears for woman's sufferings; relieves the tension of emotions with a timely humorous incident; makes you tremble for the peril of a mother passing through the lines to reach a wounded son; interests you with a faithful reproduction of Ford's Theater and the assassination of Lincoln—and when Griffith has done all these things he has just begun!

You are ushered into an antechamber in Washington where a misguided man is plotting a black regime among white people—where a mulatto woman dreams of empire. You live through a period of ruin and destruction in the country where you were born. You see the plot executed and that same country humiliated and crushed under a black heel. Former happiness is shattered by the arrogance of ignorance. You sicken at the sight of an attempt to enforce marital racial equality. Again and again the unbearable hideousness of the days of Reconstruction is borne in upon you. History repeats itself upon the screen with a realism that is maddening. You could shriek for a depiction of relief and—yes, retribution. Thus, over and over, does the picture grind and pound and pulverize your emotions.

But the end is not yet.

The insufferable reason for the Ku Klux Klan has been shown. Next, with a wealth of detail and an intimate knowledge that is astonishing, Griffith brings the spectral army into being before your eyes.

Omit these details of dangerous and mysterious night meetings of men, and of the perils of women secretly making strange white garments with crosses emblazoned upon them.

Comes then an appointed night when two men—men and horses garbed in white from head to hoof—ride out from behind an ordinary country barn that you have seen a hundred times, and canter off down the road. At the top of a hill they stop. One holds high a cross of fire. Upon a distant hill other figures catch the signal. Now a group of white-clad horsemen has foregathered. The scene shifts to a great open field at night. There is a blood-curdling trumpet blast from the orchestra pit, pitched in a minor key. A troop of white figures upon spirited horses dashes at breakneck speed into the picture and wheels into position. There is a cheer from the audience. Comes another blood-curdling trumpet call and another troop, and then another and another and another. Men grimly determined upon a last desperate chance to rescue women and homes and civilization from an unspeakable curse are gathering for the work at hand. At last as far as the camera's scope can gather is assembled a vast, grim host in white. One more troop—they are a little late; you think they have come a long distance—wheels into place, right in the camera's very eye!

The "Little Colonel," hero of the story, and such a hero!—takes his place at the head of the white multitude. Again the trumpet blast. The "Little Colonel" rises in his stirrups and holds aloft a cross of fire. The host moves forward.

The awful restraint of the audience is thrown to the winds. Many rise from their seats. With the roar of thunder a shout goes up. Freedom is here! Justice is at hand! Retribution has arrived!

The scene is indescribable.

The Birth of a Nation is built to arouse your emotions, and it does it. It is designed to educate you, and it does so more than many hours of studying books. It is not designed to arouse your prejudices, and if you are fair-minded and not predisposed, it will not do so.

Any mention of *The Birth of a Nation*, however, is not complete with comment on the picture alone. The picture is not all. There is with the picture an orchestra of a score or more pieces and it is a good orchestra. The music is wonderfully adapted to the picture. The score of an opera could not more perfectly express the sense of the lines than does this music interpret the situations, thought, and spirit of *The Birth of a Nation*. When the theme is love the music breathes romance. From a lullaby, the music surges upward to the crashing crescendo of battle in the next scene. Comes now the wild, barbaric strain of half-breed lust and unjustified ambition. When you would resist the tears of the picture, the orchestra will not let you. When you would be silent under the tremendous strain of the situation on the scene, the orchestra wrests a cry from your throat.

The Birth of a Nation has been criticized and attempts have been made to suppress it. If history should be suppressed in schools for children, *The Birth of a Nation* should be suppressed in a theater of thinking people. The picture is vindicated by historical facts, and does not attempt to misinterpret or warp these facts for the purpose of dragging from their graves prejudices that have been dead long since.

The world has long waited for the American Hugo who could write the *Les Miserables* of the War between the States. Many writers have tried and failed. But the great novel of the Civil War has at last arrived —and when it got here it was a moving picture and not a book!

HARLOW HARE

❖❖

One of the most effective features of *The Birth of a Nation* production is its really brilliant musical setting. During the two hours and a half which the big film requires, the orchestra plays an arrangement which perfectly fits the unfolding story and which includes many of the finest bits of melody extant. The library of the old masters and the collections of songs and ballads of the 60's have alike been rifled to make up the score of *The Birth of a Nation*.

When the beaux and belles of '61 danced the small hours away, they did not have the hesitation, the tango or the fox trot, but a waltz or polka tune, a schottische or a lancers, or perhaps the Virginia reel put rhythm in the feet and the tingle in the blood. So David W. Griffith, in his marvelous reproduction of the Piedmont ball in *The Birth of a*

From the Boston American, *July 18, 1915.*

Nation, has the young people dancing to the strains of "Comin' Thro' the Rye" changed to waltz time.

 On this lovely, almost sensuously intoxicating scene is brought the tattered flag that had been through the first Battle of Bull Run when the Confederates drove the Federals headlong before them and baptized the Stars and Bars in glory.

How the Johnny Rebs exult and how the women cheer as the flag is displayed and one hears the strains of the "Bonnie Blue Flag" succeeding the waltz music! But soon comes the news that the young officers at the ball must go to the front. A scene of wild confusion follows upon the joyous, orderly dance, and at daybreak, when everyone is racing about the streets, the chaos and alarm approaching strife are reflected by the strains of Suppe's "Light Cavalry Overture." The little town of Piedmont has its early share of the horrors of war. Weber's "Freischutz Overture" reproduces them to the ear as the pictures on the screen reproduce to the eye.

MUSIC AND SPECTACLE

A wonderful art, this, the marriage of music and spectacle, and one wonderfully achieved by Mr. Griffith and the man who put together the score, a composite of great themes suitable to Griffith's great ideas rather than an original work. It is, however, comparable to the way European composers like Liszt, Chopin and Dvorak take the melodies of the common people, the folk music, so to speak, and combine and elaborate them with more erudite themes.

Thus the big moments of the early part of *The Birth of a Nation,* laid in the Southland, revert to "Dixie," "My Maryland," "Marching through Georgia," "Tramp, Tramp, Tramp! the Boys are Marching," "Kingdom Coming," "Girl I Left Behind Me," and "Home, Sweet Home." To what other tune should the Southerners bound for war march than to the ever familiar "Dixie"? What more splendidly typifies the rescue of the Piedmonters from the guerrilla troops by their own men than the glorious "Maryland, My Maryland."

Of course, "Marching thro' Georgia" sets the pace for the extraordinarily vivid depiction of Sherman's March, but it is a "Marching through Georgia" with a sad antiphony—wails of the victims in minor keys answering the marching song of the conqueror. "Taps" for the deep tragedy of war's peace; "The Star Spangled Banner" to mark the grand victory of the North, and the inspiring strains of "America" for reunion of North and South in a greater nation when Grant and Lee clasped hands at Appomattox—such is the appropriate, if somewhat obvious, instrumentation of patriotic scenes.

ELSIE'S MELODY

When piquant little *Elsie Stoneman* decides to become a nurse and solace gallant wounded youths back to health, even as Cabinet officers' daughters have done in the present war [World War I] her goings and comings are accompanied by a most adorable little air which she is supposed not only to sing but also to pick on the banjo. In the close-ups you can see the dainty lips fashioning the words of the song and in the full figure you can see her working the banjo a little over time, while the handsome sufferer on the pillow manages to turn his head about three-quarters in order to get a look at her. Many persons have asked what this tune is. It is Henry E. Work's "Kingdom Coming," otherwise known as "Massa's Jubilee," one of the most fetching ditties that was ever picked out of banjo or guitar.

To return to the great war scenes. There is a magnitude about Griffith's representation of war and battle that demands the most elaborate effects. The scenes themselves are enormous, panoramic; the action is both marvelously complex and marvelously vivid; the music must reproduce this immensity, complexity and thrill at once. Thus one is not surprised that Grieg's "Peer Gynt" suite, "In the Hall of the Mountain King," is used for the terrific pictures of "the torch against the breast of Atlanta"; that Wagnerian operatic crashes accompany the cannonading and infantry charging at Petersburg; and that even when a national army tune like "Tramp, Tramp, Tramp" is used, it is elaborate and built up into a great, overwhelming symphonic movement. So, too, in the scene of Lincoln's assassination in Ford's Theatre, Washington, April 14, 1865. The appearance of the emancipator is greeted, as it was greeted on that occasion, by the well-known strains of "Hail to the Chief." But the fatal crisis of that hour can only be rendered by classical music of enormous complexity and power such as Bellini's "Norma Overture," which is the work selected.

TENDER LOVE MOTIF

Three distinctive strains or motifs run through the second half of the picture, emphasizing by contrast the three elements of which it is composed. For the loves of *Ben Cameron,* the little Confederate colonel, and *Elsie Stoneman,* the dainty Northern heroine, we have Breil's "Perfect Song," an original composition for this play and now published in sheet form. It is one of the most beautiful love themes that has ever been invented. It returns and returns with peculiar increasing effectiveness, but perhaps it is sweetest in the outdoor scene when *Elsie* kisses the dove and *Ben* repeatedly tries to steal a few for himself while she is doing so.

Then there is the wild, chaotic-seeming tune that marks the entry of the negro carpet-bagger mobs and the racket of the rioters. Perhaps Mr. Griffith got this out of the semi-musical cries of the negro dancers on the old plantation in Kentucky when he was a boy. It is certainly original so far as can be learned. It does not represent the negro of today by any means. For the last negro motif in the play is Hermann's beautifully liquid, enticing "Cocoanut Dance" to the strains of which the Hampton Institute films are shown.

But above all and everything else, the biggest thing in the second part of *The Birth of a Nation* and indeed of the whole play is the welcome Ku-Klux-Klan Call, the signal that the Fiery Cross of St. Andrew has been borne from South to North Carolina and back again and that the little band of oppressed whites, including the hero and heroine of the story, are to be saved by these Highlanders from the fury of the riotous elements unloosed upon them. The call makes the welkin ring at the opening of each part of the film. It strikes across the moments of agony, horror and suspense like a clarion note of rescue from another world. The call is not original, but an adaptation of the famous call in Wagner's "Die Walkure."

STIRRING KU-KLUX CALL

Just a flash of the ghostly horsemen, the big Ku-Klux call, and the spectators become almost frenzied in their applause. Often the call has a weird effect, as when the thin-voiced oboe plays it alone. Often it comes stridently powerful against entirely different notes.

The final Piedmont scenes of *The Birth of a Nation* are very strenuous. It seems almost impossible to conceive how Griffith could have got action of such lightning-like speed, involving such enormous numbers of people and carried on with such apparent defiance of the rules of order yet with a strange logic of its own. While these big flights, riots and rescues are going on we have the appropriately big music of Tschaikowsky's "1812 Overture," Wagner's "Rienzi Overture," the "Zampa Overture," the Fire Music from "Die Walkure" and "The Ride of the Valkyries." It all ends up, as good adventure stories should, with the triumph of the heroic characters and thus naturally with the parade of the returning clansmen for which of course "Dixie" is the tune. Then after the scenes depicting negro progress above referred to, which are enlivened by the "Cocoanut Dance," the double honeymoon by the sea is shown and the strains of "In the Gloaming" are followed by Breil's "Perfect Song."

REMARKABLE FINALE

The finale of the picture is Griffith's remarkable conception on the one hand of the "human salad" of War with the blonde brute on a horse in the background striking at his helpless victims, and, on the other hand, of a Utopian brotherhood of love and peace, with some of the folks like Koreans and others like early Romans, and the figure of the Saviour blessing the glad assembly.

These fine bits of allegory are accompanied by the "Gloria" from Haydn's Mass in C, and as the last Utopian scene fades out and the immortal words of Daniel Webster on Liberty and Union appear on the screen, "The Star Spangled Banner" rings out in all its splendor, and the scenes that have made *The Birth of a Nation* are done.

COMMENTARIES

The Making of
THE BIRTH OF A NATION
LILLIAN GISH

One afternoon during the spring of 1914, while we were still work-ing in California, Mr. Griffith took me aside on the set and said in an undertone, "After the others leave tonight, would you please stay."

Later, as some of the company drifted out, I realized that a similar message had been given to a few others. This procedure was typical of Mr. Griffith when he was planning a new film. He observed us with a smile, amused perhaps by our curiosity over the mystery that he had created.

I suspected what the meeting was about. A few days before, we had been having lunch at The White Kitchen, and I had noticed that his pockets were crammed with papers and pamphlets. My curiosity was aroused, but it would have been presumptuous of me to ask about them. With Mr. Griffith one did not ask; one only answered. Besides, I had learned that if I waited long enough he would tell me.

"I've bought a book by Thomas Dixon, called *The Clansman*. I'm going to use it to tell the truth about the War between the States. It hasn't been told accurately in history books. Only the winning side in a war ever gets to tell its story." He paused, watching the cluster of actors: Henry Walthall, Spottiswoode Aitken, Bobby Harron, Mae Marsh, Miriam Cooper, Elmer Clifton, George Siegmann, Walter Long, and me.

"The story concerns two families—the Stonemans from the North and the Camerons from the South." He added significantly, "I know I can trust you."

He swore us to secrecy, and to us his caution was understandable. Should his competitors learn of his new project, they would have films

From Lillian Gish: The Movies, Mr. Griffith, and Me *by Lillian Gish with Ann Pinchot (Englewood Cliffs, N.J.: Prentice-Hall, Inc., 1969), pp. 131–47.* © *1969 by Lillian Gish and Ann Pinchot. Reprinted by permission of Lucy Kroll Agency and Prentice-Hall, Inc. Title sup-plied.*

on the same subject completed before his work was released. He discussed his story plots freely only over lunch or dinner, often testing
them out on me because I was close-mouthed and never repeated what
anyone told me.

I heard later that "Daddy" Woods had called Mr. Griffith's attention
to *The Clansman*. It had done well as a book and even better as a play,
touring the country for five years. Mr. Griffith also drew on *The Leopard's Spots* for additional material for the new movie. Thomas Dixon,
the author of both works, was a Southerner who had been a college
classmate of Woodrow Wilson. Mr. Griffith paid a $2,500 option for
The Clansman, and it was agreed that Dixon was to receive $10,000
in all for the story, but when it came time to pay him no more money
was available. In the end, he reluctantly agreed to accept instead of
cash a 25 percent interest in the picture, which resulted in the largest
sum any author ever received for a motion-picture story. Dixon earned
several million dollars as his share.

Mr. Griffith didn't need the Dixon book. His intention was to tell his
version of the War between the States. But he evidently lacked the con-
fidence to start production on a twelve-reel film without an established
book as a basis for his story. After the film was completed and he had
shown it to the so-called author, Dixon said: "This isn't my book at
all." But Mr. Griffith was glad to use Dixon's name on the film as
author, for, as he told me, "The public hates you if it thinks you wrote,
directed, and produced the entire film yourself. It's the quickest way
to make enemies."

After the first rehearsal, the pace increased. Mr. Griffith worked, as
usual, without a script. But this time his pockets bulged with books,
maps, and pamphlets, which he read during meals and the rare breaks
in his hectic schedule. I rehearsed whatever part Mr. Griffith wanted to
see at the moment. My sister and I had been the last to join the company, and we naturally supposed that the major assignments would
go to the older members of the group. For a while, it looked as if I
would be no more than an extra. But during one rehearsal Blanche
Sweet, who we suspected would play the romantic part of Elsie Stoneman, was missing. Mr. Griffith pointed to me.

"Come on, Miss Damnyankee, let's see what you can do with Elsie."

My thin figure was quite a contrast to Blanche's ripe, full form. Mr.
Griffith had us rehearse the near-rape scene between Elsie and Silas
Lynch, the power-drunk mulatto in the film. George Siegmann was
playing Lynch in blackface. In this scene Lynch proposes to Elsie and,
when she rebuffs him, forces his attentions on her. During the hysteri-
cal chase around the room, the hairpins flew out of my hair, which
tumbled below my waist as Lynch held my fainting body in his arms.
I was very blonde and fragile-looking. The contrast with the dark man

evidently pleased Mr. Griffith, for he said in front of everyone, "Maybe she would be more effective than the more mature figure I had in mind."

He didn't tell us then, but I think the role was mine from that moment.

At first I didn't pay much attention to Mr. Griffith's concept of the film. His claim that history books falsified actual happenings struck me as most peculiar. At that time I was too naive to think that history books would attempt to falsify anything. I've lived long enough now to know that the whole truth is never told in history texts. Only the people who lived through an era, who are the real participants in the drama as it occurs, know the truth. The people of each generation, it seems to me, are the most accurate historians of their time.

Soon sets were going up; costumes arrived; and mysterious crates, evidently filled with military equipment, were delivered. As we gradually became aware of the magnitude of the new project, we grew even more anxious than usual about being assigned roles in the film. All the young players wanted to prove their worth before it was too late. This distress from young girls in their teens may seem strange today, but the photography of that time aged one so drastically that we believed that by the time we reached eighteen we would be playing character roles.

When the final casting was announced, we learned that Ralph Lewis was to play the Honorable Austin Stoneman, the "uncrowned king of Capitol Hill." The character of Stoneman, a fiery political fanatic from the North, was patterned after the real-life Thaddeus Stevens, one of the legislators whose harsh policy toward the South wrecked President Lincoln's postwar plans.

Bobby Harron and Elmer Clifton were to play Stoneman's sons, and I was given the role of his daughter Elsie. Mary Alden was to be Stoneman's mulatto mistress Lydia Brown, whom Dixon described as "a woman of extraordinary animal beauty and the fiery temper of a leopardess."

George Siegmann was awarded the part of Silas Lynch, who, according to Dixon, was "a Negro of perhaps forty years, a man of charming features for a mulatto, who had evidently inherited the full physical characteristics of the Aryan, while his dark yellowish eyes beneath his heavy brows glowed with the brightness of the African jungle." Walter Long was to be the renegade Negro Gus, and Elmo Lincoln, a magnificent strong man who would later swing through the trees as Tarzan, played the Negro who attacks Wallace Reid, the stalwart blacksmith.

There were practically no Negro actors in California then and, as far as we knew, only a few in the East. Even in minstrel shows, the parts were usually played by whites in blackface. The only scenes in which actual Negroes appear in *The Birth of a Nation* are those in which the

Stoneman boys, visiting the Southern Camerons, are taken out to the plantation to see Negroes working in the cotton fields, and, later, in which blacks are shown dominating the postwar South Carolina legislature.

But one young Negro woman did play in the film—Madame Sul-Te-Wan. (We never did discover the origin of her name.) She was first employed to help us keep our dressing rooms clean at the studio. She was devoted to Mr. Griffith, and he in turn loved her. Later, when Madame was having financial difficulties, he sent her money to help herself and her small sons. She was one of the few friends near him when he died years later in Hollywood.

The faithful mammy was played by Jennie Lee, who also became a recipient of Mr. Griffith's generosity in later years. When she was taken ill, D. W. had Mae Marsh send her some money, saying that Jennie had been the inspiration for a story he had sold to a magazine and asking her to please accept half the payment.

Henry B. Walthall was a natural choice for the part of Ben Cameron, the "Little Colonel." He was a slight man, about five feet six, fine-boned, with the face of a poet and a dreamer. Indeed, when he played a part patterned on Edgar Allan Poe in *The Avenging Conscience,* he had resembled that romantic figure. Like Thomas Dixon and Mr. Griffith, Walthall came from the South. He had been born in Alabama and was proud that his father had fought the Union troops at Vicksburg. "Wally," as he was affectionately called, was everything in life that his "Little Colonel" was on the screen: dear, patient, lovable. His only fault was that he had no conception of time. Consequently, a man was hired for the purpose of getting him into makeup and to work on time for this film.

Mr. Griffith was fond of Wally, but Wally did cause him considerable anxiety. The bodyguard was assigned to Wally not only to get him on the set on time but also to keep him from inbibing too freely. On one occasion, Wally managed to give the guard the slip. He was finally traced to a hotel room, where he was found, not drinking, but simply exhausted and trying to get some sleep.

Wally was a bit too old—Mr. Griffith thought—to be playing opposite me, so Mr. Griffith tried to bridge the difference in our ages by having Wally keep a hat on during the filming.

The rest of the Cameron family was represented by Josephine Crowell and Spottiswoode Aiken as the parents; the dark-haired classic beauty, Miriam Cooper, as Ben's sister Margaret; Mae Marsh as the little sister Flora, all fluctuating emotions and the essence of girlhood; and André Beringer and Maxfield Stanley as the two younger Cameron brothers.

For President Lincoln, Mr. Griffith chose Joseph Henabery, a tall, thin man who could be made up to resemble Lincoln. The search for an appropriate Mary Todd Lincoln ended when he found a woman with an uncanny similarity to the First Lady working in wardrobe. Raoul Walsh was picked for the role of John Wilkes Booth. Members of Mr. Lincoln's cabinet were chosen on the basis of facial resemblance to the historical characters. The other historical characters were re-created by Donald Crisp as General Grant, Howard Gaye as General Lee, and Sam de Grasse as Senator Sumner.

For the new film we naturally rehearsed longer than we had for any other film up to that time.

During his six years with Biograph, Mr. Griffith had taken strides toward his ultimate goal: filming his version of the Civil War. He had made a number of early pictures that touched on the War between the States. But it was soon obvious to everyone that this film was to be his most important statement yet. Billy Bitzer wrote of that time: *"The Birth of a Nation changed D. W. Griffith's personality entirely. Where heretofore he was wont to refer in starting on a new picture to 'grinding out another sausage' and go at it lightly, his attitude in beginning on this one was all eagerness. He acted like here we have something worthwhile."*

Although fact and legend were familiar to him, he did meticulous research for *The Birth*. The first half of *The Birth*, about the war itself, reflects his own point of view. I know that he also relied greatly on Harper's *Pictorial History of the Civil War*, Matthew Brady's *Civil War Photographs: Confederate and Union Veterans—Eyewitnesses on Location*; the Nicolay and Hay *Abraham Lincoln: A History*; and *The Soldier in Our Civil War: A Pictorial History of the Conflict 1861–1865*. For the second half, about Reconstruction, he consulted Thomas Dixon, and *A History of the American People* by Woodrow Wilson. President Wilson had taught history before going into politics, and Mr. Griffith had great respect for his erudition. For Klan material, he drew on a book called *Ku Klux Klan—Its Origin, Growth and Disbandment* by John C. Lester and D. L. Wilson. But he did not use the uniform that is worn by Klan members today. Instead he used the costumes that, according to Thomas Dixon, were worn by the earlier Klans—white and scarlet flowing robes with hood and mask to hide the features of rider and horse.

Brady's photographs were constantly consulted, and Mr. Griffith re-staged many moments of history with complete fidelity to them. The photographs were used as guides for such scenes as Lee's surrender at Appomattox, the signing of the Emancipation Proclamation, and Sherman's march to the sea. He telegraphed a newspaper in Columbia, South Carolina, for photographs of the interior of the state Capitol, which held a majority of Negro representatives after the war, and constructed the legislative chamber according to the photographs.

The largest interior was Ford's Theater, the setting of the assassination scene, which was done in one day on the lot. So great was Mr. Griffith's obsession with authenticity that he unearthed a copy of *Our American Cousin,* which had been performed at Ford's Theater on the night of the assassination, and restaged parts of it. In the actual filming, as Raoul Walsh, gun ready, steals into the presidential box, the lines being spoken on the replica of the stage are precisely those spoken at the fateful moment on the night of April 14, 1865. This fidelity to facts was an innovation in films.

Mr. Griffith knew the terrain of the battlefields, and he hired several Civil War veterans to scout locations similar to the original ones. After exploring the Southern California country, they chose what later became the Universal lot for the countryside around Petersburg, Virginia, site of the last prolonged siege and final battle of the war.

He had studied maps of the major battles of the Civil War and, with the help of the veterans, laid out the battlefields. Trenches, breastworks, roads, brooks, and buildings were constructed to duplicate those of the actual battlefields. Troop movements were planned with the advice of the veterans and two men from West Point Military Academy. Civil War artillery was obtained from West Point and the Smithsonian Institution, for use when the camera was close.

Mr. Griffith also sent to the Smithsonian for historical records and then went over the documents with his advisers. But in the end he came to his own conclusions about historical facts. He would never take the opinion of only one man as final.

The street in Piedmont on which the Cameron house was located was complete with brick walls and hitching and lamp posts. A small set, it achieved scope from violated perspective—an old stage technique in which each successive house and street lamp is a little shorter, so that the setting seems to "recede" without actually taking up much space or requiring the use of expensive lumber.

We had no stage designer, only the modest genius of a carpenter, Frank Wortman, known as "Huck." Huck, a short, rather heavy set man in his forties, with friendly blue eyes and a weakness for chewing tobacco, didn't talk much, but listened intently to Mr. Griffith. Even before rehearsals started Mr. Griffith explained to him what he wanted in the way of sets. He would show Huck a photograph that he wanted copied, or point out changes to be made in the reproduction. They would decide how the sun would hit a particular building three, four, even five weeks from then.

Men during the Civil War era were rather small in stature (it was before the age of proper nutrition), so genuine uniforms could not be used by the later generation. Uniforms for *The Birth* were therefore made by a small struggling company, which has since become the famous Western Costume Company.

The Brady photographs also served as models for the soldiers' hair styles.

To absorb the spirit of the film, we came down with a case of history nearly as intense as Mr. Griffith's. At first, between making other films during the day and rehearsing *The Birth* at night, we had scant time for reading. But Mr. Griffith's interest was contagious, and we began to read about the period. Soon it was the only subject we talked about. Mr. Griffith didn't ask us to do this; it stemmed out of our own interest. We pored over photographs of the Civil War and *Godey's Ladies' Book,* a periodical of the nineteenth century, for costumes, hair styles, and postures. We had to rehearse how to sit and how to move in the hoop skirts of the day.

My costumes were specially made. One of them had a tiny derby with a high plume. When I saw it, I rebelled.

"The audience will laugh at me," I protested.

But Mr. Griffith insisted that I wear it. He wanted the audience to be amused. "It's a darb!" he said, smiling.

As always, sunlight controlled the shooting schedule. Preparations began at five or six in the morning. The actors rose at five in order to be ready at seven, when it was bright enough for filming. Important scenes were played in the hard noon sun. I remember that we used to beg to have our close-ups taken just after dawn or before sunset, as the soft yellow glow was easier to work in and much more flattering. We continued to work—often without a break for lunch—until sundown.

At that time young actors were learning not only to act but also to direct. When they weren't acting, George Siegmann and Bobby Harron served as assistant directors. All the young people, in fact, were at Mr. Griffith's elbow to help in any way that he chose to use them.

To economize, Mr. Griffith used many of the actors in more than one role. Bobby Harron, for instance, might play my brother in the morning, and in the afternoon put on blackface and play a Negro. Madame Sul-Te-Wan played many small parts, with the help of various costumes. In the battle scenes several featured actors rode horses—but in the distance, well away from the camera. For many small roles, members of the company who happened to be working on other films came on the set of *The Birth* for a day or two.

The entire staff came on set to watch us, particularly Joe Aller and the men from the laboratory, so that they would know the effects that Mr. Griffith was seeking. This was of utmost importance, for each scene was shot only once. The only scene that was taken twice was the one in which Mae Marsh as the little sister leaps to her death from a cliff.

In those days there was no one to keep track of what an actor was wearing from scene to scene. He was obliged to remember for himself what he had worn and how his hair and makeup had looked in a previous scene. If he forgot, he was not used again. When the death scene was filmed, Mae forgot to tie the Confederate flag, which she'd been wearing in the previous scene, around her waist, and the scene had to be retaken. How we all envied her a second chance in a big moment!

In filming the battles, Mr. Griffith organized the action like a general. He stood at the top of a forty-foot tower, the commander-in-chief of both armies, his powerful voice, like Roarin' Jake's, thundering commands through a megaphone to his staff of assistants. Meetings were called before each major filmed sequence and a chain of command was developed from Mr. Griffith through his directors and their assistants. The last-in-command might have only four or five extras under him. These men, wearing uniforms and taking their places among the extras, also played parts in the film.

Griffith's camera was high on the platform looking down on the battlefield, so that he could obtain a grand sweep of the action. This camera took the long shots. Hidden under bushes or in back of trees were cameras for close-ups.

When the din of cannons, galloping horses, and charging men grew too great, no human voice, not even Mr. Griffith's, was powerful enough to be heard. Some of the extras were stationed as far as two miles from the camera. So a series of magnifying mirrors was used to flash signals to those actors working a great distance away. Each group of men had its number—one flash of the mirror for the first group, two for the second group, and so on. As group one started action, the mirror would flash a go-ahead to group two.

Care was taken to place the authentic old guns and the best horsemen in the first ranks. Other weapons, as well as poorer horsemen, were relegated to the background. Extras were painstakingly drilled in their parts until they knew when to charge, when to push cannons forward, when to fall.

Some of the artillery was loaded with real shells, and elaborate warnings were broadcast about their range of fire. Mr. Griffith's sense of order and control made it possible for the cast and extras to survive the broiling heat, pounding hoofs, naked bayonets, and exploding shells without a single injury. He was too thoughtful of the welfare of others to permit accidents.

In most war films it is difficult to distinguish between the enemies unless the film is in color and the two sides are wearing different-colored uniforms. But not in a Griffith movie. Mr. Griffith had the rare technical skill to keep each side distinct and clear-cut. In *The Birth,* the Confederate army always entered from the left of the camera, the Union army from the right.

One day he said to Billy, "I want to show a whole army moving."

"What do you mean, a whole army?" Bitzer asked.

"Everyone we can muster."

"I'll have to move them back to get them all in view," Billy said. "They won't look much bigger than jackrabbits."

"That's all right. The audience will supply the details. Let's move up on this hill, Billy. Then we can shoot the whole valley and all the troops at once."

They never talked much, but they always seemed to understand each other. People around Mr. Griffith didn't bother him with idle talk.

When daylight disappeared, Mr. Griffith would order bonfires lit and film some amazing night scenes. Billy was pessimistic about the results; he kept insisting that they would be unsuccessful. But Mr. Griffith persisted. One big battle scene was filmed at night. The subtitle was to read, "It went on into the night." Nothing like it had ever been seen before. Those of us who had time were there—the women to watch, the men to help.

Although everything was carefully organized, whenever he saw a spontaneous gesture that looked good—like the soldier's leaning on his gun and looking at me during the hospital scene—he would call Billy over to film it.

In that scene, the wards were filled with wounded soldiers, and in the background nurses and orderlies attended their patients. In the doorway of the ward stood a Union sentry. As Elsie Stoneman, I was helping to entertain the wounded, singing and playing the banjo. The sentry watched me lovingly as I sang and then, after I had finished and was passing him, raised his hangdog head and heaved a deep, love-sick sigh. The scene lasted only a minute, but it drew the biggest laugh of the film and became one of its best-remembered moments.

The scene came about in typical Griffith fashion. We players had no one to help us with our costumes. We had to carry our various changes to the set, as we could not afford the time to run back to our dressing rooms. Those period dresses, with their full skirts over hoops, were heavy. A kind young man who liked me helped me with my props and costumes. The young man, William Freeman, was playing the sentry, and he simply stood there, listening, as I sang. Seeing his expression, Mr. Griffith said to Bitzer, "Billy, get that picture on film right away." He knew that it would bring a laugh, which was needed to break the dramatic tension.

Since the release of *The Birth of a Nation,* I have often been asked by fans what happened to the sentry in the hospital. After *The Birth* was finished, I didn't see William Freeman again until the first World's Fair in New York. It was the day of the fair's closing. I happened to be riding on a float for charity, and there, walking toward the float, was William Freeman. I recognized him immediately.

"My son is here," he said after we had greeted each other. "I would like you to meet him."

He disappeared into the crowd and returned shortly with a bright four-year-old, whom he proudly introduced to me. Then we said good-bye, and I haven't seen him since.

One morning, when we assembled for work as usual, Mr. Griffith was missing. This was unheard of. Nothing short of disaster had ever taken him away from the studio. Activity came to a standstill.

"Where's Mr. Griffith?" everyone asked. "Is he ill? Did someone die?"

But slowly one story gained strength, and by late morning the word was on everyone's lips. "Money. It must be money."

When Mr. Griffith finally appeared after lunch, he explained nothing. Instead he said wearily, "All right, let's get to work."

On payday, there were no checks for his company.

"There just isn't any money," "Little" Epping explained to us with a weak smile. "But give us a little more time, and we'll have the checks."

While Mr. Griffith was working for the Aitkens, Johannes Charlemagne Epping, whom we called "Little" Epping, was his financial shadow. If ever a man needed a business manager, it was David Wark Griffith. Mr. Epping, who had been Biograph's accountant and who went with Mr. Griffith when he moved to Mutual, was a good businessman. He was to make wise investments in the future and retire to Switzerland in 1925 a prosperous man. He tried to share his knowledge with his boss, but Mr. Griffith would not accept his advice. Mr. Griffith always insisted on managing his money himself, with disastrous results. He spent it unwisely, invested it foolishly, and sometimes squirreled it away and forgot all about it. But fortunately Mr. Epping did manage secretly to withhold funds from Mr. Griffith and to invest them as non-revocable annuities, so that Mr. Griffith did not have to spend the last years of his life penniless. Yet Mr. Griffith seemed to consider Mr. Epping his adversary, someone to be outsmarted, instead of his protector and friend. Agnes Wiener remembers that he sometimes authorized days off for the actors with the warning, "Don't tell 'Little' Epping."

The day after Mr. Epping's announcement, Mother told me that she had offered Mr. Griffith help.

"Mr. Griffith, I'd like to buy into the picture," she said. "Three hundred dollars' worth."

"How much money do you have saved, Mrs. Gish?" he asked.

"Three hundred dollars."

"Mrs. Gish, I can't let you do it. You'd be taking too great a risk."

Had he allowed it, of course, she would have made hundreds of thousands of dollars.

We didn't receive our checks for several weeks, although we all knew that when Mr. Griffith got the money we would be paid. We continued to work every day, if not on *The Birth,* then on other pictures.

Mr. Griffith tried to make light of the situation.

"Come on, let's shoot this scene," he would say to the actors. "If we don't get it today, there's no money to make it tomorrow."

Although he joked, we knew how worried he was.

Harry Aitken, as president of the Mutual Film Company, had originally put up $25,000 for *The Birth,* but his directors, learning of the subject matter and the scope of the film, had panicked and demanded that the backing be withdrawn. Aitken had then raised the sum himself. But as the money dwindled perhaps Mr. Griffith was ashamed to ask Aitken for more, and felt obliged to raise the additional sum himself.

We heard from someone who had overheard him talking to "Little" Epping that he had gone to see a Mr. Talley, the owner of a large moving-picture theater in Los Angeles. He didn't get the needed amount, so he went off to see department-store owners—in fact anyone who might conceivably lend him cash. Meanwhile, what little money there was had to go to the extras.

Then one day during that tense period a stranger appeared on the lot. Rumor spread that he was William Clune, owner of Clune's Auditorium, the largest theater in Los Angeles. (It is now the Philharmonic Auditorium.) Clune was proud of his theater and even prouder of his thirty-piece orchestra, which played in it.

For Clune's benefit, Mr. Griffith staged an impressive scene from the film, the marching of the Confederate soldiers down the street to war. Henry Walthall led the procession. Clune watched intently as Walthall passed on his charger; he saw the swinging rifles, the farewells of wives and mothers, and the flutter of Stars and Bars.

Mr. Griffith had been able to engage a small brass band to play "Dixie" as the procession marched along.

"That's not much of a band," Clune said, looking pained.

"No, it's not," D. W. agreed. "But think of how that tune would sound if your orchestra played it."

"I've got the best orchestra west of Mississippi," Clune boasted.

"Think of how 'Dixie' would sound in *your* auditorium with *your* orchestra!" Mr. Griffith repeated. "Why, you'd charm the audience right out of their seats! All we need is fifteen thousand more to finish the film. What do you say?"

"Well, that's quite a sum."

They walked out of earshot toward Mr. Griffith's office, and when they reappeared both men were beaming. After Clune's departure Mr. Griffith rounded up his staff.

"Let's start shooting right away. Clune may change his mind. And for heaven's sake send that band away."

Mr. Griffith was back in production.

Once again, he was working against time. Clune's money meant that he could go on with the film, but not without watching his expenditures. To demonstrate that he was being frugal he walked around with a hole in his shoe, declaring to us that he wouldn't "buy new shoes until we start getting money back at the box office."

Even Mr. Clune's contribution proved not to be enough. Before production was completed, Mr. Griffith had to call upon his friends for money to complete the film.

In going through Mr. Griffith's papers recently, I came across some "facts" about *The Birth of a Nation* that read like most press releases of that day. Robert Edgar Long, in his soft-cover book *David Wark Griffith: A Brief Sketch of His Career,* published in 1920, suggests that professors of history from at least a half-dozen universities were called upon for facts and figures, so that no errors would mar the film's authenticity. He says that Mr. Griffith had plans to shoot some 5,000 scenes; to use 18,000 men as soldiers; to make 18,000 Union and Confederate uniforms for these men; to hire 3,000 horses; to build entire cities and destroy them by fire; to buy real shells that cost $10 apiece in order to reenact the greatest battle of the Civil War; and to select fragments from about 500 separate musical compositions to synchronize perfectly with various scenes. Many scenes, he says, were photographed from fifteen to twenty times before Mr. Griffith was pleased with the results. He adds that the scene of Lincoln's assassination was rehearsed at least twenty times before it was actually filmed.

I know that in later years Mr. Griffith himself was prone to exaggerations that were a press agent's dream. Perhaps he too believed that these gross overstatements and inaccuracies would enhance the film's prestige.

It seems to me, however, that the truth is a much finer tribute to Mr. Griffith's skill. In the battle scenes there were never more than 300 to 500 extras. By starting with a close-up and then moving the camera back from the scene, which gave the illusion of depth and distance, and by having the same soldiers run around quickly to make a second entrance, Mr. Griffith created the impression of big armies. In the battles, clouds of smoke rising from the thickets gave the illusion of many soldiers camouflaged by the woods, although in actuality there were only a few.

The scene of Sherman's march to the sea opened with an iris shot
—a small area in the upper left-hand corner of a black screen—of a
mother holding her weeping children amid the ruins of a burned-out
house. Slowly the iris opened wider to reveal a great panorama—
troops, wagons, fires, and beyond, in the distance, Atlanta burning.
Atlanta was actually a model, superimposed on the film.

The entire industry, always intensely curious about Mr. Griffith,
was speculating about this new film. What was that crazy man Griffith
up to? He was using the full repertoire of his earlier experiments and
adding new ones. He tinted film to achieve dramatic results and to
create mood. In the battle scene at Petersburg, the shots of Union
and Confederate troops rushing in to replace the dead and wounded
are tinted red, and the subtitle reads "In the red lane of death others
take their places." And, at the climax of the film, there were the thrilling rides of the Klan. These rides were beautifully handled—first, the
signal riders galloping to give warning; then, one by one and two by
two, the galloping hordes merging into a white-hooded mass, their
peaked helmets and fiery crosses making them resemble knights of a
crusade.

Before the filming of this scene Mr. Griffith decided to try a new
kind of shot. He had a hole dug in the road directly in the path of
the horsemen. There he placed Billy and the camera, and obtained
shots of the horses approaching and galloping right over the camera,
so that the audience could see the pounding hoofs. This shot has since
become standard, but then it was the first time it had been done, and
the effect was spectacular. Billy came through safely, and so did his
precious camera, as Mr. Griffith must have known it would. He would
never have taken a chance with a camera; it was far too costly.

Among the obstacles that cropped up during the filming was a lack
of muslin needed for Klan uniforms. There was also a shortage of
horses for battle scenes. Both were war scarcities. When the war in
Europe broke out, the Allies were rounding up horses and shipping
them to France. Mr. Griffith found himself in competition with French,
English, Russian, and Italian agents, all in search of horses. Acting as
his own agent, he was obliged to rent horses at higher prices from a
dealer in the West.

We had outstanding riders like the Burns Brothers, who led the
Klan riders and supervised any scene involving horses. Henry Walthall
was a superb horseman, as were some of the other actors. The cowboy
and circus riders beneath the Ku Klux sheets did a superb job. In the
mob scenes they reared their horses until clouds mushroomed, but not
one of them was hurt.

What I liked most about working on *The Birth* was the horses.

I could always borrow a horse from the set, and during my lunch hour I would canter off alone to the hills.

I saw everything that Mr. Griffith put on film. My role in *The Birth* required about three weeks' work, but I was on call during the whole time that it was being filmed. I was in the studio every day—working on other films, being available for the next scene if needed, making myself useful in any way that was required.

My dressing room was just across the hall from the darkroom, where Jimmy Smith and Joe Aller worked. Whenever I had a few minutes I would join them, watching them develop the film and cut it. I would view the day's rushes and tell Jimmy my reactions to them. I saw the effects that Mr. Griffith obtained with his views of marching men, the ride of the Klan, the horrors of war. Watching these snatches of film was like trying to read a book whose pages had been shuffled. There was neither order nor continuity. Here was a touching bit from a scene with Mae; there was a long shot of a battle. It made me realize the job that Mr. Griffith had ahead of him after the filming was done.

The shooting was completed in nine weeks, but Mr. Griffith spent more than three months on cutting, editing, and working on the musical score. I still remember how hard he worked on other films during the day and then at night on *The Birth*. Of all his pictures up to that time, none was more beset with difficulties. Without his spirit and faith, it might never have been completed.

D. W. Griffith Recalls the Making of
THE BIRTH OF A NATION
HENRY STEPHEN GORDON

What Debussy and Richard Strauss and Puccini have done for music, what Monet and Manet did for painting with their "pleen air" im-

From "The Story of David Wark Griffith, Part V," by Henry Stephen Gordon, The Photoplay Magazine, 10 (October 1916): 86–94. Reprinted by permission of Photoplay Magazine, a Macfadden-Bartell publication.

placable to translation of fact into art, what William Dean Howells accomplished when he published *Silas Lapham,* a touch of Rodin's vivifying boost of sculpture, Buckle's miracle of making history a science, something of the same as all these breaking of the fetters which made their respective arts hobble along the ruts, was done when Griffith created *The Birth of a Nation.*

For he had first sown and harvested a complete and perfect technique all his own; he applied this technique to an epical theme and a masterpiece panoplied in beauty sprang from his brain.

It has taken in receipts so far well up into seven figures. How many we can only guess on the basis that as royalty Mr. Dixon has received something probably in the hundreds of thousands.

And it is still a-going, with three-quarters of the world left as uncropped region.

This picture was the first to invade the White House.

On February 15, 1915, it was displayed in the East Room of the White House for the president, the cabinet, Miss Wilson, and the wives and daughters of the cabinet ministers.

On the following evening a similar production was made attended by the chief justice and associate justices of the Supreme Court, the diplomatic corps, and senators and congressmen—an audience of five hundred.

In recording the history of this picture, Frank Woods again takes the center of the stage as the . . . [movie's] Impulse.

It was in 1913 that Mr. Woods suggested to Mr. Griffith the value of the Dixon book as a feature picture.

A year or so before, based on a scenario by Mr. Woods, the Kinemacolor people had made what was called a *Clansman* film.

But the picture was so bad, from the difficulties of photography and lack of discriminating direction, that it was never assembled for exhibition.

Griffith inclined to the idea and reread the book and—but here is his own little story of the undertaking:

"When Mr. Woods suggested *The Clansman* to me as a subject it hit me hard; I hoped at once that it could be done, for the story of the South had been absorbed into the very fiber of my being.

"Mr. Dixon wrote to me suggesting the project, and I reread the book at once.

"There had been a picture made by another concern, but this had been a failure; as the theme developed in my mind, it fascinated me until I arrived at the point where I had to make the picture; if I had known that the result would mean disaster I do not think it would have mattered to me; truly I never was sure that the result would be a success; that first night showing at the Auditorium, if anyone had offered me just a shade over what it had cost, I would have taken the money just as quickly as I could reach for it.

"There were several months lost in the negotiations for the rights, as by that time other producers had gained the same idea, like myself, undeterred by one failure having already been made.

"As I studied the book, stronger and stronger came to work the traditions I had learned as a child, all that my father had told me. That sword I told you about became a flashing vision. Gradually came back to my memory the stories a cousin, one Thurston Griffith, had told me of the Ku Klux Klan, and that regional impulse that comes to all men from the earth where they had their being stirred potently at my imagination.

"But there was nothing of personal exhilaration required to make a picture out of that theme; few others like it in subject and power can be found, for it had all the deep incisive emotionalism of the highest patriotic sentiment.

"I wouldn't say that the story part of that picture can ever be excelled, but as for the picture itself, there will be others made that will make it appear archaic in comparison.

"For the feaure picture has just begun to come into its own; my personal idea is that the minor pictures have had their day; the two- and three- and four-reel ones are passing, if not gone.

"As I worked, the commercial side of the venture was lost to my view; I felt driven to tell the story—the truth about the South, touched by its eternal romance which I had learned to know so well.

"I may be pardoned for saying that now I believe I did succeed in a measure in accomplishing that ambition.

"It all grew as we went! I had no scenario, and never looked again at some few notes I made as I read the book, and which I read to my company before we began. Naturally the whole story was firmly in my mind, and possibly the personal exuberance of which I have told you enabled me to amplify and to implant in the scenes something of the deep feeling I experienced in that epoch that had meant everything, and then had left nothing to my nearest, my kin, and those about me.

"There was not a stage star in my company; 'Little Colonel' Walthall had been out with Henry Miller, and had achieved some reputation, though by no means of stellar sort. Possibly he felt a bit of the impulse of locality, for his father was a Confederate colonel.

"Miriam Cooper, the elder Cameron sister, was a perfect type of the beauty prevalent below the Mason-and-Dixon line, and Mae Marsh was from the same part of the [country], while Spottiswoode Aitken— Dr. Cameron—was related to a large group of distinguished Southern families.

"These people were not picked because of place of birth or of their personal feeling about the story; still, it was a fortunate incident that they were what they were; it is hard to figure exactly how far what is bred in the bone will shine through the mind.

"The casting frankly was all done by types; Miss Cooper, for instance, I kept in the company for all the months between the idea that I might make the picture until the work began, because I knew she would be an exact Cameron girl.

"Every one of the cast proved to be exactly what was required.

"When I chose Lillian Gish as Stoneman's daughter, she seemed as ideal for the role as she actually proved herself to be in her acting. Mae Marsh had driven her quality so thoroughly into the estimation of the public in *The Escape* that I felt absolutely sure of her results. It was the same with Robert Harron and Elmer Clifton, for Stoneman's sons, and Ralph Lewis as Stoneman lived exactly up to what his personality promised when he was selected. And there were George Siegmann, the mulatto lieutenant-governor, and Walter Long as the awful Negro Gus, and Mary Alden, Stoneman's mulatto housekeeper.

"There has been question as to why I did not pick real Negroes or mulattos for those three roles.

"That matter was given consideration, and on careful weighing of every detail concerned, the decision was to have no black blood among the principals; it was only in the legislative scene that Negroes were used, and then only as 'extra people.'

"There were six weeks of rehearsals before we really began. I think it took something like six months to make the picture—that is, the actual photography; but in all I put in a year and a half of work.

"It was a big venture in numbers at that time; I suppose from first to last we used from 30,000 to 35,000 people.

"That seemed immense at that era, but now, in the piece we temporarily call *The Mother and the Law* [Mr. Griffith's huge new feature, . . . named *Intolerance*], we have used since the first of January about 15,000 people a month, (this statement was made in the latter part of April), and I cannot see even the beginning of the end as yet.

"With *The Clansman* it was not alone the first expense, but the incessant fighting we had to do to keep the picture going, that cost.

"We spent over $250,000 the first six months, combatting stupid persecution brought against the picture by ill-minded censors and politicians who were playing for the Negro vote.

"Lawyers had to be retained at every place we took the picture, and we paid out enough in rents for theaters where we were not allowed to show the picture to make an average film profitable.

"But we finally won.

"Now we are showing the picture with no hindrance, and most of those who opposed us at first are now either admirers of the picture or quiescent.

"While on this censorship, this drooling travesty of sense, I want to say something that I have said before, but which is essential to a right understanding of my purposes and work.

"The foremost educators of the country have urged upon moving-picture producers to put away the slapstick comedies, the ridiculous sentimental 'mush' stories, the imitation of the fiction of the cheap magazines and go into the fields of history for our subjects.

"They have told us repeatedly that the motion picture can impress upon a people as much of the truth of history in an evening as many months of study will accomplish. As one eminent divine said of pictures, 'They teach history by lightning!'

"We would like very much to do this, but the very reason for the slapstick and the worst that is in pictures is censorship. Let those who tell us to uplift our art invest money in the production of a historic play of the life of Christ. They will find that this cannot be staged without incurring the wrath of a certain part of our people. 'The Massacre of St. Bartholomew,' if reproduced, will cut off the toes of another part of our people.

"I was considering the production in pictures of the history of the American people. This got into the papers. From all over the country I was strongly advised that this was not the time for a picture on the American Revolution, because the English and their sympathizers would not take kindly to the part the English played in the War of the American Revolution, and that the pro-Germans would not care to see the Hessians enact their harsh roles in the narrative of our freedom.

"Bernard Shaw spoke fatefully and factfully when he said: 'The danger of the cinema is not the danger of immorality, but of morality; people who, like myself, frequent the cinemas testify to their desolating romantic morality.'"

"Do you anticipate a similar fight when your *Mother and the Law* picture is produced?" Griffith was asked.

"That depends upon what degree of success I achieve in my efforts to portray Truth in the picture."

That remark sounds as if it had been made by Columbus, Socrates, Christ, Galileo, Robert Emmett, Joan of Arc, Guttenberg, and the others of the holy and noble army of martyrs of sodden, stupid, bleareyed disgust at Truth, inevitably frowned at first by the mass of human-kind.

After all Mr. Griffith only uttered a commonplace.

Try it yourself! If you have a glimmering of a great fact, if you can prove that a certain line of thought or action has been wrong, pitch your truth to the world and then turn tail and run like hell fire, or you will be immersed in that very same!

"If I approach success in what I am trying to do in my coming picture," continued the creator, "I expect a persecution even greater than that which met *The Birth of a Nation*."

Out and about Los Angeles, people still talk about the making of *The Clansman*.

Some of Griffith's stockholders also still talk and mourn over his exactitude—and its cost.

Something over 150,000 feet of negative was exposed in the making of this, and of this about 30,000 was "assembled for the making of the thirteen reels," from which the final production—less than 12,000 feet —was selected.

All the technical science used was Griffith's own devising. A new feature was the taking of battle scenes at night by the use of deftly placed artificial lights. These scenes look simple enough in the picture, but they were the object of repeated experiments and they caused all manner of excitement; the light illuminated the skies, and the explosions were the basis for many interesting rumors of foreign fleets attacking the California coast.

Watching D. W. Griffith Shoot
THE BIRTH OF A NATION
SELWYN A. STANHOPE

◆◇◆

In every branch of industry there is some one man who towers above all others. Usually he is an innovator. Often his ideas were so new, until he had proved them, that they seemed ridiculous to his rivals. And only repeated successes have made his name an established trademark of individuality and excellence. Such a man is David W. Griffith.

From "The World's Master Picture Producer," by Selwyn Stanhope, The Photoplay Magazine 7 *(January 1915): 57–62. Published with the permission of* Photoplay Magazine, *a Macfadden-Bartell publication.*

Though almost unknown to the millions of movie fans throughout the world, David W. Griffith is not only the peer of the photoplay producers of the world, but also the founder of modern motion-picture technique. For more than six years he has been contributing to the public's incessant demand for an ever-changing array of motion-picture entertainment. He is directly responsible for a greater number of photo dramas than any other man in the world. During the very short time that he has been experimenting with the possibilities of the new art he has accomplished a multitude of amazingly big things. If you were measuring the films in miles, you would find them long enough to girdle the globe a number of times. But mere quantity is beside the point. It is quality that has made Mr. Griffith's reputation.

I have talked with more than a hundred men who are big in the realm of the movies and I have yet to hear one man deny David W. Griffith the right to be known as the world's foremost director of motion-picture plays, be it either drama or comedy. . . .

Director Griffith is one of those strange combinations, a realist in action and a mystic in temperament, who sees clearly the beauty about him and can transfer his artistic impressions to others because of that side of him which is eminently practical. He was a playwright by tendency, an actor by opportunity, and he became a motion-picture actor and director by force of circumstance. He would have succeeded as a dramatist—he was valiantly working toward that end in spite of hunger and the need of clothes—but, while he was looking out of the front door for histrionic fame to drive up in a coach and four, there came a modest knock at the back door, and a poor, little, ragged, half-starved new art was there begging for a wee bit of stimulus and a spark of the fire of genius to keep it from freezing to death. That half-starved new art was the motion-picture play. It was a most fortunate day indeed when David W. Griffith was forced to listen to it. . . .

As this is being written he is engaged in producing *The Clansman,* by Thomas W. Dixon. If my readers could gain admittance to the big lot across from the Mutual studio on Sunset Boulevard, Los Angeles, he would probably see a whole line of little Negro cabins of befo' the war days, and more than a hundred colored and white people mingling about waiting for Director Griffith to start things.

A good-natured roar comes from the middle of the crowd. One turns to look upon a tattered straw hat, from under the edge of which protrudes a big, commanding nose. He sits on a wooden platform with a megaphone to his lips, and begins wheedling, coaxing, and joshing his actors up to dramatic heights they do not realize themselves.

No scenario, no notes are in his hands as he works. He has studied his production thoroughly before starting the company on it. He directs with his right hand, which always clutches a huge, black, burned-out cigar. He always has the cigar. He lights it after breakfast and it does for all day. In his left hand he holds a megaphone. He waves either cigar or megaphone at his people and they obey. That cigar serves him as the baton serves an orchestra director.

For *The Clansman* he built two villages. One depicts a Southern village during the Reconstruction period, showing a street lined with houses and a church in the background. Foliage and flowers have been transplanted to places along a picket fence and they look as if they had been growing there for years; the village itself looks as if it had been standing for years, though the paint is scarcely dry.

In this street the visitor will see old-fashioned street lamps, the hitching posts and racks of the old days. When this village is peopled with film actors and actresses in suitable costumes, one is transported back to the days of the period and feels the atmosphere of it. Because of this atmosphere thus created, better work is done.

The other village is a group of negroes' cabins, the negroes' quarters of the Old South. Director Griffith was producing a scene here when first I saw him. Two hundred people were before him; two hundred more were behind the ropes watching. Negroes of every age were at work rehearsing. Mule carts were being driven back and forth. Banjo players were there, barefooted negro dancers, old colored men, picka-ninnies under foot. His eyes watched them all.

And the methods that make him a $100,000-a-year director are as characteristic as the man. He sits in a chair on a little platform in front and a little to the side of the camera, wearing a tattered straw hat, his cigar and his megaphone in action. A half-dozen negro boys are "act-ing" in the foreground. He doesn't scream to them that that will not do. His hand dives into his pocket; it comes forth full of dimes. He tosses a dozen into the group.

"Scramble for 'em!" he calls. "That's it! Laugh and cut up! Now, there's another dime for each of you if you do it again, and do it right. That's it!"

Then his eye travels two hundred feet away, the megaphone comes to his lips:

"Out a little more back there! Hit it up, Bill! You two men near the cabin get to dancing! That's it!"

Back to the foreground again:

"Take the hat off that banjo player—it shades his face. Now—all ready! Dance, there—dance! That's it! You children run right back through the crowd now. You white folks come up to the center! You— in that chair! Put back your head—go to sleep and snore!"

It is a real snore that answers him. The snore is not depicted on the film, of course, but it gives atmosphere, and that is worth its weight in gold. And these details are not in the scenario.

Now he looks down the street and spies an aged negro man. The camera has ceased to whirr. That particular scene is finished. He sends a subdirector for the old darky, looks him over from head to foot and smiles. He has found a type.

This aged negro, who is but an extra, has struck Director Griffith's eye. He is "made," though he doesn't know it yet. He is placed in the foreground with the dancers. The music and the dancing begin again. Griffith tells the cameraman to get busy. The aged negro dreams of the days of his youth. He dances better than the young men. He dances the old plantation steps. He pats the top of his bald head with the palm of his hand. He forgets he is working before a movie camera— he is back in the old days and these folk around him are his people.

Wait until you see *The Clansman* and you'll see the aged negro dancing up to the front of the screen, the look of enthusiasm on his face. If you didn't know you would say he was a great actor. But he isn't. He isn't an actor at all. He is simply an old negro living over again the days of his youth, the spirit of youth dragged from him again by the genius of D. W. Griffith—and that is why that particular scene will be so effective.

Even in early Biograph days Director Griffith much preferred the untrained actor with talent to the actor with a reputation, and many interesting stories are told by those who were associated with him at the Biograph studio regarding the methods used to make his people rise to sufficient heights of emotion during the playing of their first important parts. As illustrated by the old darky incident, Director Griffith's ability to make people act approaches real genius, and he will go to almost any length to get an actor to give him the effect demanded.

In the early days of Mary Pickford's career, when she was engaged to her present husband, Owen Moore, who was working with her in Biograph productions, Director Griffith would charge Moore with lack of intelligence. Miss Pickford, you must remember, was only a child —just sixteen years old. She would lose her temper and become angry. Then he would turn quickly to the cameraman and whisper, "Go ahead! Grind!"

The result was always an exhibition of temperament on the part of "Little Mary" that exactly fitted the character she was portraying. *Wilful Betty,* a Mary Pickford-Biograph revival, was made under such circumstances.

Some insight into the secret of Director Griffith's success may, perhaps, be gained by noting that although he demands the hardest kind of work from his players and is most exacting during the making of a picture, the regard in which he is held by them amounts almost to worship. It is not unusual to hear his people, by whom he is affectionately called "Larry," claim that he is the greatest man this country has produced.

And here another incident of the visit to the Mutual studio comes to my mind, one which illustrates just why his people love him. Miss Mae Marsh was standing near him just before he gave the cameraman the word to start grinding. Calling her to him, he commanded:

"Look down the line and see what you think of it!" He knew that four eyes, in matters of that kind, were better than two. I think he told her so at the time.

Miss Marsh suggested that the clothes of one of the darkies looked too new and unsoiled.

"That's right," shouted Director Griffith. "Go get some older-looking clothes!" he commanded the negro.

"Anything else, Miss Marsh?" he asked.

Someone else whispered that the insignia on one of the officers' uniforms was not correct. The military expert was called, the mistake corrected, and other mistakes in detail were looked for. Two or three changes here and there, all at the suggestion of his players, and the scene was begun. You see, though he gets $100,000 a year he takes advice and suggestions from anyone from the office boy to the "stars." This advice is applied scientifically, and he doesn't waste many seconds applying it. That's why he is valuable and successful, why his players love him, why his films are different, and finally, why he is the highest-paid and most-talked-of man in all filmdom.

THE BIRTH OF A NATION: An Editorial

◆◆◆

Several years ago a "professional southerner" named Dixon wrote a sensational and melodramatic novel which has been widely read.

From The Crisis *10 (May–June 1915): 33. Reprinted by permission of the publisher. Title supplied.*

Eight years ago Dixon brought out his novel as a sordid and lurid melodrama. In several cities the performance of this play was prohibited because of its indecency or incitement to riot. Recently this vicious play has been put into moving pictures. With great adroitness the real play is preceded by a number of marvelously good war pictures; then in the second part comes the real *Clansman* with the Negro represented either as an ignorant fool, a vicious rapist, a venal and unscrupulous politician or a faithful but doddering idiot. By curious procedure this film received the preliminary approval of the National Board of Censors. It was put on in Los Angeles and immediately the fine organization of the N.A.A.C.P. was manifest. The facts were telegraphed to us from our Los Angeles Branch. We started at the Board of Censors. The proprietors of the film fought madly but the Censors met, viewed the film and immediately withdrew their sanction. Many of them were astonished that any committee of their board had ever passed it. The owners of the film promised to modify it but the modifications were unimportant. Yet this remarkable Board of Censors met a third time and passed the film over the protests of a minority of nine persons. Among these nine, however, was the chairman and founder of the board, Frederick C. Howe, Commissioner of Immigration at the Port of New York and several others equally influential. In other words, the board of censorship is now practically split in two. The Association was not discouraged but immediately took steps on the one hand to bring the matter into court and on the other hand to interview the mayor. The interview with the mayor was after some difficulty arranged. The delegation of five hundred of the most prominent white and colored people in the city filled the Council Chamber at City Hall and for an hour in terse, tense speeches urged the mayor to act. The mayor promised to have the two rape scenes cut out immediately and to go further than this if the play still seemed objectionable from the point of view of public peace and decency.

This action while commendable is not sufficient. The whole second half of the play ought to be suppressed and the Association will continue to work to this end. It is gratifying to know that in this work we have the cordial co-operation of all elements of colored people. The New York *Age* and the CRISIS worked hand in hand with Harlem. Brooklyn and Jersey City. We know no factions in the righting of this great wrong.

It is sufficient to add that the main incident in *The Clansman* turns on a thinly veiled charge that Thaddeus Stephens [*sic*], the great abolition statesman, was induced to give the Negroes the right to vote and secretly rejoice in Lincoln's assassination because of his infatuation for a mulatto mistress. Small wonder that a man who can thus brutally falsify history has never been able to do a single piece of literary work that has brought the slightest attention, except when he seeks to capitalize burning race antagonisms.

Fighting Race Calumny

◈◈

February 12–26

We are advised by our Los Angeles Branch that *The Birth of a Nation,* a picture play founded on Dixon's *Clansman,* is running in that city and that the branch has been unable to suppress the play because it has the approval of the National Board of Censorship, located in New York.

Advance announcement of this performance in New York appears in the local press.

We go to the office of the Board of Censorship and request:

The names of the committee who approved the picture so that we may ascertain its character from someone who has seen it; the names and addresses of the National Board of Censorship; a list of the cities where the film has been released; the possibility of arranging for an advance performance when the film could be reviewed by the entire Board of Censorship and a committee from our Association.

The office of the Board of Censorship reply that there is nothing objectionable in the picture and refuse to give us the names of any of the committee who have approved it. They also refuse the addresses of members of their board and advise us not to communicate with them. They say that since the picture has been passed by the Board, no advance preformance can be arranged in New York and nothing can be done about it.

We appeal to the Chairman of the National Board of Censorship, Mr. Frederic C. Howe, for an advance performance and it is arranged.

February 27

We write a letter to the members of the National Board of Censorship stating our position in regard to the picture.

From The Crisis 10 *(May–June 1915):* 40–42, 87–88. *Reprinted by permission of the publisher.*

The National Board of Censorship and a committee from our Association are invited to attend the advance performance on March 1. We were at first promised twelve tickets; later the number is cut to two by the office of the Board of Censorship and *colored people are excluded.*

March 1

The National Board of Censorship meet after the performance and (according to their Chairman, Dr. Howe), disapprove certain incidents in the first section of the film and practically the entire second part. No communication in regard to this action is sent from the office of the Board of Censorship to the N.A.A.C.P.

March 3

The owner and producer of the film are summoned by the N.A.A.C.P. to the Police Court on the grounds that they are maintaining a public nuisance and endangering the public peace. They are represented by Martin W. Littleton. Chief Magistrate McAdoo rules that it is not within his jurisdiction to stop the performance unless it actually leads to a breach of the peace.

March 8

We write for a statement of the disapproval of the play by the Board of Censorship. We do not get it. We request all our members in New York and vicinity to write letters of protest to the press.

March 9

We again write to the Board of Censorship for a statement of their disapproval of the film and also request a copy of the statement of release which is being sent to other cities, and a list of the states where bills for public censors are pending.

We are advised by a member of the Board of Censorship that the action of the Board on March 1 in disapproving the film was not official. No communication on the subject comes from the office of the Board.

March 10

Prominent members of our Association, Mr. Jacob H. Schiff, Miss Jane Addams, Dr. Jacques Loeb, Miss Lillian D. Wald, as well as several prominent white Southerners, see the play. All agree in condemning it.

March 10

The National Association brings criminal proceedings against Aitken and Griffith, owner and producer of the film, and retains James W. Osborne as attorney.

March 11

We send a letter to the moving picture trade calling their attention to the action of Aitken and Griffith in producing this play after it has been disapproved by the National Board of Censorship.

March 12

We appeal to the Commissioner of Licenses to stop the performance under that section of the penal code which applies to public nuisances.

We are advised that the Board of Censorship is seeing the play in its revised form. We attend the same performance and find that only slight changes have been made.

March 13

Miss Jane Addams who has witnessed the play at our request, gives an exclusive interview condemning it to the *Evening Post*, which is sent out by the National Association to the press of the country. None of the New York papers carried this except the *Post* which, we understand, is the only paper in New York that has refused the advertising for *The Birth of a Nation*.

March 15

We are officially advised by the office of the National Board of Censorship that the film has been approved by the Board. Some of the members present tell us that the producer was even cheered when he came into the room.

March 16

We are asked by the Board of Censorship to retract our letter sent to the moving picture trade. We do not.

We request of the Board of Censorship the addresses of their committees and again ask for a list of the cities where the film has been released and a list of states where bills for public censors are pending. We do not get this information.

March 19

We write the Mayor requesting him to use his authority to suppress the play as an offense against public decency and as endangering public morals; also on the ground that the effect of the picture is likely to lead to a breach of the peace.

March 23

A review of the play in the *New Republic* for March 20 published under the title "Brotherly Love," [1] is mailed by the N.A.A.C.P. for editorial comment to five hundred newspapers.

March 24

The New York press breaks its silence by publishing the "story" of the split on the Board of Censorship over the vote on this film.

March 26

We are advised by the Mayor that he will receive a delegation from our Association. We invite all churches, clubs, and organizations interested, in New York and vicinity, to unite with us in appearing at this hearing.

March 27

We attempt to arrange a procession to the Mayor's office. License is refused on the ground that it might lead to a breach of the peace.

March 29

The National American Woman Suffrage Association refuses to co-operate with the National Board of Censorship in working against the bill for a public censor pending in Pennsylvania, because of the action of the Board on this play.

March 30

Hearing before the Mayor with following speakers: Dr. Frederic C. Howe, Chairman of the National Board of Censorship; Dr. William H. Brooks, Pastor of St. Mark's M. E. Church; Dr. W. E. B. Du Bois, Editor of the CRISIS; Dr. Stephen S. Wise, Rabbi of the Free Synagogue; Mr. Fred R. Moore, Editor of the *New York Age;* Mr. George E. Wibecan, President of the Brooklyn Citizens' Club; and Mr. Oswald Garrison Villard, President of the New York *Evening Post* Company, and Vice President of the N.A.A.C.P.

The following organizations were represented: The colored and white ministry of Greater New York, the Citizens' Club of Brooklyn, the Committee of One Hundred of Hudson County, N.J., the National League of Urban Conditions Among Negroes, the United Civic League, the Columbus Hill Civic League, and the Northeastern Federation of Women's Clubs.

The Mayor told the delegation which overflowed the Council Cham-

---

[1] [Editor's note: See this volume, pp. 84-86.]

ber that he had seen the film and that he agreed with all that had been said about it. He felt that it might perhaps incite to breaches of the peace and had already so advised the management of the theatre and the owners of the film; the latter had consented to cut out the two scenes which had been particularly objected to and the play would be produced in that form for the first time that night. This, the Mayor was careful to say, had been done without any attempt on his part to exercise any power he might be given by statute. The breadth and force of such powers were in doubt, he said, but if it was found necessary to take the matter up again he would take such steps as were authorized by law.

March 31

We adjourn our legal case with the idea of discontinuing it if the changes promised by the Mayor are made in the film.

April 1

We see the play in its second revised form and find again that only unimportant changes have been made and that the two particularly objectionable scenes still remain the motif of the second part.

We again appeal to the Mayor calling his attention to the fact that these scenes which he promised the delegation should be eliminated have not been cut out.

April 2

Miss Rosalie Jonas, a native of New Orleans, with other prominent Suffragists in New York, file a protest with the Mayor against the play.

We are advised by the Mayor that he has been assured by the producers of the film that they will meet his wishes in the matter of elision.

PART II

We gave last month a chronology of the fight of the National Association for the Advancement of Colored People against Tom Dixon's latest libel. This is a continuation of that narrative.

The Birth of a Nation is now being shown in New York, Boston, Los Angeles, San Francisco, and is booked for Chicago for the summer. In each place our branches have protested. In Los Angeles they got no results. In San Francisco a few objectionable scenes were eliminated.

In Des Moines, Iowa, the play cannot be presented because of the fact that Mr. S. Joe Brown some years ago introduced an ordinance which was passed prohibiting plays arousing race feeling.

In Ohio, Cleveland and Toledo branches and other agencies co-
operating, kept out the play, *The New Governor,* and think they can
keep this out of the State.

The center of the fight has been Boston.

April 6

The film interests attack The Crisis as an "incendiary" publication.
They explain Jane Addams' criticism by declaring that she saw only
half the film, which is absolutely false; and they declare that the film
had the endorsement of the President of the United States, George
Foster Peabody, Senator Jones of Washington and others.

April 9

A hearing was held before Mayor Curley. Many prominent persons
took part. A letter to us saying:

When the hearing was over a little bout occurred between Moorfield
Storey and Griffith. It seems in the Boston papers that Griffith had
promised Mr. Storey $10,000 for any Charity he would name if he
could find a single incident in the play that was not historic. Mr.
Storey asked Mr. Griffith if it was historic that a colored lieutenant
governor had locked a white girl into a room in the Capitol and
demanded a forced marriage in South Carolina? Mr. Griffith only
answered, "Come and see the play" and held out his hand to Mr.
Storey. Mr. Storey drew back and said, "No sir," refusing to shake
hands with him.

April 15

George Foster Peabody, in a public letter, calls the film "unfair to
the Negro and to the white equally and a traversity [*sic*] on sound peace
principles." Senator Jones writes: "I never endorsed it," and con-
tinues, "the character of the second part of the play became evident
before it began and I did not stay to see it." The Rector of Trinity
Church, Boston, calls the film "untrue and unjust." Persons uncon-
nected with this organization threw rotten eggs at the screen in New
York City.

April 17

A new feature is added to the film in Boston "portraying the advance of Negro life." A prominent New York lawyer informs us that
this was done at the suggestion of Mr. Booker T. Washington. Colored
citizens of Boston are refused tickets to the first exhibition of the film.
The colored people persist in demanding tickets and eleven of them

are arrested including Mr. W. M. Trotter, editor of the *Guardian*, and the Rev. Aaron Puller. All were discharged except the two mentioned.

April 19

Great protest meeting in Faneuil Hall presided over by Frank B. Sanborn. Governor Walsh of Massachusetts promised to advocate a law which will enable such films to be suppressed.

April 20

The state police of Massachusetts refuse to permit *The Birth of a Nation* to be exhibited on Sunday.

April 21

The Massachusetts court orders elimination of the rape scene in the film. Large hearing before the legislature.

April 28

Mrs. Carter H. Harrison, wife of the former mayor of Chicago, denies that she ever approved the film. "It is the most awful thing I have seen. It would arouse racial feeling. I am a southerner and you naturally would expect me to oppose such pictures as this."

April 29

Clergymen representing six Protestant denominations protest against the film.

April 30

The secretary to the President of the United States replying to W. H. Lewis of Boston, and to Bishop Walters, writes:

Replying to your recent letter and enclosures, I beg to say that it is true that *The Birth of a Nation* was produced before the President and his family at the White House, but the President was entirely unaware of the character of the play before it was presented and has at no time expressed his approbation of it. Its exhibition at the White House was a courtesy extended to an old acquaintance.

A committee of the Massachusetts legislature reports a bill which is a compromise between several proposals. This bill places unlimited powers of censorship in the hands of the Mayor, the police commissioner and the chief justice of the municipal court. This bill has passed the lower House and is before the Senate.

May 2

Mass meeting of 2,500 persons at Tremont Temple to protest against the film. Ex-President Eliot, Dr. S. M. Crothers, Dr. F. M. Rowley, Miss

Adelene Moffat and Mr. Ralph Cobleigh were among the speakers. A mass meeting was also held on Boston Common. Mr. Cobleigh declared that Dixon had told him that the object of the film was the ultimate deportation of 10,000,000 Negroes from the United States, and the repeal of the war amendments. President Eliot said that this proposal was "inconceivable and monstrous" and "an abominable outrage." He continued:

> A more dangerously false doctrine taught by the play is that the Ku-Klux-Klan was on the whole a righteous and necessary society for the defence of Southern white men against black Legislatures led by Northern white men. This is the same sort of argument being used by the Germans to-day, that a contract may be destroyed as a military necessity. Undoubtedly, grievous conditions existed in the South, but they did not justify the utter lawlessness and atrocities which marked the trail of the Ku-Klux. There can be no worse teaching, no more mischievous doctrine than this, that lawlessness is justified when necessary.

May 5

The Rev. A. W. Puller was discharged by the court while Mr. Trotter was fined for assult on a policeman, but entered an appeal. The judge blamed the ticket seller chiefly for the disturbance.

May 15
Telegram from the Chicago Branch, N.A.A.C.P.:

> *Mayor Thompson has unqualifiedly refused license to the photoplay* Birth of a Nation.

Capitalizing Race Hatred

❖❖❖

In view of the splendors of national reunion what should be the attitude of every right-minded person toward attempts to revive the passions of the Civil War period, relight the fires of sectionalism, and

From the New York Globe, *April 6, 1915.*

intensify race prejudices that are unhappily still much alive? The questions sufficiently answer themselves, and when they are answered there is no reason to ask the further question of whether it is desirable, for purely sordid reasons, to exhibit such a moving-picture film as the so called *The Birth of a Nation*.

Few of us are competent to pass judgment with respect to the tangled facts of the Reconstruction period. A fair and impartial narrative has never been written and probably never will be. But certain big facts shine out in the confusion. One is that never in human history did a victor show more consideration for the defeated. Men but lately in arms were restored to full citizenship, states in rebellion were received back in the sisterhood of the states. Let us rejoice that the Stonemans of Washington were magnanimous, but let us not dishonor ourselves by calling in question their great merit by presenting them as the paramours of quadroon mistresses, moved by petty spite. It is insulting to every man of Southern birth to assume that he is pleased by misrepresentation so colossal.

Another big fact of the Reconstruction period is that the 4,000,000 former slaves, suddenly emancipated but with no way of earning their livelihood except by working at small wages for their former masters, displayed, all things considered, the most exemplary patience. They had protected the women and children on the plantations while the struggle went on which was to decide whether they were to become men or to remain as chattels, and the great body of them continued to exhibit, under the most trying circumstances, docility and kindliness. To present the members of the race as women-chasers and foul fiends is a cruel distortion of history. Bad things occurred, but what man will say that the outrages of black on white equalled in number the outrages of white on black? Which race even to the present day has the better right to complain of the unfairness and brutality of the other?

The very name of *The Birth of a Nation* is an insult to Washington, who believed that a nation, not merely a congeries of independent states, was born during the common struggles of the Revolutionary War, and devoted himself to cementing the union. It is an insult to Lincoln and the great motives inspiring him when he was called on to resist the attempt to denationalize a nation. This nation of ours was not born between 1861 and 1865, and no one will profit from trying to pervert history.

White men in this country have never been just to black men. We tore them from Africa and brought them over as slaves. For generations they toiled without recompense that their white owners might have unearned wealth and ape the ways of aristocracy. The nation finally freed them, but has but slightly protected them in the enjoyment of the legitimate fruits of their freedom. We nominally gave them the vote, but looked on inactive when the right was invaded. We do not, in any state of the Union, grant to the Negro economic and political economy. No white man of proper feeling can be proud of the record. The wonder is that the Negro is as good as he is. Then to the injury is added slander. To make a few dirty dollars men are willing to pander to depraved tastes and to foment a race antipathy that is the most sinister and dangerous feature of American life.

Reply to the *New York Globe*
THOMAS DIXON

◆◆

Editor of the *Globe,* Sir—As a reader of your paper may I claim the courtesy of a reply to your editorial attack of yesterday on *The Birth of a Nation?*

As author of the book and play on which the larger film drama is based I accept the full moral responsibility for its purpose and its effects on an audience.

We have submitted *The Birth of a Nation* to a jury of three representative clergymen of New York—the Rev. Thomas B. Gregory, Universalist; the Rev. Charles H. Parkhurst, D.D., Presbyterian, and the Rev. John Talbot Smith, D.D., Roman Catholic, editor of *The Columbian,* organ of the Knights of Columbus.

They did not suggest a single change or cut, but fully agreed with the high praise given by the dramatic critic of the *Globe.*

They declare in substance that the play in its final impression on the audience does six things: (1) It reunites in common sympathy and love all sections of our country. (2) It teaches our boys the history of our nation in a way that makes them know the priceless inheritance our fathers gave us through the sacrifice of civil war and reconstruction. (3) It tends to prevent the lowering of the standard of our citizenship by its mixture with Negro blood. (4) It shows the horror and futility of war as a method of settling civic principles. (5) It reaffirms Lincoln's solution of the Negro problem as a possible guide to our future and

From the New York Globe, *April 10, 1915.*

glorifies his character as the noblest example of American democracy. (6) It gives to Daniel Webster for the first time his true place in American history as the inspiring creator of the modern nation we know today.

The most important point on which I take issue with your editorial is found in the sentence: "Let us rejoice that the Stonemans of Washington were magnanimous, but let us not dishonor ourselves by calling in question their great merit by presenting them as the paramours of quadroon mistresses, moved by petty spite."

Who has ever dared to declare that Thaddeus Stevens, B. F. Butler, and Benjamin Wade, the leaders of Congress during this reign of terror, were magnanimous?

Abraham Lincoln was magnanimous, and his mighty spirit brooded over the Capitol after his death pleading for generous treatment of the South.

The magnanimity extended was in spite of Stevens and his associates, not through them.

The established facts are that Stevens, who lived and died a bachelor, separated a quadroon Negress from her husband of her youth and kept her in his house for thirty-six years. For this woman he became a social outcast in Washington and at the last moment lost his place in Lincoln's cabinet, the appointment suddenly going to Simon Cameron, his rival.

He left this woman, Lydia Brown, an annuity in his will and was buried in a Negro cemetery in Lancaster, Pa., that he might sleep beside her in death.

Do you question these facts? If so, I will submit them to a jury of three historians of established character, and if they decide against me I will agree to withdraw *The Birth of a Nation* from the stage.

Was Mr. Stevens magnanimous even when the shadow of death was upon him in the last year of his life?

Read his famous bill to confiscate the remaining property of the stricken, starving South and give it to the Negroes, two years after Lee's surrender!

If you still doubt that he was ungenerous, read his awful speech in the *Congressional Record* pressing this pet measure, House Bill No. 29, to a vote. Nothing so fierce, cruel, and vindictive was ever uttered on the floor of the House of Representatives in our history, before or since.

The stricken South was only saved from this act of brutal vengeance by Mr. Stevens's death. No other man had the ability to pass such a measure.

I am not attacking the Negro of today. I am recording faithfully the history of fifty years ago. I portray three Negroes faithful unto death to every want and two vicious Negroes, misled by white scoundrels. Is it a crime to present a bad black man, seeing we have so many bad white ones?

Reply to the New York Globe
D. W. GRIFFITH

◆◆◆

Editor of the *Globe*, Sir—In an editorial in your issue of April 6, 1915, under the heading: "Capitalizing Race Hatred," you undertake to label our picture *The Birth of a Nation* with alleged feelings of sectional difference between the North and South. You ask yourself questions and proceed to answer them in the same old way that the same things have been gone over and over again. Where I must take issue with you is that you intimate that these old differences have been raised and exhibited "for purely sordid reasons," to quote your own words.

In presenting this motion-picture story before the intelligent theatergoers of New York City, in a regular theater, which has been well advertised, I thought the moving drama told its own story. My associates have maintained a dignified silence in the face of an organized attack of letter writers, publicity seekers, and fanatics against our work. We have traced this attack to its source, and know the reasons for it. Without wishing to tell any newspaper its business, permit me to suggest that a cub reporter in one hour could find out that this attack is an organized effort to suppress a production which was brought forth to reveal the beautiful possibilities of the art of motion pictures and to tell a story which is based upon truth in every vital detail. Our story states, as plainly as the English language can express a fact, the reasons for this presentation. In our captions we reiterate that the events depicted upon the screen are not meant as a reflection upon any race or people of today.

I demand to know the authority upon which you base your intimation that this work of art has been exhibited "for purely sordid

From the New York Globe, *April 10, 1915*.

reasons." I further demand that failing to establish this authority you retract your statement in as prominent and direct a manner as you have given publicity to the opinions of the writer of your editorial.

Our picture tells its own story and we are willing to stand upon the verdict of the New York public as to the fitness of this work of art to be judged as a drama of action based upon the authenticated history of the period covering the action of our plot.

The succeeding paragraphs of your editorial are political generalities which have nothing in common with the truths and purposes of the motion picture, *The Birth of a Nation.* Our picture does show historic events which you undertake to use for an entirely different argument. We have contrasted the bad with the good and following the formula of the best dramas of the world we establish our ideals by revealing the victory of right over wrong.

I do not agree with your statements regarding the history of slavery and the Reconstruction period of this nation, but that is not a matter of importance in this connection. Most well-informed men know now that slavery was an economic mistake. The treatment of the Negroes during the days of Reconstruction is shown effectually and graphically in our picture. We show many phases of the question and we do pay particular attention to those faithful Negroes who stayed with their former masters and were ready to give up their lives to protect their white friends. No characters in the story are applauded with greater fervor than the good Negroes whose devotion is so clearly shown. If prejudiced witnesses do not see the message in this portion of the entire drama we are not to blame.

Your editorial is an insult to the intelligence and the human kindness of nearly 100,000 of the best people in New York City, who have viewed this picture from artistic interests and not through any depraved taste such as you try to indicate. Among those you have insulted are your contemporaries on the newspapers of New York, whose expert reviewers were unanimous in their praise of this work as an artistic achievement. Included in this list is your own able critic, Mr. Louis Sherwin, of the *Globe.*

We have received letters of the heartiest commendation from statesmen, writers, clergymen, artists, educators, and laymen. I have in my possession applications for reservations from the principals of ten schools, who having seen the picture, are desirous of bringing their pupils to view it for its historic truths.

The Rev. Dr. Charles H. Parkhurst,[1] the Rev. Father John Talbot Smith, and the Rev. Thomas B. Gregory are among the clergy who have given us permission to use their names in approval of this picture

---

[1] [Editor's note: See this volume, pp. 102–3.]

in its entirety. Parents have asked us to make reservation for them that they may bring their children to see it. In every walk of life there are men and women of this city who have expressed their appreciation of this picture. Do you dare to intimate that these voluntary expressions of approval were voiced "for purely sordid reasons"?

The attack of the organized opponents to this picture is centered upon that feature of it which they deem might become an influence against the intermarriage of blacks and whites. The organizing opponents are white leaders of the National Association for the Advancement of the Colored People, including Oswald Garrison Villard and J. E. Spingarn, who hold official positions in this prointermarriage organization.

May I inquire if you desire to espouse the cause of a society which openly boasts in its official organ, *The Crisis,* that it has been able to throttle "anti-intermarriage legislation" in over ten states? Do you know what this society means by "anti-intermarriage legislation"? It means that they successfully opposed bills which were framed to prohibit the marriage of Negroes to whites.

Do you know that in their official organ, *The Crisis,* for March, 1915, they brand 238 members of the Sixty-Third Congress as "Negro baiters" because these Representatives voted to prohibit the marriage of Negroes to whites in the District of Columbia?

You close your editorial, in which by inuendo you link our picture to your own assertions, with this sentence:

"To make a few dirty dollars, men are willing to pander to depraved tastes and to foment a race antipathy that is the most sinister and dangerous feature of American life."

That statement is obviously a generality, but it is printed at the end of an editorial which is a covert attack upon our picture, *The Birth of a Nation.* As the producer of that picture, I wish to say if the man who wrote it meant one iota of the sentence just quoted to apply to our picture he is a liar and a coward.

Whether this was the intent of the sentence quoted it could not fail to create an impression in the minds of your readers, damaging my reputation as a producer. Therefore, as a matter of justice, I ask that you publish my statement of the facts.

Why I Oppose THE BIRTH OF A NATION
ROLFE COBLEIGH

◆◆

I, Rolfe Cobleigh, of Newton, in the County of Middlesex and Commonwealth of Massachusetts, being duly sworn depose and say, that:

I am associate editor of *The Congregationalist and Christian World,* published at 14 Beacon St., Boston, where our offices are located.

My attention was attracted to the moving-picture play entitled, *The Birth of a Nation,* by editorials which appeared in the New York *World,* the New York *Evening Post,* the New York *Globe,* and other newspapers condemning the production when it was first shown in New York. Several of my friends, who saw the show in New York, soon reported to me their disapproval on the grounds that it incited race prejudice against the Negro race, that it glorified lynching and falsified history. Influenced by this evidence I wrote a letter to Mr. D. W. Griffith, who was advertised as the producer of the film, and protested against the exhibition of such a series of moving pictures as these were represented to be. I received in reply a letter from Mr. Thomas Dixon, whose interest in *The Birth of a Nation* was indicated by the paper upon which he wrote, the letterhead being printed with the words: "Thomas Dixon's Theatrical Enterprises," under which was *"The Birth of a Nation,* with D. W. Griffith," following the titles of five other plays written by Mr. Dixon. He said in the letter referring to "our picture": "The only objection to it so far is a Negro society which advises its members to arm themselves to fight the whites." He also wrote that Rev. Charles H. Parkhurst, D.D., was "making a report on this work," and that if I would "await Dr. Parkhurst's report" he would send it to me. This letter was dated March 27.

Under date of April 3, I wrote in reply: "I shall await Dr. Parkhurst's report, which you say you will send me, with interest." I asked

From Fighting a Vicious Film: Protest Against *The Birth of a Nation* (*Boston: Boston Branch of the National Association for the Advancement of Colored People, 1915*). *Title supplied.*

for the name of "a Negro society which advises its members to arm themselves to fight the whites."

Mr. Dixon wrote again under date of April 5, enclosing Dr. Parkhurst's report of which he said: "As this letter has been forwarded to Mayor Curley by Dr. Parkhurst I will appreciate it if you will publish it in *The Congregationalist,* with any comment you may make. Also Dr. Gregory's letter except one clause." Both the Parkhurst and Gregory letters were in approval of *The Birth of a Nation.* Mr. Dixon referred to his opponents as a "Negro intermarriage society," a term used in Mr. Gregory's letter to Mayor Curley and he gave the name of the organization as the National Association for the Advancement of Colored People, and suggested that it might produce a play to answer him, and that, "The silly legal opposition they are giving will make me a millionaire if they keep it up." I did not reply to this letter.

On the morning of April 9, 1915, Thomas Dixon called at my office and I had a long talk with him about *The Birth of a Nation.* He tried to convince me that it deserved my approval. He referred especially to the favorable reports of Dr. Parkhurst and Mr. Gregory. Mr. Dixon asked what I thought of Dr. Parkhurst's approval of the play. I replied that the evidence which had come to me was so strongly against the play that I was not influenced by Dr. Parkhurst, but that I would try to judge the play impartially when I saw it. He talked at length with reference to the artistic and dramatic merits of the play and of its value for the teaching of history, and ridiculed those who disapproved it. In reply to my questions with reference to the treatment of the Negro race in the play, he said that the subject was a debate, that he presented one side and that those who disagreed were at liberty to present the other side.

Mr. Dixon admitted that some of the scenes as originally presented in New York were too strongly suggestive of immorality and that he told Mr. Griffith they went too far.

I asked Mr. Dixon what his real purpose was in having *The Birth of a Nation* produced, what he hoped to accomplish by it. He began to read from the copy of Thomas B. Gregory's letter to Mayor Curley six things that Mr. Gregory said the play did in its effect on an audience. I interrupted to say, "Yes, but what is your chief purpose, what do you really want to accomplish through the influence of this play?" He replied in substance that he wanted to teach the people of the United States, especially the children, that the true history of the Reconstruction period was as it was represented in *The Birth of a Nation.* He said that in the play he presented the historical fact that Thaddeus Stevens became dictator of the United States government immediately after the death of President Lincoln, and that he appeared in the play under the name of Stoneman. Mr. Dixon said that one purpose in the play was to suggest Stevens' immorality in his relationship to his colored mistress for many years. He said the alleged sensual character of this woman, who in the play is called "Lydia Brown, Stoneman's mulatto housekeeper," was emphasized. Mr. Dixon described bad conditions in the South during the Reconstruction period, alleging that the Negroes gained control politically incited chiefly by Thaddeus Stevens, that the white Southerners were insulted, assaulted, robbed, and disfranchised and that white girls and women were in constant danger of assault by colored men. He emphasized the alleged dominant passion of colored men to have sexual relations with white women and said that one purpose in his play was to create a feeling of abhorrence in white people, especially white women against colored men. Mr. Dixon said that his desire was to prevent the mixing of white and Negro blood by intermarriage. I asked him what he had to say about the mixing of the blood outside marriage and if it was not true that white men had forced their sexual relations upon colored girls and women all through the period of slavery, thus begetting children of mixed blood outside marriage, and if it was not true, as I am creditably informed, that such conditions prevail to a wide extent even among white men who occupy high social and political positions in the South today.

Mr. Dixon hesitated and finally answered that there was less of such conditions than there had been. Mr. Dixon said that the Ku Klux Klan was formed to protect the white women from Negro men, to restore order, and to reclaim political control for the white people of the South. He said that the Ku Klux Klan was not only engaged in restoring law and order, but was of a religious nature, as represented in the play, having religious ceremonies and using the symbol of the cross. He said that the best white men of the South were in it, that Mr. Dixon's father was a Baptist minister in North Carolina and left his church to join the Ku Klux Klan, and that he remained with the organization until it was disbanded.

I asked Mr. Dixon what solution of the race problem he presented in *The Birth of a Nation* and he replied that his solution was Lincoln's plan. He said this was the colonization of the Negroes in Africa or South America, which he said President Lincoln favored during the last of the Civil War. Mr. Dixon said that he wished to have that plan carried out, that he wished to have all Negroes removed from the United States and that he hoped to help in the accomplishment of that purpose by *The Birth of a Nation*.

I suggested the difficulty of getting ten million people out of the country, and asked if he seriously advocated such a scheme. He replied with great earnestness that he did, that it was possible to create public sentiment such that a beginning could be made in the near future, that a large faction of the Negroes themselves would cooperate in the enterprise and that within a century we could get rid of all Negroes.

Mr. Dixon informed me that the first presentation of *The Birth of a Nation* in Boston would be given that evening for censorship before the mayor and other city officials and newspaper critics and gave me two tickets for that exhibition. He said that in anticipation of a hostile demonstration he and his associates would have thirteen Pinkertons scattered through the audience at the first performance and that as many or more Pinkertons would be employed in the Tremont Theater at the exhibitions that would follow in Boston, with orders to rush anyone into the street instantly who started any disturbance. He said that he had feared there would be trouble in New York and that many Pinkertons were employed when the show was presented in New York, but that up to the time I saw Mr. Dixon there had been no disturbance in the Liberty Theater, where the play was presented in New York. Mr. Dixon said that he owned a one-fourth interest in the "Birth of a Nation" Company.

I asked Mr. Dixon to what cities the show would be taken next and he replied that all plans had been held up until they knew the result of the protests in Boston. He said he regarded Boston as the critical point for their enterprise, that it was more likely to object to such a play than any other city and that he and his associates believe that if they could get by in Boston they would be able to go anywhere else in the country with the show without trouble.

As he went away he asked me to let him know what I thought of the play after I had seen it and expressed the hope that I would approve it.

I saw *The Birth of a Nation* that evening, April 9, and saw it again three weeks later, after omissions had been made to comply with the decision of Judge Dowd. I have expressed my disapproval of *The Birth of a Nation*, following each view of it on the grounds of falsifying history, in a riot of emotions glorifying crime, especially lynching, immorality, inviting prejudice against the Negro race, falsely representing the character of colored Americans, and teaching the undemocratic, unchristian, and unlawful doctrine that all colored people should be removed from the United States. I especially disapprove the play because Mr. Dixon frankly explained to me that his purpose in the play was to promote a propaganda with the desire to accomplish the results that I have stated.

ROLFE COBLEIGH

Personally appeared Rolfe Cobleigh and made oath to the truth of the foregoing affidavit by him subscribed before me in Boston, Massachusetts, this 26th day of May, A.D. 1915.

GEORGE R. BRACKETT,
Notary Public

Brotherly Love

FRANCIS HACKETT

◆◆

If history bore no relation to life, this motion-picture drama could well be reviewed and applauded as a spectacle. As a spectacle it is stupendous. It lasts three hours, represents a staggering investment of time and money, reproduces entire battle scenes and complex historic events, amazes even when it wearies by its attempt to encompass the Civil War. But since history does bear on social behavior, *The Birth of a Nation* cannot be reviewed simply as a spectacle. It is more than a spectacle. It is an interpretation, the Rev. Thomas Dixon's interpretation, of the relations of the North and South and their bearing on the Negro.

Were the Rev. Thomas Dixon a representative white Southerner, no one could criticize him for giving his own version of the Civil War and the Reconstruction period that followed. If he possessed the typical Southern attitude, the paternalistic, it would be futile to read a lecture on it. Seen from afar, such an attitude might be deemed reactionary, but at any rate it is usually genial and humane and protective, and because it has experience back of it, it has to be met with some respect. But the attitude which Mr. Dixon possesses and the one for which he forges corroboration in history is a perversion due largely to his personal temperament. So far as I can judge from this film, as well as from my recollection of Mr. Dixon's books, his is the sort of disposition that foments a great deal of the trouble in civilization. Sometimes in the clinical laboratory the doctors are reputed to perform an operation on a dog so that he loses the power to restrain certain motor activities. If he is started running in a cage, the legend goes, he keeps on running incessantly, and nothing can stop him but to hit him on the head with a club. There is a quality about everything Mr. Dixon has done that reminds me of this abnormal dog. At a remote period of his existence it is possible that he possessed a rudimentary faculty of self-analysis. But before that faculty developed he

From The New Republic 7 *(March 20, 1915)*: 185. *Reprinted by permission of Mrs. Signe Toksvig.*

crystallized in his prejudices, and forever it was stunted. Since that time, whenever he has been stimulated by any of the ordinary emotions, by religion or by patriotism or by sex, he has responded with a frantic intensity. Energetic by nature, the forces that impel him are doubly violent because of this lack of inhibition. Aware as a clergyman that such violence is excessive, he has learned in all his melodramas to give them a highly moral twang. If one of his heroes is about to do something peculiarly loathsome, Mr. Dixon thrusts a crucifix in his hand and has him roll his eyes to heaven. In this way the very basest impulses are given the sanction of godliness, and Mr. Dixon preserves his own respect and the respect of such people as go by the label and not by the rot-gut they consume.

In *The Birth of a Nation* Mr. Dixon protests sanctimoniously that his drama "is not meant to reflect in any way on any race or people of today." And then he proceeds to give to the Negro a kind of malignity that is really a revelation of his own malignity.

Passing over the initial gibe at the Negro's smell, we early come to a negrophile senator whose mistress is a mulatto. As conceived by Mr. Dixon and as acted in the film, this mulatto is not only a minister to the senator's lust but a woman of inordinate passion, pride, and savagery. Gloating as she does over the promise of "Negro equality," she is soon partnered by a male mulatto of similar brute characteristics. Having established this triple alliance between the "uncrowned king," his diabolic colored mistress, and his diabolic colored ally, Mr. Dixon shows the revolting processes by which the white South is crushed "under the heel of the black South." "Sowing the wind," he calls it. On the one hand we have "the poor bruised heart" of the white South, on the other "the new citizens inflamed by the growing sense of power." We see Negroes shoving white men off the sidewalk, Negroes quitting work to dance, Negroes beating a crippled old white patriarch, Negroes slinging up "faithful colored servants" and flogging them till they drop, Negro courtesans guzzling champagne with the would-be head of the Black Empire, Negroes "drunk with wine and power," Negroes mocking their white master in chains, Negroes "crazy with joy" and terrorizing all the whites in South Carolina. We see the blacks flaunting placards demanding "equal marriage." We see the black leader demanding a "forced marriage" with an imprisoned and gagged white girl. And we see continually in the background the white Southerner in "agony of soul over the degradation and ruin of his people."

Encouraged by the black leader, we see Gus the renegade hover about another young white girl's home. To hoochy-coochy music we see the long pursuit of the innocent white girl by this lust-maddened Negro, and we see her fling herself to death from a precipice, carrying her honor through "the opal gates of death."

Having painted this insanely apprehensive picture of an unbridled, bestial, horrible race, relieved only by a few touches of low comedy, "the grim reaping begins." We see the operations of the Ku Klux Klan, "the organization that saved the South from the anarchy of black rule." We see Federals and Confederates uniting in a Holy War "in defence of their Aryan birthright," whatever that is. We see the Negroes driven back, beaten, killed. The drama winds up with a suggestion of "Lincoln's solution"—back to Liberia—and then, if you please, with a film representing Jesus Christ in "the halls of brotherly love."

My objection to this drama is based partly on the tendency of the pictures but mainly on the animus of the printed lines I have quoted. The effect of these lines, reinforced by adroit quotations from Woodrow Wilson and repeated assurances of impartiality and good will, is to arouse in the audience a strong sense of the evil possibilities of the Negro and the extreme propriety and godliness of the Ku Klux Klan. So strong is this impression that the audience invariably applauds the refusal of the white hero to shake hands with a Negro, and under the circumstances it cannot be blamed. Mr. Dixon has identified the Negro with cruelty, superstition, insolence, and lust.

We know what a yellow journalist is. He is not yellow because he reports crimes of violence. He is yellow because he distorts them. In the region of history the Rev. Thomas Dixon corresponds to the yellow journalist. He is a clergyman, but he is a yellow clergyman. He is yellow because he recklessly distorts Negro crimes, gives them a disproportionate place in life, and colors them dishonestly to inflame the ignorant and the credulous. And he is especially yellow, and quite disgustingly and contemptibly yellow, because his perversions are cunningly calculated to flatter the white man and provoke hatred and contempt for the Negro.

Whatever happened during Reconstruction, this film is aggressively vicious and defamatory. It is spiritual assassination. It degrades the censors that passed it and the white race that endures it.

Censorship: The Curse of a Nation

◆◇◆

The framers of the organic law of the Commonwealth concluded their contribution to human happiness with the purposeful phrase: "To the end it may be a government of laws and not of men." Upon Massachusetts therefore rests a peculiar obligation to oppose the tendency of the times to change by class legislation and executive censorship a government of laws to a government of men. The passion to limit by legislation or executive order the freedom of the individual is today the curse of the nation. . . .

The Sullivan petition would deliver a blow at religious freedom, the rights of the individual, and the liberty of the press. It puts a premium on violence by making it possible for any two men who engage in a fisticuff in the lobby of a theater to force the authorities to stop the show or entertainment over which the fisticuff occurred. Were such a statute in operation today our citizens of German sympathies could prevent by resolutions of protest or threats of violence the exhibition of any film showing the devastation in Belgium; our Catholic citizens could shut down any theater whose entertainment failed to receive the approval of the cardinal; our Jewish citizens could prohibit a performance of *The Merchant of Venice*; our Christian Science citizens could place their veto upon any film whose portrayal of pain or of the efficacy of medical aid they found conflicted with the tenets of their creed; our Protestant citizens could end the exhibition of any film extolling the usefulness of the parochial school system or portraying the awful persecution of the priests and nuns in Mexico; our mill owners could drive off the stage any play or from the screen any film portraying the horrors of child labor; our saloonkeepers could force the Prohibitionists to give up the use of the film in their crusade; our citizens of Southern origin could have the license of any theater revoked where a picture was exhibited in illustration of the hideous conditions to which helpless Negro prisoners are today subjected in some of the Southern states. In short, the usefulness of the theater either as a place of amusement or of education would be reduced to a ridiculous minimum were the law enforced as Mr. Sullivan would write it.

From the Boston Evening Transcript, *April 23, 1915.*

No city or town officials in Massachusetts today lack power under existing law to revoke the license of any theater giving an exhibition which, in the opinion of the authorities, is obscene or immoral or tends to injure the morals of the community. Where the decision of the mayor or, in the case of Boston, of the mayor and the head of the police jointly, is not satisfactory, an appeal can be taken to the courts. Such an appeal has just been made in this city and the court decision was promptly complied with by the theater management and acquiesced in by the city officials. No further legislation is necessary to protect the public morals of any community, and no further legislation is warranted which would set up over any community a racial or religious censorship. If it be found that the city authorities are not enforcing existing laws with respect to motion pictures, it may well be that the responsibility for such enforcement will sooner or later be transferred either to the State Board of Education, or better still to a national board under the direction of the secretary of the interior, which is provided for in a bill favorably reported to the House of Representatives at the last session of Congress. But we must keep in mind that to license a theater is no more to sanction its exhibition than to license a bookstore is to approve the contents of the books sold over its counters. Any sort of censorship is irritating to the spirit of our people, and only that regulation which is in the essential interest of public decency and public morals should ever be tolerated, if we are to preserve the handiwork of the fathers in the form they wrought—"a government of laws and not of men."

Defense of THE BIRTH OF A NATION and
Attack on the Sullivan Bill
D. W. GRIFFITH

◆◆◆

The conflict over the film play, *The Birth of a Nation,* was renewed today at a legislative hearing on the bill introduced by Representative Lewis R. Sullivan, which would make it a criminal offence to produce

From the Boston Journal, *April 26, 1915.*

Colonel Ben Cameron (Henry B. Walthall) leads the Piedmont troops to war.

Ben Cameron commands his troops to charge. Courtesy the Museum of Modern Art Film Stills Archive.

A lovesick sentry (William Freeman) moons over Elsie Stoneman at the hospital. Courtesy the Museum of Modern Art Film Stills Archive.

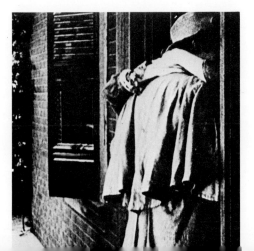

Ben Cameron returns home. Courtesy the Museum of Modern Art Films Stills Archive.

The Camerons (Henry B. Walthall, Mae Marsh, Spottiswoode Aitken, Josephine Crowell, and Miriam Cooper) grieve for the assassinated Abraham Lincoln — The Great Heart. Mammy (Jennie Lee) stands in the background. Courtesy the Museum of Modern Art Film Stills Archive.

Newly enfranchised Negroes elected to the South Carolina House of Representatives. (One of the shots following the title "Historic incidents from the first legislative session under Reconstruction.") Courtesy Arthur Lennig.

Cameron rejects Silas Lynch (George Siegmann), the mulatto protégé of Austin Stoneman (Ralph Lewis). Courtesy the Museum of Modern Art Film Stills Archive.

Gus (Walter Long), the renegade Negro, captured by the Klan for attempting to rape Flora and driving her to her death. Courtesy the Museum of Modern Art Film Stills Archive.

The Klan restores order to Piedmont. Courtesy the Museum of Modern Art Film Stills Archive.

Ben Cameron and Elsie Stoneman contemplate their future together. Courtesy the Museum of Modern Art Film Stills Archive.

D. W. Griffith on the Ford's Theater set. Courtesy the Museum of Modern Art Film Stills Archive.

Peoria, Illinois, 1916. Courtesy the Museum of Modern Art Film Stills Archive.

any "show or entertainment which tends to excite racial or religious prejudice or tends to a breach of the public peace."

D. W. Griffith, author and proprietor of the photoplay, issued a statement defending his production and attacking the Sullivan bill. He said:

"The Sullivan bill is astounding! Actually an effort is being made to rush through the general court, under suspension of the rule, House Bill No. 2,077 which would make it a criminal offence to produce 'any show or entertainment which tends to excite racial or religious prejudice, or tends to a breach of the public peace.' Not only have the rules been suspended to jam it through, but the second section provides that, immediately and without further notice to any property rights involved, 'this act shall take effect upon its passage.'

"Probably it has never occurred to the supporters of this measure that universal dramatic art is practically impossible without the excitation of some degree of race or religious feeling. How unwise to drag race or religion into the realm of censorship! It is unwritten law that neither of these matters belong to legislative regulation, but are reserved within the clause of the Constitution that grants freedom of speech. If the Sullivan bill be enacted, the civic authorities and the courts will find themselves in very deep waters. They will be censoring racial and religious matters that do not possibly concern them.

CITES RECENT PLAYS

"The Jew that finds himself prejudged in the eyes of the community by *The Merchant of Venice* or *The Children of the Ghetto,* the German whose sensibilities are offended by *The Hypen* or *Marie-Odile* or *Inside the Lines* of this season's plays, the Italian stung by *The Vendetta,* the Irishman who dislikes Bernard Shaw's *John Bull and His Other Island,* the Yankee disliking *Way Down East* caricatures, the Russian miffed by *The Yellow Ticket,* and the Oriental hurt by *The Typhoon* or *Mr. Wu* will rush into the courts of the Commonwealth for sympathy, vengeance, and redress.

"I do not mean that all the representatives of the various American stocks will do this, but the opportunity opened up for petty persecution and spite against the theatrical producers and managers is almost endless.

"On the religious side, the consequences will be more momentous and lamentable. Even the great religious operas will be barred from the opera house. From the wonderful *Passion Play* of Oberammergau to the latest drama dealing with the spirit world or some faith cult, not one but is open to objection from its more bitter opponents. One man's orthodoxy is another man's heterodoxy. One man's 'judgment' is another man's 'prejudice.' Why, then, this idle talk of 'religious prejudice'?"

Object Is to Destroy Play

"The truth is hardly anyone seems to have considered seriously the far-reaching consequences of this rash project. The clause, 'tending to a breach of the public peace' opens up the way for any disgruntled or venomous adversaries to start a disturbance in a theater lobby and thereby get a play suppressed. The real purpose of the bill is to destroy one film play, *The Birth of a Nation*.

"Shall this magnificent Civil War and Reconstruction drama be stopped in Boston at the behest of an insignificant minority? Shall Lewis and Trotter and Puller and Wilson tell the legislators of Massachusetts and the people of Boston what to do?

"We respect the colored people of this city and Commonwealth. But in this controversy those who have tried to rush class legislation of the above character, for the arbitrary purpose of suppressing one play, have been most badly advised. No good will ultimately come to the race through an attempted hushing-up of Reconstruction memories.

"Special class legislation should not be allowed for one instant in the free state of Massachusetts. The senators and representatives should not make themselves the laughing stock of the country by enacting such a travesty of law and justice."

Fair Play for THE BIRTH OF A NATION
THOMAS DIXON

To the Editor of the Boston *Journal*—For more than twenty years I have studied the history of the period of Reconstruction. In *The Birth of a Nation* I have given to the world the results of my work in

an honest, earnest, and dignified presentation of the life of that turbu-
lent era.

The courts of Massachusetts, in the face of the most persistent campaign of slander and personal vilification, have sustained the play
squarely on its merits.

The critics who still differ with my views of history and philosophy,
unable to answer them, have introduced a bill into the legislature to
silence me by a special statute.

Whatever may be said or thought of my book, *The Clansman,* or *The
Birth of a Nation,* founded on it, there can be but one opinion among
thoughtful men and women on the character of such vicious special
legislation. It is the violation of every principle of freedom and democracy for which the grand old Commonwealth has stood for 200 years.
I cannot believe that the supreme lawmaking assembly of the state will
deliberately deny to a Southern white man freedom of speech on
Boston Common merely because a few negro agitators differ from his
historical conclusions.

Still more dangerous than any play would be the establishment of
such tyranny in censorship of opinion.

MEAN CONFISCATION

Such a law would have suppressed *Uncle Tom's Cabin.* Such a law
established in New England will reduce at one stroke the whole drama
to the dead level of negro minstrelsy and musical comedy. No author
will dare to write on any great theme in our history or life about
which there can be any difference of opinion. Under such a statute any
man who differed from him could walk into the theater, create a disturbance, and have the play stopped. Under such a law two-thirds of
all the serious drama at present running in America could be instantly
confiscated, its authors and promoters beggared.

Whatever a few negro agitators in Boston may think about *The
Birth of a Nation,* it expresses the passionate faith of the entire white
population of the South. If I am wrong, they are wrong. The number
of white people in the South who differ from my views of the history of
Reconstruction could be housed on a half-acre lot.

Moorfield Storey, president of the negro society leading their fight in
Boston, in a lame article attacks the historical accuracy of the play:

All over the South conditions were substantially the same—the
negro everywhere reduced to a condition of slavery—as was abun-
dantly shown by a report made by Carl Schurz, who was sent down
by President Johnson to examine and report. This was the state of

the South which confronted Congress when, on December 4, 1865, it met for the first time after Mr. Lincoln's assassination. White Reconstruction had been tried and had failed disastrously.

The first act which assured the negroes the right to vote by setting aside the existing state governments and providing that no seceded state should be readmitted to the Union unless its constitution gave the suffrage to white and black alike was not passed till about February 15, 1867. It was not till after May, 1868, that acts were passed admitting the Southern states, and the last of three, Virginia, Mississippi, and Texas, were not admitted till 1870. Only after these acts were passed, and after the fundamental conditions which they imposed were complied with, did the governments of the Southern states come under the control of the colored voters. The Ku Klux Klan had really run its course before the colored voters exercised any substantial power.

This simple chronological statement could be much amplified, but it is sufficient to show how absolutely false is the view of history presented by this play.

FEAR TO FACE HISTORY

The play is a faithful record of the origin of our present, united nation through the agony of Civil War and the still greater agony to the South in Reconstruction. The trouble with Mr. Storey and his negro society is they dare not face the truths of history. So they ask the people of Massachusetts to deny me a hearing.

He tells you that Andrew Johnson became president in April, 1865, and that by December 1 white Reconstruction had been tried in all the South and proved a failure. The last Southern army did not surrender until May. The army of occupation held the South in a grip of steel from the James to the Rio Grande. The little finger of a Southern white man could not be lifted during these months except by the consent of the military authorities, and yet this historian informs us that the white Reconstruction of civil government in the entire South was tried and was a complete failure from May to December, 1865—exactly seven months.

The assertion that the white South, with 1,000,000 Federal bayonets at their throats, attempted during these months to pass laws to re-enslave the negro is merely a bald campaign lie of the year 1868.

Besides the Federal army to protect the negro, the Freedman's Bureau of blessed memory was always there. This bureau, established by Federal power and protected by Federal bayonets, had absolute control of the relations of negroes and whites. No contract could be made without the approval of these armed guardians.

Every law passed by a Southern legislature during this period before negro enfranchisement was done under the direct superintendence and advice of the Freedman's Bureau, and every law relating to the adjustment of the newly emancipated slaves to their new duties was copied from Northern states.

A CAMPAIGN LIE

The assertion that the Freedman's Bureau and the army could not protect the negro from his former master was a malicious lie, which would have been invented only in the heat of a presidential campaign. The laws of vagrancy and apprenticeship were all enacted with the advice and cooperation of the bureau in an attempt to make a lot of joyous Negroes go back to work and quit trying to live on the free rations furnished by the United States government.

Mr. Storey consults a very bad memory both for his facts and his principles.

President Johnson, on receiving Carl Schurz's report of the condition of the South—did what? Certainly he did not join with Thaddeus Stevens and his radical associates in their program of placing the white South under negro rule! Thaddeus Stevens tried to remove Johnson from the office of president and set up a dictatorship on the ruins of the republic because the president stood firmly by Abraham Lincoln's plan of Reconstruction and refused to place the South under the rule of a million ignorant negroes who had just emerged from slavery.

Johnson honestly tried to carry out the martyred president's policy. In a letter to Hahn, his Reconstruction governor of Louisiana, on negro suffrage Lincoln said: "You are about to have a convention which, among other things, will probably define the elective franchise. I barely suggest for your private consideration whether some of the colored people may not be let in—as, for instance, the very intelligent and especially those who have fought gallantly in our ranks" (See Hay and Nickolay). [1]

For standing by this principle of the murdered president, Stevens swore to impeach Johnson, remove him from office, and hang him from the balcony rail of the White House! Stevens failed to impeach

[1] [Editor's note: Nickolay and Hay, *Abraham Lincoln: A History,* one of Griffith's biographical sources. See Lillian Gish's account of the making of *The Birth of a Nation* included in this volume, pp. 42–55.]

President Johnson by one vote. By that one vote we were saved the shame of a dictatorship under Ben Wade, whom Stevens had selected for the position—although Mr. Wade had the effrontery to vote for himself for that office in the final test on the issue of removing the president.

HAY APPROVED BOOK

In my work on the history of Reconstruction I have mastered the contents of more than 4,000 volumes forming the sources of the history of that period. The Hon. John Hay, while secretary of state, corrected the proofs of *The Clansman*. Mr. Hay gave the book his unqualified indorsement in the State Department at Washington. Walter Hines Page, the publisher of the book, can testify to the truth of my statement.

One date and fact Mr. Storey gets correct. He says that universal negro suffrage was not passed until February 15, 1867. Just so, and Gen. N. B. Forrest organized the Ku Klux Klan into a political power during the summer of 1867 to meet the conditions of social hell into which this measure plunged the South. Up to this time the Ku Klux Klan was merely a college boy's prank which started at Pulaski, Tenn., the year before.

That a condition of social anarchy followed the enactment of this law, enfranchising a million ignorant blacks and disfranchising the men whose fathers created this republic, is amply proven by the sworn testimony in ten enormous volumes of the *Ku Klux Klan Conspiracy*, a United States government document, which Mr. Storey has evidently never seen.

"GUS" INCIDENT REAL

I refer him to the volume entitled *North Carolina* for the sworn record of the incident of "Gus" in *The Birth of a Nation*. This crime was typical of thousands. It was this crime which took my father, the Rev. Thomas Dixon, from the pulpit into the ranks of the Klan. It was this crime which led my brother, the Rev. A. C. Dixon, D.D., pastor of the Metropolitan Tabernacle of London, former pastor of the Ruggles Street Baptist Church of Boston, to join the Klan and ride one of those white-robed horses you see in our play.

My great-grandfather, Lieut. Col. Frederick Hambright, poured out his blood at King's Mountain to create this republic and gave you the South—the South with her beautiful valleys, her blue mountains, and glorious skies. Your fathers fought at Bunker Hill and gave to me rock-ribbed New England, her foaming seas and shining shores. It's mine today as the South is yours. I claim with you the right to free speech on Boston Common; in short, not to fix a black censorship of opinion for 80,000,000 white men and women. If you don't like my views of history and philosophy, use my weapons, Reason and Truth, with which to answer—don't try to silence me with a club in the hands of an officer of the law.

Edward Sheldon's play, *The Nigger,* is a bold argument for the marriage of blacks to whites. This play has just been given in Boston. No white man was silly enough to demand its suppression. This play is peculiarly distasteful to the South, yet it was permitted in every Southern state and no crank attempted to suppress it. It was written in answer to *The Clansman.* I scorn the contemptible cowardice which would invoke the law to protect me from its argument.

I modestly suggest to Moorfield Storey that this is a free country and that only a negro or his color-blind associate could be child enough to ask such protection from historical discussion.

The plain truth is that every Negro associated with Mr. Storey in the Intermarriage Society, which is conducting this persecution, hates *The Birth of a Nation* for one reason only—it opposes the marriage of blacks to whites.

A Faithful Record

This play was not written to stir race hatred. It is the faithful record of the life of fifty years ago. It is no reflection on the cultured, decent negro of today. In it are sketched good negroes and bad negroes, good whites and bad whites.

I received the first recognition of my life work in the call extended to me by the Dudley Street Baptist Church in Boston twenty-seven years ago. I got from the people of New England a cordial welcome and early learned to love and admire them.

I refuse to believe that the Commonwealth of Massachusetts at this late hour will pass a special law for the sole purpose of denying to a Southerner freedom of speech in the discussion of our national history. The enactment of such a bill, it seems to me, would be an incredible insult to the 25,000,000 of Southern white people whom I represent, whose cause I am pleading and with whom the people of New England hold the most cordial business and social relations.

The Motion Picture and Witch Burners
D. W. GRIFFITH

◆◇◆

"The most beautiful picture ever on canvas, the finest statue ever carved is a ridiculous caricature of real life compared with the flickering shadow of a tattered film in a backwoods nickelodeon."
The above assertion was made by Dr. E. E. Slossen of the Columbia University in an article entitled "The Birth of a New Art" and published in the *Independent* on April 6, 1914.

Primitive man emerging from a dark cave; evolving atoms abortively struggling in the first man's brain cell; unformed dreams, the crying out of which we call the soul in man's beginning attempting expression; carved rude images on stone, find expression in rhythmic shouting, progressed through the centuries until we had the written word.

The written word became, and perhaps still is, the best means of getting that wild something evolving in the inner man, out of the mouth of his clay carcass into expression.

The old carving on stone developed into the making of beautiful and godlike statues in the hands of the Greeks. The written word enabled the world to know and see and feel and believe in a Buddah, a Confucius, and a Christ. The written word enabled us to know the mornings and the nights of a struggling soul and all souls from Shakespeare, Goethe, Emerson, and a list too long to name.

Evolution, building up from rough carving in granite, and the pitiful expression on softer stone to Homer dashing his brains out against a world; to Shakespeare splashing beautiful dreams over a canvas that seems to be able to live forever. Yet the time it would take a modern prototype of Shakespeare to write a history, say, for instance, of the tragedy of the civil war in our own country, would take you days to read, would take a series of plays running a week to perform. Man ever groping for expression, discovered a new form—the motion picture.

This article, written for a syndicated column entitled "Flickerings from Film Land by Kitty Kelly," appeared in numerous newspapers throughout America as part of the film's publicity.

The same things that would take the greatest modern writing brains we know, from Woodrow Wilson to Rudyard Kipling, years to write and days to be read, can be shown in a moving picture in three hours' time.

According to men of the standing of Metcalf, the cynical critic of *Life*, including besides such people as the Rev. Thomas Gregory, Dorothy Dix, Burns Mantle, Louis Defoe, in fact, all the great dramatic critics of New York, aided in this line by twenty-one members of the United States House and Senate, Richard Harding Davis, Booth Tarkington, two such international characters as the Rev. Father John Talbot Smith to Dr. Charles Parkhurst,[1] enthusiastically indorse (I quote this as an instance) the motion picture play *The Birth of a Nation*.

An outsider, knowing of this, would imagine these people would be capable of having and expressing judgment, which the average audience would accept as trustworthy. They would on any other subject in the world and receive attention, but *The Birth of a Nation* is a motion picture, and the motion picture is at present the witch of modern times, and at all times there must be witches to be burned.

The old witch of the Salem Commons, who made a horrible clamor as she was being tortured, had nothing on the new art of the motion picture in this respect.

I think it is generally agreed that the motion picture is at least on a par with the spoken and written word as a mode of expression.

The motion picture has progressed. It is capable of conveying a given message in many ways enormously more effectively than any mode of expression the world has ever possessed. It is already performing this work.

It is softening the hard life of the plain citizen with beauty and sweetness: it keeps men away from saloons and drink, because it gives them a place of recreation in pleasant surroundings: it brings to the poor who are unable to travel away from their own dingy surroundings the beauty and poetry of moving foreign scenes, of flowers, waving grasses, the beauty of uplifted mountain crests, and the wonders of nature. The great outdoors and beauty of dreams have uplifted man slowly and painfully with much torture and aching of joints out of the state of beasts.

The motion picture will help as no other art has done in this work, if it is given a chance. We understand that all new things must go through an inquisitorial gate. Why not make the passage of the moving picture less brutal than has been that of all other arts?

The printing press was called "an instrument of the devil" by the

---

[1] [Editor's note: See this volume, pp. 102–3.]

ignorant masses of that day. Should we put ourselves on the plane of
the unenlightened people of that day? . . .

In the name of common sense and public decency can't there be an
understanding of this case? The ordinary theater, in which four or five
different plays are shown a night, where the bill is changed nightly,
where the audience before entering cannot possibly be aware of the
nature of each performance, must of necessity have some watch put
over it.

Growing children with unformed minds must be guarded. To that
we all agree. But the new motion picture, as a form of art, running the
same length of time as the play, playing to exactly the same theaters
in which the play is performed, charging the same admission, advertised in exactly the same manner, with its prospective audience told
far ahead of the kind and manner of performance they are to see; in
other words, the moving picture put in exactly the same place as a
play, playing to exactly the same class of people, should be allowed at
least the same fair reception and treatment.

The witch burners, who burn through the censorship of the motion
picture today, when they have nothing left but the charred and black-
ened embers of that which promised once to be a beautiful art, when
this grisly work is finished, where will they turn their attention next?
They have established a precedent. The stage will be the next victim.
After the stage, the press. After the press and free speech are van-
quished, then Russia.

All drama must of necessity be conflict—battle, fight. How are we to
depict the right unless we show the wrong? Unless we show the evils
of a vicious past how are we allowed to be the means of guiding the
footsteps of the present generation?

When you apply the method of censorship to these arts, what possible dream can we have of progress in the future? Had these witch
burners built beech logs around the written word, setting fire to which
made possible our literature and our drama, where would we be
today? They are beginning their work now. It is for us to look to the
present and the future.

If moving pictures properly done of the horrors of war had been
inoculated in all the nations of Europe, there would be no bodies of
men lying on European battlefields.

The greatest field which the motion picture has is the treating of
historic subjects: as a great man has said of a certain motion picture,
"It is like teaching history by lightning."

The witch burners will make this impossible. History is a story of
conflict. You could not even portray the drama of the days of '49 to '70
in the golden west. If you tell the story of this period, you must show
the atrocities committed by the Indians against the whites. Some

public-seeking fanatic would protest that it was an injustice to the Indians and might raise feeling against them.

These people revel in objections. There could be no story of the American revolution. Certainly the English do things which the American does not think proper. Those of English descent in our country would protest, and so on down the line with all nationalities and all grades of people. It would be impossible to present anything.

The Future of the Two-Dollar Movie
D. W. GRIFFITH

◆◇

While there has been a vast amount of comment regarding the advent of the two-dollar motion picture, it seems to me that there really is no occasion for surprise that a picture should be produced which vies with the best offerings of the dramatic stage. After all it is nothing but the old first law of nature—the survival of the fittest. The remainder is purely a question of selection and execution.

When it was first announced that we intended to present *The Birth of a Nation* in a regular Broadway theater, which had never played a picture attraction before, the wiseacres of the theater world said it would not succeed. You see, they knew nothing of pictures. Most people had looked upon a motion picture drama as a ten-cent proposition. They measured everything by the standard of price. It was not surprising that they overlooked the fundamental facts in the case and were unprepared to pass judgment upon this undertaking. But in all truth there was nothing daring or venturesome in it. You see, we knew what we had. That was an advantage which the other fellow had never taken into consideration.

The significance of this is in the proof of the big picture being an undoubted success. There will be many two-dollar pictures. The success will depend entirely upon how well they are done, and reverts back solely to a question of merit. It takes great care, time and an enor-

This article appeared in numerous newspapers as part of the publicity surrounding the film.

mous expense to produce a picture which will compare with the best
the spoken drama can bring forth. But, given the theme, the understanding and the ability to project his ideals, the moving picture director has a material advantage over the stage director who puts on a
comedy or a drama of comtemporary life. The latter is confined and
limited in his scope. He can show only certain scenes in the limits of
three walls, and at best has only a few square feet in which to place
his characters. For his background he must depend upon painted
scenery and manufactured effects, which are, after all, only miserable
imitations of natural objects. I do not mean this in a spirit of criticism.
There are fundamental ideals of the spoken drama which make it the
aristocrat of the arts. Every one of us has pleasant recollections of great
moments when true dramatists enjoyed the privileges of artistic inter-
pretations. When a great actor throws the best there is in him into the
principal role of a fine play you have a combination which is irresisti-
ble. I have been impressed deeply by such performances upon several
visits to the theater. What painting or piece of sculpture stands out in
your memory to compare with this living, breathing thing you are part
of for a single evening. Long years afterward in pleasurable reveries
you recall the play and the player. Who ever saw Irving's matchless
work in *Louis XI,* can forget that wonderful scene when he urged the
images on his cap to listen to him and yet was equivocating at the same
time? Or can one ever quite efface from memory the majestic manner
with which Mansfield, as Cyrano de Bergerac, tossed his purse to the
crowd? These are specific instances to illustrate my meaning.

It was the art of interpretation glorified. The player and his mood
became the great figure in such cases. With the moving picture it is
different. The poetic simulation, the tour de force which arrests attention and makes memories that are to live, is a silent power. The brain
behind this art is never revealed. It lends itself to that concealment
which is one of the rarest attributes of true art. The living thing is
subjective. There is no rivalry with the spoken drama. Each has its
niche and, if artistically done, will live. The mere presentation may
be ephemeral but the ideas and the recollections go on and on as long
as life lasts.

In motion pictures we have a larger field in which to operate. On
the stage these so called "effects" are imitations at best. In the film play
we show the actual occurrence and are not hampered by the size of our
stage or the number of people we can crowd into the scene. If our story
traverses to a battlefield we show an actual battlefield. If it means that
10,000 people were part of this conflict we engage 10,000 people, rehearse them in minute detail, and when we are ready we show you that
scene as realistically as if you were looking down from a hilltop and
watching an engagement of contending forces.

Let us look into the cost of this. This scene for a motion picture might cost you in the neighborhood of $75,000. But the cost ends with the taking of the original negative. There are no salaries after this, and the only expense is the comparatively slight one of making new copies from the original negative.

A big spectacle on the stage can at the utmost employ 400 people in a scene. This is an unusually large number. It takes the same time and pains to rehearse them that it does to handle 10,000 people in a motion picture scene, and the salaries and costuming of the supernumeries run up to $2,500 a week, so that at the end of two seasons these forces have cost easily $150,000. Here you have twice the outlay for 400 people that it costs a motion picture director to employ 10,000. If there is any significance in these figures they point an important moral without need of further explanation. In the same way we can go afield and get anything we want. If there is a shipwreck we show the angry sea and the restless waves. For a lovers' tryst we have but to pick out some sylvan dell and bring our players there and let them act as two people in love would act under a given circumstance, and the great audiences weave their own romances and do the larger share of the acting for that scene. Along the sidelines we can have roses blooming in the sunlight with a snow-crusted mountain in the background. In our drama the trees wave in the breezes and blades of grass damp with real dewdrops are none too insignificant to become a part of the action. You see, an observing director has the world for his studios. The centuries have been piling up those inexhaustible productions for him. He has but to use artistic sense in the matter of selection.

The motion picture is no longer an infant art. It is the newest and most powerful form of dramatic expression and there is no end to which it can be carried. I firmly believe the day will come when great poetic pictures will not only compare with the best of the legitimate stage, but will be upon a parity with the greatest productions of grand opera and at corresponding prices. Remember, a few years ago it was the limit of extravagance to spend $500 on a moving picture production. At that time we played to five-cent audiences. Now we spend $500,000 on a picture, and we crowd the theaters everywhere at two dollars a seat. By this ratio what is to hinder the superproducer from spending three times that amount and getting five dollars a seat for it.

THE BIRTH OF A NATION
REV. DR. CHARLES H. PARKHURST

◆◇

It is impossible to witness the film drama *The Birth of a Nation,* now being shown at the Liberty Theater, and not want to say something about it.

Every one who has seen it is saying something about it. When one has been crowded upon, pressed down and run over it is against nature not to make some kind of an outcry.

That is the way one feels when coming out of the Liberty Theater. The thing is vast. It is overwhelming. Nothing like it has ever before been put upon the stage.

The tension of the performance is but a single feature of it, but it is that which one feels most poignantly after three straight hours. It begins in an easy way, but commences soon to find its muscle and goes on to the end, pounding upon one's senses with blows that come heavier and heavier, more and more rapid.

It is not apparent what are the grounds of the objections urged against it nor what is the animus of those who are scheming to have the exhibition prohibited.

The national board of censorship has approved it and reaffirmed its approval. The popular endorsement which the play has since received by the thousands who are seeing it daily will require more than small prejudices or moral eccentricities to disturb. In the meantime efforts to suppress it are thus far successful in nothing so much as in giving it wider and more remunerative publicity.

The intimate familiarity which David W. Griffith has shown with the events of the Reconstruction period along with the detailed scholarly study which he has made of the wider territory of events which the play covers renders the production one of surprising educational value to those who were either young children still or even unborn in the stirring years of 1860 to 1870. A boy can learn more true history and get more of the atmosphere of the period by sitting down

This review appeared in numerous newspapers throughout America as part of the film's publicity.

for three hours before the film which Mr. Griffith has produced with such artistic skill than by weeks and months of study in the classroom. This drama is a telling illustration of the possibilities of motion pictures as an instrument of instruction in history.

The criticism that it exhibits the negro in an unfortunate light and that it is calculated to engender racial animosity is fully met by the consideration that it represents the negro, not as he is now at all, but as he was in the days when he had just had the chains broken from him and when he was rioting in the deliciousness of a liberty so new and untried that he had not yet learned to understand it and was as ignorant as a baby of the way to use it. It is in this respect exactly true to history, and if it reflects upon the negro as he was then it is a compliment to the black man of today. An exhibition of lawlessness might not have been proper thirty or forty years ago. Such proprieties change with the passing of time.

The battle scenes which Mr. Griffith has depicted are of surpassing power and realism. Every lover of peace must experience a certain painful gratification that just at this time the ghastly horrors of carnage can be brought so closely home to the eye. It is one thing to read about the trenches, the killing and the corpses. It is quite another thing to have them bodily pressed before the eye, with all the demoniac fury that marks conflict at close range. A well-written description of a battlefield allows the place, and the occasion to be invested with features of magnificence, with the heroism of the contestants and the glory of the victors. On Griffith's screen we see the real thing. There is no magnificence, no glory, but horror, brutality, and stark butchery. It sickens with the sense of man's inhumanity to man. It makes war despicable and devilish. It conveys an indelible lesson to all who have been bewitched by those who have decked out the naked hideousness of war with tinsel drapery.

There are also scenes of surpassing dignity and beauty done by a master artist's hand—the signing by the president of the proclamation for volunteers which marked the end of the old regime, the surrender of Lee to Grant and the assassination of the president in Ford's Theater.

The tender affection in which Mr. Lincoln is held was manifested in the way the great audience received the scene of a heartbroken southern mother pleading with him for her son, sentenced to death as a guerilla. Every eye was dim with tears in the strangling hush that fell on the theater. What might not our country have been saved had the problem of Reconstruction been left to the great heart—the one man who compassed within himself the resources of the intelligence, experience, breadth and sympathy of Abraham Lincoln!

The Birth of a Nation has my unqualified approval.

•◦{ ESSAYS }◦•

BIRTH OF A NATION
or White Power Back When
by ANDREW SARRIS

The Paris Cinematheque recently screened D. W. Griffith's *Birth of a Nation* in connection with Lillian Gish's arrival in the city for a lecture, and so I decided to take another look at this fountainhead film in the history of the medium. Classic or not, *Birth of a Nation* has long been one of the embarrassments of film scholarship. It can't be ignored in even the most basic curriculum, and yet it was regarded as outrageously racist even at a time when racism was hardly a household word. What to do? One academic solution is to honor Griffith's contributions with a screening of *Intolerance,* itself an act of alleged atonement on Griffith's part for any bad impression fostered by *Birth of a Nation.* Anyway, the Old Left film historians have always insisted that it was *Intolerance* and not *Birth of a Nation* that inspired Eisenstein, Pudovkin, and the other Russians to make their montage masterpieces, and since the cinema attained its ideological-aesthetic peak with *Potemkin,* we were told further, *Intolerance* could be safely studied as a relatively primitive influence on *Potemkin.* The fact that *Intolerance* was as much a popular failure as *Birth of a Nation* was a popular success carried little weight with the left-wing revisionists. "Popular" merely meant "commercial" in the lexicon of Marxist film history, and everyone knew that commericial success in the cinema usually involved the manipulation of the ideologically innocent masses by the evil exploiters.

My own attitude toward *Birth of a Nation* and *Intolerance* is one of reluctant respect without great affection. I much prefer the Griffith of *True Heart Susie, Broken Blossoms, Way Down East,* and even *The White Rose* to the Griffith of the monumental superproductions of

From The Village Voice, *July 17 and July 24, 1969, 45; 37, 45. Copyright 1969 by The Village Voice, Inc. Reprinted by permission of the publisher.*

1915 and 1916. Not only do I have an ingrained bias in favor of small, personal visions to big, social spectacles; I feel also that Griffith was more at home (literally and figuratively) with domestic details than with cosmic configurations. Indeed, there is more of eternity in one anguished expression of Mae Marsh or Lillian Gish than in all of Griffith's flowery rhetoric on Peace, Brotherhood, and Understanding. Another factor in my not booking *Birth of a Nation* and *Intolerance* for my classes is the three-hour running time of each picture, a rather long stretch for a silent movie nowadays, particularly when no musical accompaniment is provided. Henri Langlois, superpurist that he is, never has music played at the Cinematheque for silent films, a position I consider illogical to the extreme in that silent movies were always accompanied by music, and *Birth of a Nation* in particular was released with an elaborate score for the guidance of its exhibitors.

The pioneering marvels represented in *Birth of a Nation* and *Intolerance* present an increasingly more troublesome challenge to the film lecturer. The more we get to know about the period from 1896 to 1915, the more subtly ambiguous Griffith's position becomes in terms of easily identifiable technical and stylistic contributions. Also, the neoantiquarianism of Welles and the nouvelle vague directors has taken from Griffith some of the patina of his pastness. Griffith's editing, for example, is not nearly as sophisticated as film histories would have us believe, certainly not by the surrealistic standards of Eisenstein. Griffith's artificial masking and iris framing *is* fairly primitive next to Eisenstein's functional framing in *Strike* through which the dynamic movements of machinery and architectural forms vary the visibility ratios on the screen. Or so we thought until Welles reintroduced the iris dissolve as an expression of nostalgia in *The Magnificent Ambersons* in 1942, and Ophuls reinvented artificial masking and framing in *Lola Montes* in 1955 to make CinemaScope more supple, and Godard expressed his fleeting narrative instinct with an iris fade-out in *Breathless* in 1960. With everything again possible, nothing seems antiquated, Griffith least of all, and if the criteria for Griffith's shot sequences seem relatively literary and theatrical next to Eisenstein's, who is to say that "literary" and "theatrical" are necessarily pejorative expressions in this period of more flexible film aesthetics.

On the level of content, however, *Birth of a Nation* was an infinitely more influential political event than either *Intolerance* with its well-meaning abstractions and sentimentalities [or] *Potemkin* with its for-export-only exhortations to revolution. Indeed it was naive for Griffith to imagine that the platitudinous generalities of *Intolerance* could ever atone for the plastic specifics of *Birth of a Nation*. The best that could be said for Griffith was that he was not fully conscious of all the issues involved in his treatment of Reconstruction after the Civil War.

Certainly, Griffith could not have been overly sensitive to the absurdity of casting his blackest black villains with whites in blackface while showing authentic negritude in the ranks of the Reconstruction extras. Hence, we have blackness itself (apart from the "loyal" Mammy and Tom blackface servants) as an index of social and sexual presumption, and the hero gets the inspiration for the Ku Klux Klan robes from watching white children frighten black children with white sheets representing the ghosts that were to make a whole generation of Negro screen comics roll their eyes in abject fear and ritualistic servitude. But I am describing the visual Manicheanism of Griffith's racism in mere words, black type or print on white paper, a medium in which "black" and "white" are in themselves equivalently colorless sensations to the eye. To witness whiteness and blackness on the screen is to witness the birth of a color taboo that has not been shattered to this day. Griffith aggravated the problem by thrusting the coyest of coy Victorian heroines into the most sordid situations a Southern sentimentalist could imagine. Curly-haired child-women who resisted their own upper-class sweethearts suddenly became the prey of uppity blacks, and the poor innocents either fainted with lascivious modesty or jumped off cliffs with commendable honor. It is as if an army of black Uriah Heaps were unleashed on an array of Agneses meant for the snobbish fantasies of a Dickens and nowhere else. Griffith, like Dickens, had no adult conception of social organisms and class structures. Unlike Gance and Eisenstein, Griffith relied more on a theory of character than a theory of history. What happened after *Birth of a Nation* was in many ways more dispiriting in its hypocrisy than the racist shock of *Birth of a Nation* itself and even so-called progressives were not immune to this hypocrisy.

The Birth of a Nation opened officially at the Liberty Theater in New York on March 3, 1915, preaching peace at a time when most of the world was at war. President Woodrow Wilson, who honored the film with an unprecedented screening in the White House, is reported to have remarked, "It is like writing history with lightning." At that, Wilson's blurb came under the heading of noblesse oblige since Griffith's titles for *Birth of a Nation* quote Woodrow Wilson, the historian, on more than one occasion for historical evidence of the evils of Reconstruction. Wilson, born a Southerner, like Griffith, was a liberal Democratic president in an era when most of the Negro vote, North and South, went to the Republicans virtually by default. Hence, there is no reason to believe that he felt unduly menaced by the race riots in Northern cities or the political protests from such lingering abolitionists as Jane Addams and President Charles E. Eliot of Harvard.

Unfortunately, the outcries against *Birth of a Nation* served merely to drive racism underground without confronting the specific issues involved. By arguing that Griffith was being unfair to Negroes, the white liberals succeeded in preventing any sequels to *Birth of a Nation,* but they failed completely and perhaps deliberately to counter the impact of *Birth of a Nation* with a positive picture of the Negro on a scale comparable to Griffith's negation of Negritude. For decades, Southern theater owners exercised veto power over the slightest intimation of black-white miscegenation, and this veto power was never challenged even by supposedly Stalinist-swimming-pool-Hollywood screenwriters of the '30s and '40s. The Left was always good for a few pickets to protest racial slurs in *Gone with the Wind* and *Song of the South,* but there never seemed to be any countering scripts to restore sexual dignity to the Negro. Indeed, liberal tolerance was counterproductive to the extent that it blocked out any consideration of race-sex taboos as potentially harmful to the Negro race. Even *Birth of a Nation* has failed to receive the detailed analysis it deserves because liberal and Left activists prefer to dismiss the entire film as a distortion and thereby evade the politically dangerous issues involved. If it isn't true, nice people will say, why discuss it at all? The answer is of course that a work of art need not be true for it to be deeply felt and fervently believed.

Marxist critics have been particularly handicapped in this particular controversy by their reluctance to open the Pandora's box of sexual mythology. To argue, however, as Griffith does, that no black man can ever aspire to any white woman goes beyond the boundary of political partisanship into racial tabu, and tabus must be broken at least metaphorically before they can poison the body politic. Certainly, out of all the stories that have unfolded on the American continent, Griffith himself could have found some black-white version of *Broken Blossoms* if he had been truly sincere in his professed desire to atone for *Birth of a Nation.* But though there were many movies on the forbidden loves of whites and Orientals, whites and Indians, not to mention the intramural tabus among whites themselves, there were no movies until very recently to romanticize even one example of black-white miscegenation from the millions that must obviously have occurred. *Birth of a Nation* not only upholds the lily-white mythology of the Aryan Southland; it imputes to Thaddeus Stevens (alias Stoneman) sordid sexual motives to explain his vendetta against the defeated Confederacy dear Abe Lincoln wants only to caress and forgive. Thus the ghost of Lincoln is allied with the formidable cultural presences of Griffith and Wilson in a blanket condemnation of black arrogance. Significantly, the uppity mulatto maid who seduces Stoneman merely by baring one of her shoulders is played by a white actress in blackface. The effect of blackface in white-oriented iconography is to emphasize the treacherous incongruity of darting white eyes and daggerlike white teeth. And the use of blackface performers makes blackness itself a state of being so inferior that blacks themselves are incapable of interpreting and communicating its inescapable baseness. Hence, an American screen tradition is born in *Birth of a Nation* to the effect that no authentic black man younger than Bill "Bojangles" Robinson will ever place his hand on the flesh of any white woman older than Shirley Temple. This taboo has remained in force so long that even as late at 1957 Joan Fontaine was deluged with poison-pen mail for merely holding hands with Harry Belafonte in *Island in the Sun,* and only this year [1969] a TV functionary admitted cutting a bit of television tape in which Petula Clark was shown touching the still presumably untouchable Belafonte.

Curiously, *Birth of a Nation* has gained more ambiguity over the years than its professed bias would indicate. Mae Marsh, in particular, seems more than the conventional victim of black lust. Even by Griffith's outraged Victorian moral standards, Miss Marsh's fierce virgin overreacts hysterically to every emotional challenge until, finally, she is doomed not so much by the relatively restrained blackface pursuer who keeps insisting that he merely wants to talk to her as by her own increasing inability to cope with all the demands made on her feelings. Mae Marsh and Lillian Gish are brilliantly directed by Griffith because he believed in all their Victorian-American affectations as sublime manifestations of white womanhood, and he could not bear to see them buffeted about by the disorder represented by Reconstruction. His small-town agrarian vision of the world is intellectually inadequate by any standard, but there is no point suppressing *Birth of a Nation.* It marks not only where we were, but where it's still at. And it remains to be answered on the screen in its own terms, not by Marxist metaphors of the class struggle.

The Reaction of the Negro to the Motion Picture, BIRTH OF A NATION

by THOMAS R. CRIPPS

In the decade before Woodrow Wilson's first administration the reforms of urban Progressives were essentially for whites only. Despite the Negro's rising wealth and increasingly successful struggle with illiteracy, the tenuous *rapprochement* that a few Negro leaders had with Theodore Roosevelt, the formation of active and influential agencies of reform like the National Negro Business League, and (at the behest of several white liberals) the National Association for the Advancement of Colored People and the Urban League, the Wilson years represented the continuation of a decline. Residential segregation was increasing; the ballot box was a distant memory to many Negroes; Jim Crow had become the custom in public accommodations. For the Negro there was a denial of reform even before the resurgent Democratic party brought to Washington a return to Southern ideals.[1]

Typical of the ascendency of the ideology of the white South was the circulation of *Birth of a Nation,* a spectacular twelve-reel film, much of which was drawn from *The Clansman,* a romantic, angry novel of the fate of the ideals of the antebellum South during Reconstruction. Its author was Thomas Dixon of North Carolina, a sometime preacher, a professional Southerner, and a fretful Negrophobe. The novel—which constituted the basis of only the last half of the film—is based on an attempt by a group of defeated Southerners to reassemble the traditional power structure of the South. Hindered and thwarted in their efforts by Stoneman, a thinly disguised Thad Stevens, who with his mulatto mistress rules America after Appomattox, they turn natu-

From The Historian *26 (1963): 344–62. Copyright 1963. Reprinted by permission of the publisher.*

[1] See George C. Osborn, "The Problem of the Negro in Government, 1913," *The Historian,* XXIII (May 1961), 330–47 for the most recent study of the Negro's plight in the Wilson years.

rally to extralegal means of political expression: the Ku Klux Klan.[2] The director of the film, David Wark Griffith, son of a Confederate soldier, had an affinity for the Lost Cause and a fondness for portraying in melodrama "the pale, helpless, slim-bodied heroines of the nineteenth-century poets" being attacked by Negroes. It was Griffith who wrote the first half of the film, a Southern view of the Civil War.[3]

The film was significant for other reasons. Artistically, it was the finest work the cinema had ever produced. Socially, it was reflective of the depth of hostility that many white Americans felt toward Negroes and of the degree to which this feeling might be fed by film propaganda and its accompanying mass advertising. It also presented Negro leaders with a dilemma. They could ignore the film and its hateful portrayal, knowing not what damage it might do. They could urge censorship. Or, and at least likely, they could finance and make their own films propagandizing favorably the role of Negroes in American life.

Films with an essentially regional tone and even an anti-Negro bias had been made previously. In 1915, the year of *Birth of a Nation*, Paramount was circulating *The Nigger*, another heavy-handed racist film. Griffith himself had made *The Battle*, a Civil War picture of earlier vintage. *The Clansman*, too, had been shot earlier, starring Griffith's wife; in 1906 as a play it had been labeled "as crude a melodrama as has ever slipped its anchor and drifted westward from Third Avenue." [4]

Why was this one film so powerful and so fiercely resented? Aside from the flaws that offended Negroes and some film aesthetes, the picture made far greater use of advertising than was normal and consequently drew far larger crowds than earlier films. But the movie created the greatest stir chiefly because it was the nearest to fine art that the cinema had achieved. It reached a technical brilliance, an "art by lightning flash," a kind of visual music with its own rhythm and logic. Its tempo was varied by editing together numerous shots into

[2] Thomas Dixon, Jr., *The Clansman* (New York, 1907) is one of several editions. A print of *Birth of a Nation* is in the Museum of Modern Art Film Library, New York City (copyright no. LP 6677).

[3] Iris Barry, *D. W. Griffith: American Film Master*, in the *Museum of Modern Art Film Library Series No. 1* (New York, 1940), pp. 7–10, 15–21; Arthur Knight, *The Liveliest Art* (New York, 1959), pp. 31, 35; Nicholas Vardac, *Stage to Screen: Theatrical Method from Garrick to Griffith* (Cambridge, Mass., 1949), pp. 64, 199, 208; Seymour Stern, "Griffith: Pioneer of Film Art," in Lewis Jacobs, *Introduction to the Art of the Movies* (New York, 1960), pp. 158–59. For a new scholarly treatment with many fresh insights and sound criticism of earlier students see Edward Wagenknecht, *The Movies in the Age of Innocence* (Norman, Okla., 1962), pp. 99–109.

[4] A review in the Harvard Theater Collection, January 8, 1906, cited in Vardac, *Stage to Screen*, p. 64.

a montage that could evoke large-than-life images of past reality. Early critics spoke of this effect as "panoramic drama" or "outdoor drama" which could create "crowd splendor" and "crowd passion" rather than private passion so that "the Ku Klux Klan dashes down the road as powerfully as Niagara pours over the cliff . . . [and] the white leader . . . enters not as an individual, but as . . . the whole Anglo-Saxon Niagara." Audiences became mobs "for or against the Reverend Thomas Dixon's poisonous hatred of the Negro." Few viewers could distinguish between art and ax-grinding, technique and content. Only a few critics like Vachel Lindsay could admire the film as "a wonder in its Griffith sections" with its "mobs splendidly handled, tossing wildly and rhythmically like the sea," while pointing out the pathological flaws of Dixon's script.[5]

No earlier American film had been so impressive. Even the producers referred to their redundant, unimaginative nickelodeon entertainments as "sausages." And when *Birth of a Nation* was made, the Mutual Company, which had helped finance production, did not take it seriously enough to back its distribution; Griffith, his cameraman Billy Bitzer, and a friend and film producer named Harry Aitken had to form the Epoch Company to circulate the film. Other distributors did not want it for fear of hurting the receipts of their own films, some of which were also racist.[6]

Art, technology, advertising, the racism of Dixon—all fell together into what Negroes took to be a malicious conspiracy. "Every resource of a magnificent new art has been employed with an undeniable attempt to picture Negroes in the worst possible light" the NAACP declared in its *Annual Report*.[7] Lacking funds with which to make propaganda films of their own, Negroes of the urban North turned to censorship, an acceptable position among liberals of the time who were concerned about "vice" and its assumed cause—the nickelodeon parlors that dotted American cities showing corrupting movies.[8] Many

[5] Nicholas Vachel Lindsay, *The Art of the Motion Picture* (New York, 1915), pp. 41, 46–49.

[6] Barry, *D. W. Griffith*, p. 22. In an interview with Rolfe Cobleigh, editor of *The Congregationalist and Christian World*, Dixon claimed to own one-fourth of the picture. See Boston Branch of the NAACP, *Fighting a Vicious Film: Protest against "Birth of a Nation"* (Boston, 1915), p. 26 [Cobleigh's description of the interview is reprinted on pp. 80–83 of this volume].

[7] NAACP, *Sixth Annual Report* (n. p., 1915), p. 11.

[8] Here, as throughout the paper, the proper noun "Negro" used collectively, is shorthand for Negro pressure groups and their white allies. Ideologically, it should not suggest unanimity of opinion or action but only that these people recognized and resented certain social customs and disabilities that whites commonly imposed upon Negroes.

cities and some states had begun to censor films. Negroes turned to these agencies to stop the showing of *Birth of a Nation*.

In February 1915 the film was shown in Los Angeles and in San Francisco. A few days later advertising started in the New York newspapers; almost simultaneously the Los Angeles branch of the NAACP notified the New York office of the West Coast opening. The film should have followed a normal course eastward to the National Board of Censorship of Motion Pictures, a private agency created by the film producers who hoped that it would give the movies respectability as family entertainment and the wider market they thought would accrue to their product once they were able to squelch the sensational investigations of the nickelodeons.[9] The board, later called the National Board of Review, was one of many expressions of the intellectual climate of the time. It was unique in that it was private; yet it was admired by public censors because 80 percent of the film exhibitors were said to abide by its decisions. In Washington the year before, the House committee on the establishment of a motion-picture commission had taken considerable testimony, much of which favored public censorship. But the committee chose to heed the counsel of Frederic C. Howe, chairman of the New York board, who recommended that the existing board be permitted to continue its work without intervention from a superfluous body in Washington.[10]

Two days before the film was to be reviewed by the board, Dixon sidetracked it into Washington and showed it in the East Room of the White House to Woodrow Wilson, members of his cabinet, and their families. The night following this unprecedented event, he showed it in the ballroom of the fashionable Raleigh Hotel, with Chief Justice Edward White, the Supreme Court, and members of Congress in attendance. Both showings were granted as favors to Dixon, a former student of Wilson's at Johns Hopkins, with the stipulation that there be no publicity. Dixon stopped in Washington because he hoped to

---

[9] Investigations resulted in the creation of censoring boards in Chicago, New York, Kansas, Maryland, and Ohio. The movement entered Congress in the persons of Southern and New England Calvinists and overzealous progressives who also tended to support prohibition and suffrage for women [Terry Ramsaye, *A Million and One Nights* (New York, 1926), II, 569].

[10] U.S., Congress, House of Representatives, *Motion Picture Commission: Hearings before the Committee on Education . . . on Bills to Establish a Federal Motion-Picture Commission*, 63rd Cong., 2nd sess., Nos. 1 and 2, 1914, Pt. I, pp. 3–5, 56–62; Pt. II, p. 79; Ramsaye, *Million and One Nights*, II, 482; "Films and Births and Censorship," *Survey*, XXXIV (April 3, 1915), 4–5. For further comment on the censorship controversy see Donald Ramsay Young, *Motion Pictures: A Study in Social Legislation* (Philadelphia, 1922), pp. 21, 42, 58, 75, 98; Morris L. Ernst and Pare Lorentz, *Censored: The Private Life of the Movies* (New York, 1930); and Wagenknecht, *Movies in the Age of Innocence*, p. 100.

bolster Wilson's known Southern biases, especially his attitude toward the Negro. As he later told Joseph Tumulty, Wilson's secretary,

> I didn't dare allow the president to know the *real big purpose back of my film—which was to revolutionize Northern sentiments by a presentation of history that would transform every man in the audience into a good Democrat!* And make no mistake about it— we are doing just that thing. . . . Every man who comes out of one of our theaters is a Southern partisan for life—except the members of [Oswald Garrison] Villard's Intermarriage Society who go there to knock.[11]

Wilson, according to Dixon, liked the film and congratulated him, saying that it was "history written in lightning." [12] Justice White, before the same showing, in Dixon's words, "leaned toward me and said in low tense tones: 'I was a member of the Klan, sir. . . . Through many a dark night, I walked my sentinels' beat through the ugliest streets of New Orleans with a rifle on my shoulder. . . . I'll be there!' " Thus whenever the NAACP protested the film, Dixon could claim approval in high places. No denials came from Washington until after the New York and Boston runs had begun.[13]

Hence Dixon, even before the New York board saw the movie, had in effect secured the *imprimatur* of the president of the United States. In New York on February 20 the board allegedly wildly applauded the picture, spurring Dixon to leap to his feet, shouting that it was the "birth of a nation," and the old title, *The Clansman*, was then and there discarded. The producers, expecting no opposition, advertised the film's opening on March 3 at the Liberty Theater at a top price of two dollars.[14]

[11] Dixon to Tumulty, May 1, 1915; later Dixon let Wilson know his plans in blander terms, assuring the president that soon "there will never be an issue on your segregation policy," Dixon to Wilson, September 5, 1915, cited in Arthur Link, *Wilson: The New Freedom* (Princeton, 1956), pp. 253–54. Dixon made a similar reference to the "Negro Intermarriage Society" in an interview with Rolfe Cobleigh (NAACP, *Fighting a Vicious Film*, p. 26) [See p. 81 of this volume].

[12] Mrs. Thomas [Madelyn Donovan] Dixon to Thomas R. Cripps, June 7, 1962; telephone conversation between Mrs. Dixon and Cripps, June 6, 1962. Thomas Dixon, *Southern Horizons: An Autobiography*, ms. in the possession of Mrs. Dixon, Raleigh, North Carolina, cited in Eric Goldman, *Rendezvous with Destiny* (New York, 1956), pp. 176–77. See also Knight, *The Liveliest Art*, p. 35; and New York *Post*, March 4, 1915.

[13] Correspondence cited in Link, *Wilson*, pp. 253–54.

[14] *New York Times*, February 14, 1915. See also Lewis Jacobs, "D. W. Griffith" [see p. 154 of this volume]; Daniel Talbot, *Film: An Anthology* (New York, 1959), p. 416 for titling incident. For another version see Wagenknecht, *Movies in the Age of Innocence*, p. 99. Dixon in an interview claimed to have hired thirteen Pinkerton men for the New York run (NAACP, *Fighting a Vicious Film*, 16) [See p. 83 of this volume].

The NAACP had eleven days to persuade the board to reject the film. Earlier, the Los Angeles branch had wrung from the local mayor a commitment to cut all scenes suggestive of rape. Soon *The Crisis,* the NAACP organ, working with Fred Moore's New York *Age,* pressed for similar concessions in New York City. It was surprised upon hearing of the board's acceptance of the film in its entirety.[15]

Actually the alleged enthusiasm of the board's approval may have been exaggerated, for even with the cuts that the NAACP was to win, the vote to approve was divided. The Negroes had protested the decision on the basis of the split and had reminded the board that when *The Clansman* had been performed on the stage in Philadelphia, it had caused riots and had been banned. They were also aroused when, after the excisions, they saw that there were still close-ups of leering Negroes (many of whom were crudely made-up whites) pursuing white ingénues. But even with the omission of several shots of a "forced marriage" and a lynching sequence, most of which were poorly contrived anyway, the decision still remained at 15–8 for approval, with the chairman, Howe, among the dissenters. He refused to put his name on the board's seal of approval.[16]

The board felt that its job was not to judge historical accuracy, its job was "moral" and there was never any assumption of jurisdiction over race prejudice. Moreover, the board was a cumbersome barge that steered best in calm waters. Composed of 125 members who were placed in numerous smaller groups in order to view the vast output of films, it acted as a general committee only in case of dispute. A subcommittee had passed on Griffith's work without change; it was because of Howe's insistence that the whole board saw it and decided to pare footage from Part II, the segment drawn from Dixon's novel.[17]

After the producers failed to appeal the first deletions, the NAACP insisted that all of Part II be cut.[18] As the premiere approached, the NAACP demanded that Howe let Negroes preview the film. Howe responded by doling out two tickets, ten less than promised, for a March 1 showing with the provision that only whites use them. The Negroes pressed on, having heard that the board had vocally disapproved of the film and might be persuaded to put it in writing. Failing, they sued for an injunction on March 3, the date of the New York opening; they were refused because there had been no breach of peace. The board, in an effort to close the case, stopped an-

[15] "Fighting Race Calumny," *Crisis,* X (June 1915), 87.

[16] Frederic C. Howe to [Joseph P.] Loud in NAACP, *Fighting a Vicious Film,* p. 33; *Survey,* XXXIV (April 3, 1915), 4–5.

[17] W. D. McGuire, Jr., of the National Board of Review, "Censoring Motion Pictures," *New Republic,* II (April 10, 1915), 262–63.

[18] "Fighting Race Calumny," *Crisis,* X (May 1915), 40–42.

swering mail on the subject. But under increasing pressure, the Howe group cracked and admitted that the March 1 action had been unofficial; it decided to allow Jacob Schiff, Jane Addams, Lillian Wald, and other NAACP members to have a private showing. A few Southerners also went along. They all roundly condemned the picture with the vigor of eyewitnesses, which they had become for the first time.[19]

After the viewing the Negro group instituted criminal proceedings against Griffith and Aitken, circularized the movie industry with their case against the Epoch Company, and demanded that the New York commissioner of licenses stop the film as a nuisance.[20] Intimidated, the board consented to another viewing and two more cuts were accepted by Epoch. Then Oswald Garrison Villard, one of the founders of the NAACP, refused advertising for the film in his New York *Post.* Three days later he printed a Jane Addams review in which she saw the film as a "gathering [of] the most vicious and grotesque individuals he [Griffith] could find among the colored people, and showing them as representatives of the . . . entire race." [21] She, like Wilson, had mistaken verisimilitude for reality.

Although the board gave a final approval on March 15, the NAACP continued its work, nagging the board for the names and addresses of members and urging the mayor to stop the film as detrimental to "public decency." Failing, they sent copies of Francis Hackett's stinging review in the *New Republic* to 500 newspapers, marking the first time either side used a critic's aesthetic standards. Within the week the New York press learned of the board's division and its disclosures brought the NAACP to the mayor's office again. It tried to marshal delegations from many local churches and clubs, but Mayor John P. Mitchell, fearing a riot, refused them a license to parade.[22]

Howe, W. E. B. Du Bois of *The Crisis,* Fred Moore, Rabbi Stephen A. Wise, Villard, delegates from the colored and white clergy and the Urban League overflowed into the outer halls of the mayor's office. Mitchell told them that he had no statutory powers over the film; he then droned through his earlier assurances that slashes in the film had already been made, that riot warnings had been issued, and that he could do no more. The announcement that the picture was being shown with excisions surprised the delegates; they meekly acquiesced and departed.[23]

---

[19] Ibid.
[20] Ibid.
[21] New York *Post,* March 10, 1915, carried the last advertisement. The review appeared March 13, 1915.
[22] *Crisis,* X (May 1915), 40–42.
[23] Ibid. (June 1915), p. 87; NAACP, *Fighting a Vicious Film,* passim; *Afro-American Ledger* (Baltimore), March 27, 1915.

The mayor's conciliatory statement about cuts was achieved at the expense of Negro unity. The meeting in his office revealed the deep fissures that ran through the Negro leadership, an elite that many whites thought was sturdily cemented in common cause. Taking advantage of the strife, the "Tuskegee machine," Booker T. Washington's coterie (a group which it was thought accepted the Negro's low status) had reached the mayor ahead of the NAACP through the efforts of Charles W. Anderson, a friend of Washington and a recently resigned federal officeholder. Often antagonistic, but at times cooperative with the NAACP liberals, the Tuskegee group chose this occasion to embarrass the "Vesey Street crowd" (Anderson's name for the liberals) and "take the wind out of their sails" by demonstrating Washington's influence with those in high places. But though the Negro groups were placated, apparently unknown to Anderson, the requested cuts were not made. Thus the New York campaign was lost amid the recriminations that often marked the Negroes' efforts to unify against the bigotry that existed in the United States.[24]

When the film continued to run, the Negro groups moved to friendlier territory in Boston, home of William Monroe Trotter's *Guardian* and the liberal Boston *Post*. Starting early in April, Negro and white pulpit, press, and lectern attacked the film. Nevertheless, on the first Sunday in April Bostonians opened their papers and found a large sensational, pseudoreligious advertisement for the film which mentioned a forty-piece orchestra, 18,000 extras, and 3,000 horses. By Tuesday Mayor James Curley, who had banned movies of the Jess Willard–Jack Johnson fight, announced that he was giving public hearings to the numerous Negro societies over *Birth of a Nation*. Just before the hearings a Tremont Theater advertisement reminded the public that Wilson, George Peabody, and others had liked the film.[25] The next day accusations flew: in reply to a statement by Moorfield Storey who had accused the manager of issuing distortions, the theater called DuBois' *Crisis* "incendiary." [26] In turn, Griffith chided Storey for ignoring the historians Wilson, James Ford Rhodes, and Walter

---

[24] *Crisis,* X (May 1915), 40–42; *Afro-American Ledger,* March 3, 1915; August Meier, "Booker T. Washington and the Rise of the NAACP," *Crisis,* LXI (February 1954), 122.

[25] Ibid., X (June 1915), 87; NAACP, *Fighting a Vicious Film,* passim. See also Boston *Sunday Post,* April 4, 1915; Boston *Post,* April 6, 7, 8, 1915. The list included Dorothea Dix, Rupert Hughes, Booth Tarkington, Richard Harding Davis, Hugh Johnson, George Peabody, Senators James E. Martine, Duncan U. Fletcher, Henry Lee Myers, Thomas J. Walsh, Wesley L. Jones, Representative Claude Kitchen, the Reverends C. H. Parkhurst and Thomas Gregory. According to the NAACP Dixon's method of soliciting approval was to pass out cards between halves of the film: that is, after the predominantly Griffith parts and before his own part.

[26] NAACP, *Fighting a Vicious Film,* p. 26.

Lynwood Fleming—claiming that all would have accepted the film's thesis—and then made brilliant publicity by offering Storey $10,000 if he could prove the film distorted. They parted coolly when Storey complied; later the film interests declared that Storey had not seen the movie.[27]

Curley, perhaps sensing impending violence, promised to get the picture cut by the municipal censor. At the meeting of April 7 tempers were short. The Negroes hissed the mention of Wilson. In demanding censorship they cited the fact that the United States had banned the importation of boxing films and that the Women's Christian Temperance Union favored film censorship. They pointed to the frequent depiction of "sexual excesses" in movies, raised the fear that the film would create race hatred, and read letters from Addams, Wise, Mary W. Ovington, and other liberals. At one point Curley, piqued at the growing mountain of redundant testimony, asked if *Macbeth* tended to incite feeling against whites. Storey bristled and charged Curley with representing the "other side." The meeting broke up amid Curley's denials, Griffith's interjections on his right to film "history" as he saw it, and the mayor offering to cut a scene showing a Negro chasing a white girl.

Curley made good his offer. The chase scene, several leering Negroes, a marriage between a dissolute Negro and a white girl, the shots of Stoneman alone with his mulatto mistress, and the whole segment showing a corrupt, bacchanalian South Carolina legislature were removed. Curley made it clear, though, that the cuts were a concession and not an act of conscience.

During the second week of the film's run in Boston the *Post* began clearly to take the Negroes' position, though advertising for the film continued to run in its pages. Its writers reminded Bostonians of the murderous moods of the New York audiences observed as they left the Liberty Theater, that Curley's predecessor had stopped the stage production of *The Clansman* in 1906, and chided the producers for using clergymen as "authorities" in the advertisements.[28]

Toward the end of the week violence erupted when two hundred police were summoned because a crowd of Negroes (who were barred from theaters) attempted to purchase tickets. Eleven people were arrested. Two Negroes managed to worm their way into the theater. When one hurled an "acid bomb" and the other an egg, they were quickly arrested. Trotter personally stood bail. On Saturday afternoon rumors of riots spread through the streets. The next day a wild, hooting

---

[27] *New Republic*, III (May 5, 1915), 17; see also correspondence in NAACP, *Fighting a Vicious Film*, passim; *Broad Ax* (Chicago), June 5, 1915; Boston *Post*, April 24, 1915.

[28] Boston *Sunday Post*, April 4, 11, 1915; Boston *Post*, April 6, 7, 8, 1915.

crowd gathered at Faneuil Hall. There, Michael Jordan of the United Irish League, making common cause with the Negroes, castigated Wilson. The *Post* later gave the day's events a whole page. Hurriedly, Governor David Ignatius Walsh and Attorney General Henry Attwill met to thrash out the limits of their authority to stop the film. As the meeting progressed both whites and Negroes gathered on the steps outside to orate. The harried governor promised a delegation that he would ask the legislature to pass a censorship law covering inflammatory material. Meanwhile, he ordered the state police to stop Sunday's show. A day later he managed the excision of another rape scene while the legislature held a hearing on the film.[29]

The publicity caused a few early supporters of the film to have second thoughts. George Peabody labeled the picture "unfair" after an earlier endorsement. Late in the month Senator Wesley L. Jones of Washington, several clerics, and others publicly turned on the film. To conciliate the defectors, the producers introduced a bland prologue extolling the progress of the Negro, but Negroes were still kept from the box office.[30]

During the whole Boston affray Booker T. Washington remained aloof except for his advice and the work of his Negro Business League, which he had been having difficulty controlling. When Griffith, in mid-April, asked him to make a film about Tuskegee, Washington refused because he questioned Griffith's sincerity and did not wish to associate with the makers of the "hurtful, vicious play." Principal Hollis Frissell of Hampton Institute allowed a similar film to be made of his school for use as the prologue to *Birth of a Nation,* a decision which *The Crisis* attributed to Washington's advice. Although Washington gave no overt support, he was gratified to know that "Negroes are a unit in their determination to drive it out of Boston." At the same time he was very much aware that the campaign was increasing the picture's business, for he remembered when Negroes had been hired in 1906 to oppose *The Clansman* as a promotional "gimmick." In addition to these tactical considerations Washington kept out of the Boston affair because the Boston Negro Business League, in which he exerted considerable influence, was in a factional fight over endorsing the Griffith movie. Two members, it was reported, had already tried to endorse the film in his name. It was said that William Lewis, former United States

[29] After the riot the rest of the Boston papers began to cover the movie and its effects. None of them—the *Evening Transcript,* the *Herald,* the *Journal*—adopted a procensorship stand or seemed deeply concerned about the struggle over the film. See the issues of April 18, 1915, through April 26, 1915, particularly.

[30] Boston *Post,* April 12, 18, 19, 1915; *Crisis,* X (June 1915), 87; correspondence in NAACP, *Fighting a Vicious Film,* pp. 30–33.

assistant attorney general and a Negro, concurred in the endorsement. Fortunately for Washington the resolution to endorse was blocked in a meeting of the executive council, but even so he had to manipulate the rebel group into remaining in the organization so as to continue the public impression of Negro unity.[31]

Meanwhile the debate went on in Boston. When the Massachusetts lower house passed a censor bill, all the Boston newspapers carried large advertisements attacking it. On April 24 Trotter was arrested and fined twenty dollars when he tried to use tickets he had bought. Negroes still complained that scenes were removed for "moral" rather than racial reasons and insisted that many offensive shots remained. At a meeting at the First Unitarian Church Charles Eliot of Harvard, William Lewis, and others thrashed out the problem of legislation that would distinguish between art and propaganda—in their view *Birth of a Nation* belonged to the latter category. That this distinction was a main issue occurred to few of the antagonists. Most tried to draw a line short of "absolute freedom," to define what should be banned as "mischief," and to decide whether a "travesty of history" was censorable. Only one man at the meeting thought all censorship a "violation of freedom of the press and public expression." The Federation of Churches of Greater Boston condemned the film as "injurious to public morality." [32]

As the situation in Boston worsened, Wilson's Southern sympathies—not as deep as Dixon's—wavered; the president and the chief justice sought a way out of their endorsement as the adverse press reaction to the film spread. Tumulty suggested "some sort of letter" that would get Wilson out of a corner without appearing to have been bullied by that "unspeakable fellow [Trotter]." Finally, the president permitted Tumulty to write a letter to Representative Thomas Thacher of Massachusetts, asserting that the White House had never sanctioned the film. Although other correspondents were similarly reassured,[33] the damage had been done, for Dixon had been able to use the president's name

---

[31] Phil J. Allston to Booker T. Washington, copy, April 12, 1915; Washington to Allston, copy, April 25, 1915; Washington to Allston, copy, April 19, 1915; Charles E. [?]llason to Washington, June 1, 1915; Samuel E. Courtney to Washington, copy, April 19, 1915; Washington to Courtney, copy, April 23, 1915; Rabbi Abram Simon to Washington, confidential telegram, April 14, 1915; Emmett Scott to Simon, telegram, April 14, 1915, Booker T. Washington Papers, Box 75, Library of Congress. Washington wrote one letter of protest to the Atlanta *Independent* [NAACP, *Fighting a Vicious Film*, pp. 35–36]. See Boston *Post*, April 24, 1915, for hints that Allston himself may have expressed approval of the film.

[32] *Broad Ax*, June 5, 1915; Boston *Post*, April 24, 1915; Boston *Evening Transcript*, April 20, 1915; Boston *Herald*, April 21, 1915; *Crisis*, X (June 1915), 87.

[33] Link, *Wilson*, pp. 253–54; Goldman, *Rendezvous with Destiny*, pp. 176–77.

for commercial purposes for the better part of three months. The Thacher letter was shown to William Lewis and African Methodist Episcopal Zion Bishop Alexander Walters, who were expected to take the belated news to the Negroes who had despaired at the president's thoughtless endorsement. Thus it took three months for Wilson to approach the position of the urban weeklies that dismissed the film as a spectacle and its audiences as curiosities, that denounced the "censors that passed it and the white race that endures it," that blasted Dixon as a "yellow clergyman," and that sometimes noted the paradox of brilliant techniques perverted for specious ends.[34]

After the president's retraction the Boston fight neared the end that Negroes feared. The newly created Massachusetts Board of Censors ignored a petition of six thousand names and permitted the Tremont to continue showing *Birth of a Nation*. The board, which had been created partially because of the Negroes' lobbying, had turned on its makers. Fitfully, the squabble dragged on through the summer with *The Crisis* impotently recording minor successes with triumphant glee and failures with arch cynicism.[35] As the days grew longer the Negroes of Boston hoped that Booker T. Washington and Bishop Walters would come to town to actively aid DuBois and Trotter in keeping the pot boiling. But New York and Boston had become the scenes of bitter defeats, which were reflected across the land.

By midyear, except in a few cases, the distributors of *Birth of a Nation* could exhibit their film almost anywhere they wished. Mayor William Thompson killed it in Chicago and later in all of Illinois. In Wilmington, Delaware, the city council approved a fine of fifty dollars for showing it or *The Nigger*. In Cleveland, Harry Smith of the *Gazette* helped to keep *The Nigger* out of the city, but Mayor Newton D. Baker failed to induce the governor to keep *Birth of a Nation* out of Ohio.[36]

The film could be seen in New York, Los Angeles, San Francisco, and Boston. Agitators were at work against the picture in Baltimore;

[34] "The Civil War in Film," *Literary Digest*, L (March 20, 1915), 608–9; Francis Hackett, "Brotherly Love," *New Republic*, II (March 20, 1915), 185 [See pp. 84–86 of this volume]; see also "After the Play," ibid., V (December 4, 1915), 123; ibid., III (June 5, 1915), 125.

[35] Boston *Post*, June 5, 1915, clipping in the Washington Papers; *Crisis*, X (July 1915), 147–48 insisted there had been no hearing; ibid. (August 1915), 200–201; ibid. (September 1915), 245; "The Negro Business League," ibid. (October 1915), 280–81; "Social Uplift," ibid., 268; "*The Birth of a Nation*," ibid., 295–96. *The Crisis* claimed to have "wounded the bird" because "the latter half has been so cut, so many portions of scenes have been eliminated, that it is a mere succession of pictures, sometimes ridiculous in their inability to tell a coherent story."

[36] See correspondence in n. 31. For suggestions of the political motives of Walsh, Curley, and other Massachusetts politicians see Boston *Herald*, April 18, 26, 1915.

Charleston, West Virginia; Philadelphia; and Atlantic City with scant success.[37] Rarely did the violence and rioting that many Negroes expected occur in these cities. The press at times viewed the film as newsreel reality; often roundly condemned it for the prejudices it presented; argued over authenticity; discussed the social impact; distrusted Dixon; praised Griffith; and except for papers like the New York *Post,* whose editor was accessible to the NAACP, few took unequivocal positions one way or the other.[38] The Negro press, too, ranged from unconcern to dutiful worry and almost universally failed to see it as art or entertainment. The chief difference between the Negro and white press reactions was that some of the Negro editors were less kind to Griffith.[39]

By the latter half of the year, when the Boston rancor had waned, both the NAACP activists and the more covert Booker T. Washington group reassessed what had happened and gained insights about their functions as pressure groups. *The Crisis* conceded that Griffith was an ill-used but "mighty genius" and that negative opposition was pointless. If the film was a "cruel slander upon a weak and helpless race," DuBois wrote, then the race must learn to use its money for films, poetry, music, and its own history. In October the Negroes in Washington, D.C., began preparations for "The Star of Ethiopia," an all-Negro pageant.[40] At Tuskegee, Washington was badgered by writers who wanted him to make films which would refute the stereotypes of *Birth of a Nation* and "make wonderful propaganda for every kind of social reform." He refused, perhaps fearing the loss of face suffered by Frissell when he let Griffith use Hampton for the locale of a film

[37] *Afro-American Ledger,* May 22, 26, June 5, July 31, August 7, September 25, December 25, 1915; *New Jersey Informer,* August 21, 1915, clipping in the Washington Papers.

[38] Chicago *Tribune,* May 9, 14, 15, 1915; Baltimore *Sun,* November 1, 1915; Philadelphia *Inquirer,* March 30, September 5, 23, 26, 27, 1915; Boston *Post,* March 4, 1915; New York *American,* March 5, 1915; Vardac, *Stage to Screen,* p. 224, cites *New York Times,* June 6, 1915; New York *Sun,* March 4, 1915. See also New York *Evening Post,* February 20, March 3, 4, 13, 1915; "The Birth of a Nation," *Outlook,* IV (April 14, 1915), 854; "Negro Segregation Adopted by St. Louis," *Survey,* XXXV (March 11, 1915), 694; ibid., XXXVI (April 24, 1915), 96; ibid. (July 10, 1915), 344–45; *New York Times,* March 4, 7, 1915. See also Ramsaye, *Million and One Nights,* II, 638.

[39] Washington *Bee,* February 20, May 1, 27, June 5, 1915; St. Paul *Appeal,* October 2, 1915; *Afro-American Ledger,* March 3, 13, 20, 1915.

[40] *Crisis,* II (November 1915), 36; "The Slanderous Film," ibid. (December 1915), 76–77. *The Crisis* was probably referring to the fact that Dixon was able to weave his racism into Griffith's art with such finesse that no one could attack ideology and art separately, thus assuring Dixon an audience that he might not have gathered solely on the merits of his own work.

prologue to *Birth of a Nation*.[41] Consequently, the annual report of the NAACP for 1915 could only record a long, negative battle for censorship. Negroes had demonstrated and had broken into segregated theaters to get a hearing for their censorship pleas—a stand their leaders were coming to reject in principle but tactically were unable to replace with another weapon because of budgets already strained by litigations and demonstrations. And sometimes even censorship backfired, as in Massachusetts, where the board that the Negroes helped create eventually accepted most of the films to which the Negroes objected.[42]

For Negroes, their failure in the fight against *Birth of a Nation* was another reminder that the scant progress made in the Roosevelt years was not necessarily inevitable and that the Wilson era was a time of troubles characterized by a Jim Crow federal government, lynching, and the seed-time of a new Ku Klux Klan. The controversy also demonstrated the seriousness with which films had come to be regarded both as creators and reflectors of opinions and attitudes after only two decades of existence.

[41] Florence Sewell Bond to Washington, June 27, 1915; Washington to Bond, June 30, 1915; Washington to F. P. Hull, personal-confidential copy, April 23, 1915; Scott to J. H. Beak, St. Paul Association of Commerce, October 27, 1915; Beak to Washington, wire, October 10, 1915; Amy Vorhaus to Washington, July 9, 1915; Laurence Gomme to Emmett Scott, June 17, 1915; Scott to Gomme, copy, June 23, 1915, Washington Papers.

[42] NAACP, *Sixth Annual Report*, pp. 11–22; Vorhaus to Washington, July 9, 1915; Washington to Vorhaus, July 13, 1915, Washington Papers. For examples of later protest see Francis Grimké, *"The Birth of a Nation,"* (n.p., October 15, 1915) in Francis J. Grimké, *Addresses and Pamphlets* (n.p., n.d.); NAACP, *Fighting a Vicious Film*; Reverend W. Bishop Johnson, *"The Birth of a Nation": A Monumental Slander of American History; the Negro and the Civil War by Thomas Dixon Analytically and Critically Considered* (n.p., [1916]); Isaac L. Thomas, *"The Birth of a Nation": A Hyperbole versus a Negro's Plea for Fair Play* (Philadelphia, 1916) —all in the Moreland Library, Howard University, Washington, D.C. See also *"Birth of a Nation* Revived, Draws Protest," *Crisis*, XLV (March 1938), 84.

The Negro in THE BIRTH OF A NATION
by PETER NOBLE

*The North London Film Society opens
its new season in October, when* The
Birth of a Nation, *a classic of the silent
days, will be screened. The film will be
shown unabridged and will include the
scenes which were once banned because
they were alleged to be anti-Negro, and
which caused riots in America.*

NORTH LONDON OBSERVER,
SEPTEMBER 27, 1946

If *Uncle Tom's Cabin* was the first full-length picture to give
prominence to Negro subservience, the first important full-length film
to devote much of its content to Negro villainy was the famous *The
Birth of a Nation.* It is not my intention here to analyze D. W.
Griffith's monumental achievement in terms of its admittedly considerable artistic merit, but to concentrate solely upon one aspect—
its extraordinarily vicious anti-Negro bias. Director Griffith was himself
a Southerner, steeped in an atmosphere of racial intolerance, and
brought up with the conventional Southern states attitude to the colored
man. In the majestic sweep of Thomas Dixon's strongly partisan novel
The Clansman he probably saw perfect material for a large-scale epic.
The resultant production was technically and artistically far ahead of
any other movie of that period, for it must be acknowledged that
Griffith was a cinematic genius and certainly the pioneer in employing
a number of vital techniques in filmmaking which are in general use
in the studios today. Nevertheless, however great the workmanship,
however inspired the direction, and however remarkable the acting
and production of *The Birth of a Nation,* the fact remains that for
sheer bias and distortion this film heads the considerable list of Amer-

From The Negro in Films *by Peter Noble (London: Skelton Robinson, 1948). Copyright 1948 by Peter Noble. Reprinted by permission of
the author. Title supplied.*

ican motion pictures which have consciously maligned the Negro race. Perhaps it would be as well to deal in some detail here with this truly historic film. Its great theme covered the eventful period of the American Civil War, tracing the histories of two families, one from the North and another from the Southern town of Piedmont. We are shown the palatial homestead of the Southern family, the Camerons, with the usual pretty picture of the indulgent master and the devoted slaves. The Stoneman's the family from the Northern state, and the Camerons are good friends, and, indeed, Ben Cameron falls in love with Elsie Stoneman and their marriage seems imminent.[1] Then comes the Civil War, and the film traces their necessarily ill-fated love story, for Southerner Cameron becomes a colonel in the Confederate army, while Elsie is the daughter of a leading Northern politician, whose main political platform is the abolition of salvery. The bitterness of the Civil War drives the young lovers apart, and with the Confederate army facing defeat, their love seems destined to be destroyed. Later, Cameron, the "Little Colonel," is wounded and captured in battle by Stoneman's son, and is in danger of being shot as a traitor; but is eventually released through the intervention of Elsie, who still loves him, and his mother, both of whom plead with Lincoln on his behalf. There are many stirring scenes of the final months of the Civil War, but at last we see the final peace settlement, with the fanatical Northerners demanding harsh terms and carrying their victory into even harsher realization.

Follows the Reconstruction period, with Stoneman arriving in Piedmont with Elsie, and taking up his abode next door to the Camerons, who now regard him with distaste. The Northern politician has been appointed adviser to Silas Lynch, the lieutenant-governor of the district, and quickly he proceeds to bring his ideas of "revenge on the South and complete emancipation for all Negroes" into full play. (Incidentally, "Stoneman" is said to be based upon an actual political figure of the period, Thaddeus Stevens, who also figured more recently in William Dieterle's film *The Man on America's Conscience,* released in the United States under the title of *Tennessee Johnson.* [1943] Griffith portrayed this character with very little attention to the true facts, and Dieterle was also attacked by the Negro press for his unfair conception of the well-known abolitionist.)

The sympathy of the entire film is with the South, though this is not unnatural since Griffith was born in Kentucky; but his understandable partisanship provides no real excuse for the deliberate dis-

---

[1] [Editor's note: Although Ben first falls in love with a picture of Elsie that Phil Stoneman shows him in Piedmont, Ben actually meets her when she nurses the wounded soldiers in Washington.]

tortion and, indeed, his almost malevolent disregard of the real historical facts. His treatment of Stoneham, the progressive, liberal-minded
abolitionist, is symptomatic of his narrow and prejudiced outlook. The
Yankee politician is depicted by Griffith as a villainous careerist, ego-
tistically insincere, whose avowed plans for the betterment of Negro
life and conditions are shown to be fired only by personal ambitions
and a deep hatred of the South. With the "renegade" Negro leader,
Silas Lynch, he is seen plotting to enforce a "black stranglehold"
(Griffith's own description) on the defeated Southern states. The
mulatto, Lynch, is also shown as a character of the utmost villainy.
His lust extends not only to power, it seems, but also to Elsie, and
in the final reel of the film the inevitable rape attempt occurs, following the politician's refusal to allow the mulatto to marry his daughter.
(This latter incident provided yet another subtle dig at the "Northern
liberal," who, while fighting for Negro emancipation and considering
that blacks were the social equal of whites, still refused to allow his
daughter to marry a man with Negro blood in his veins.) The pathological obsession of some Americans with the Negro rape of white women
is remarkable, and seems to have occurred with astonishing frequency
in American literature of the past hundred years. Griffith's *The Birth
of a Nation* marked its first appearance on the screen.

His treatment of mulattos, those "unfortunates" who possess both
white and Negro blood, is interesting in its vehemence. Not only does
he depict Silas Lynch in the most unfavorable light, but he also introduces another half-caste, Stoneman's servant and mistress, who is revealed as a scheming, envious, entirely unpleasant creature, yearning
for the time when she can treat whites not as equals but as *inferiors*.
Hatred and malevolence are constantly reflected in her dark, evil face
when she meets white politicians in Stoneman's house, and in one
astonishing scene, she literally writhes with hate, spitting fury and
vowing vengeance on Stoneman's guests and friends for continuing to
treat her as a servant rather than as the politician's "unofficial" wife.
And there is much more in the same vein. Mulattos receive from
Griffith even worse treatment, it would appear, than full-blooded Negroes.

To continue with the plot of *The Birth of a Nation,* Lynch and the
politician eject all the white Southerners from positions of power and
prominence, and substitute ignorant, ill-educated Negro types. From
the program notes given out at the first performance of the film comes
Griffith's description of the following scenes: "The rule of the carpetbaggers begins. The Union League, so-called, wins the ensuing state
election. Silas Lynch, the mulatto, is chosen lieutenant-governor, and
a legislature with carpetbag and Negro members in overwhelming
majority loots the state. Lawlessness runs riot. Whites are elbowed off

the streets, overawed at the polls, and often despoiled of their possessions."

And the above is an accurate picture of events in the actual film. We see swaggering black toughs elbowing white women off the pavements and indulging in similar brutalities to all the white citizens. The new regime of "Northern progressiveness" brings, according to Griffith, an even worse tyranny than existed previously when the white landowners were in power. There follows much talk of a "Black Empire" and of Negro plans for the complete suppression of the South, and such is Griffith's directorial power that we find ourselves believing him when he draws the situation in the final reel as being fraught with hideous disaster for the formerly well-to-do, and equally well-meaning, whites in the defeated South. They are, it seems, threatened by the plundering, raping, and looting of their subhuman exslaves. But help is at hand. A new and heroic band of Southerners springs up, led by excolonel Ben Cameron, an organization of exservicemen, a group which will put to rights all the injustices of the Northern rule. This new army of courageous and chivalrous heroes will bring justice (and with it the terror of the hangman's rope) to every Negro in the South. And the name of the organization? None other than that dreaded and terrifying body, the now notorious Ku Klux Klan!

By night they ride in their white hoods, lynching, murdering, whipping, and threatening. By sheer force, intimidation, tyranny, and terrorism the black citizens of the Old South are driven from office, even from the polls, afraid to use their hard-won votes, afraid to take further advantage of their new-found privileges. Since, however, the Negroes have been depicted throughout the film's length in the worst possible light, the inevitable conclusion reached by cinemagoers is that their persecution by the Ku Klux Klan is only part of their just deserts. Indeed, audiences running into millions must have left the cinema with this conclusion.

The Birth of a Nation showed starkly that the question of historic accuracy did not trouble Griffith overmuch. There was no attempt at truth, and certainly not justice, as may be seen in the following instances. Time and again we are shown the "good niggers," the trusted and faithful Negro slaves who still cling devotedly to the Camerons through times of war and defeat, and hate the free North, preferring slavery in the South. No doubt at that period in the history of the USA these types of black retainers did in fact exist, but it was inevitable that Griffith concentrated all his patronizing sympathy upon these "Uncle Tom" characters while showing all other black men as vicious rebels and killers. Gus, for example, a "renegade" Negro, formerly employed as a servant in the Camerons' household, is seen at the end of the war as a swaggering soldier in the colored militia occupying the town of Piedmont. Inevitably he is a hard-swearing, hard-drinking, glowering, and lustful scoundrel, and just as inevitably he tries to rape the white heroine, Flora Cameron, eventually driving her to suicide in a brutal attempted-rape scene. (Gus was played by a white actor, Walter Long, noted for his tough and villainous appearance, made even more hideous, incidentally, by the liberal application on his features of what appeared to be black boot polish. Other white actors played leading colored characters, for apparently Griffith would not employ Negro actors to play parts of any significance, even though they be villains.)

Another scene shows the newly formed Negro parliament in session. Here "the new tyrants of the South" hold sway. They concern themselves with passing measures preventing white citizens from holding any important offices, lounging back in their chairs with their bare feet up on their desks, a bottle of whisky in one hand and a leg of chicken in the other. These "politicians" are not interested in affairs of state; they desire only revenge on their former white masters and content themselves with planning retaliation, the while intimidating white girls in the gallery with nods, winks, and lewd suggestions. This is how Griffith handles the first historic attempts by the former slaves to govern themselves in that tragic postwar period. His monstrous caricatures of colored politicians, officials, army officers, soldiers, and servants in *The Birth of a Nation* rival anything seen on the screen since that time.

The final reel of this monumental film sees the Ku Klux Klan riding into town and sweeping the blacks out of Piedmont, scattering the frightened Negroes in a magnificently directed crowd scene. The black bullies are tamed by the hooded heroes! In one sequence a group of colored soldiers are besieging a hut where the proud and heroic Cameron family have fled and are fighting for their lives. As the murdering blacks, with bulging eyes and frothing mouths, are breaking down the door for the final kill, the white-hooded Ku Klux Klan sweep over the hill to a burst of Wagnerian music and in an exciting and impressive sequence save the white family from the Negro terror. Such a distortion has, indeed, to be seen to be believed; many younger filmgoers who have been told about "the great film, *The Birth of a Nation*" are by no means aware of its almost unbelievable viciousness. And, although it must be admitted that Griffith's epic has an honored place in film history and may still be regarded technically as a landmark in film production, it deserves scant recognition nowadays from more enlightened cinema audiences. Even regarded as a period piece, it is still capable of causing harm.

As historian Lewis Jacobs says of *The Birth of a Nation*, in his book *The Rise of the American Film*: "The film was a passionate and persuasive avowal of the inferiority of the Negro. In viewpoint it was, surely, narrow and prejudiced. Griffith's Southern upbringing made him completely sympathetic towards author Thomas Dixon's exaggerated ideas and the fire of his convictions gave the film a rude strength. At one point in the picture a title bluntly editorialized that the South must be made 'safe' for the whites. The entire portrayal of the Reconstruction days showed the Negro, when freed from his white domination, as an ignorant, lustful villain. Negro congressmen were pictured drinking heavily, coarsely reclining in Congress with bare feet upon their desks, lustfully ogling the white women in the balcony. Gus, the Negro servant, is depicted as a renegade when he joins the emancipated Negroes. His advances on Flora, the 'Little Colonel's' sister, and Silas Lynch's proposal to the politician Stoneman's daughter, are overdrawn to make the Negro appear obnoxious and audacious. The Negro servants who remain with the Camerons, the dignified Southern family, on the other hand, are treated with patronizing regard for their faithfulness, and the necessity of the separation of Negro from white, with the white as the ruler, is passionately maintained throughout the film. The social implications of this celebrated picture aroused a storm of protest in the North." [2]

Griffith had the impudence to insert an epilogue to the film, reading—"The establishment of the South in its rightful place is the birth of a new nation. . . . The new nation, the real United States, as the years glided by, turned away forever from the blood lust of war and anticipated with hope the world millennium in which the brotherhood of love should bind all the nations." And after this production, which was an incitement to racial intolerance (and worse), Griffith went on to make the famous *Intolerance,* which condemned the very things most apparent in his previous film. Perhaps he was never fully aware of his own shortcomings?

At any rate a storm of indignation arose after the first showing of *The Birth of a Nation,* a storm which continued through the war years and well into the 1920s. It is said that later on Griffith relented somewhat concerning the cruelty of his portrayal of the Negro in this historic film; and in 1918, in his *Greatest Thing in Life,* he inserted a sequence in which a dying Negro soldier cried for his mother and a white comrade kissed him as he died. This shamelessly sentimental scene was, as Richard Watts, Jr., remarked, in *New Theater,* November 1936, "a pretty shoddy and futile effort to make up for what he had done in his film of Dixon's novel *The Clansman.*"

In New York, *The Birth of a Nation* was banned for a time, and it

---

[2] [Editor's note: Noble quotes this somewhat inaccurately. See Lewis Jacobs, "D. W. Griffith: *The Birth of a Nation*," included in this volume, pp. 154–68.]

was also refused a license for exhibition in Connecticut, Illinois, Kansas, Massachusetts, Minnesota, New Jersey, Wisconsin, Ohio, and many other states. Such prominent people as Oswald Garrison Villard, Jane Addams, and Charles Eliot, president of Harvard, spoke bitterly and often against the showing of the film. Rabbi Stephen Wise declared that it was "an intolerable insult to the Negro people." The liberal magazine *The Nation* described the film as "improper, immoral, and injurious, a deliberate attempt to humiliate ten million American citizens and to portray them as nothing but beasts." Historians were quick to point out the many inaccuracies in the film, and generally the effect upon intelligent people was one of antagonism and indignation. Griffith was shocked by this opposition and rose to the defense of his film with a pamphlet entitled *The Rise and Fall of Free Speech in America,* which included quotations from those magazines and newspapers which had endorsed the film, but which did not attempt to answer the accusations of race prejudice. He was greatly incensed by the attack on his beloved film and for many years referred to the public protest as deliberately unfair. But the movie deserves all the protests made against it, then and now.

As Dr. Lawrence Reddick points out in *The Journal of Negro Education,* Summer 1944: "The film's justification of the Ku Klux Klan was at least one factor which enabled the Klan to enter upon its period of greatest expansion, reaching a total membership of five million." A contemporary American film critic, Richard Watts, Jr., states in *New Theater*: "As a completely partisan account of a particularly ugly chapter in American history, *The Birth of a Nation* still possesses a certain stunning power. But its cruel unfairness to the Negro is an inescapable blot upon it." And the English film critic Oswell Blakeston declares, in *Close Up,* August 1929: "As a spectacle Griffith's production was awe-inspiring and stupendous, but as a picture of Negro life it was not only false, but it has done the Negro irreparable harm. And no wonder, since it was taken from a puerile novel, *The Clansman,* a book written to arouse racial hate by appealing to the basest passions of the semiliterate." Many leading critics on both sides of the Atlantic agreed with the above statement.

Prominent in the movement against the showing of the film was the National Association for the Advancement of Colored People, which did a great deal of valuable work in this direction, canalizing the protests of Negroes and enlightened white organizations and individuals everywhere. As late as 1931 the film was banned in Philadelphia after the mayor had declared it "prejudicial to peace between the black and white races." Nevertheless, in spite of all the public action taken against the film, *The Birth of a Nation* was an enormous financial success, establishing D. W. Griffith as the greatest film director of his time and exerting a considerable influence upon the millions of people who saw it. It is to be regretted that a film which still occupies something of a place of honor in the list of memorable achievements of the cinema could bear such responsibility for a great and incalculable harm. Thirty years ago it constituted an incitement to race riot, and seeing it today still tends to leave a nasty taste in one's mouth.

Incidentally, this controversial picture was revived in New York in 1942, despite the protests of Negroes everywhere, but eventually due to the opposition of the Negro press, the picture was withdrawn after a run of a few days. Afterwards Lowell Mellett, chief of the Bureau of Motion Pictures of the Office of War Information, assured the press that his office would seek to prevent future exhibition of Griffith's film; and since that time it has been shown only by film societies in the USA and Britain.

Cultural History Written with Lightning:
The Significance of
THE BIRTH OF A NATION
by EVERETT CARTER

On February 20, 1915, David Wark Griffith's long film, *The Clansman,* was shown in New York City. One of the spectators was Thomas Dixon, the author of the novel from which it was taken, who was moved by the power of the motion picture to shout to the wildly applauding spectators that its title would have to be changed. To match the picture's greatness, he suggested, its name should be *The Birth of a Nation.*[1] Only by a singular distortion of meaning could the film be interpreted as the story of a country's genesis; the birth it did herald was of an American industry and an American art; any attempt to define the cinema and its impact upon American life must take into account this classic movie. For with the release of *The Birth of a Nation* "significant motion-picture history begins."[2] Its prestige became enormous. It was the first picture to be played at the White House, where Woodrow Wilson was reported to have said: "It is like writing history with lightning."[3] By January 1916 it had given 6,266 performances in the area of greater New York alone.[4] If we conservatively estimate that five hundred patrons saw each performance, we arrive at the astounding total of over three million residents of and

From American Quarterly *12 (Fall 1960): 347–57. Copyright 1960, Trustees of the University of Pennsylvania. Reprinted by permission of the author and the publisher.*

[1] Lewis Jacobs, *The Rise of the American Film* (New York: Harcourt, Brace & Co., 1939), p. 175 [See p. 157 of this volume].

[2] Seymour Stern, "*The Birth of a Nation* in Retrospect," *International Photographer* VII (April, 1935), 4.

[3] Jacobs, p. 175 [See p. 157 of this volume].

[4] Stern, *International Photographer*, VII, 4.

visitors to New York who saw the picture, and forever viewed themselves and their country's history through its colorations. And not only does significant motion-picture history begin, but most of the problems of the art's place in our culture begin too. The picture projects one of the most persistent cultural illusions; it presents vividly and dramatically the ways in which a whole people have reacted to their history; its techniques in the narrowest sense are the fully realized techniques of the pictorial aspects of the motion picture; in the widest sense, its techniques are a blend of the epical and the symbolically realistic, and each part of this mixture has developed into a significant genre of cinematic art.

Griffith was a Kentuckian, a devout believer in Southern values, and these values, he was certain, were embodied in *The Clansman,* a sentimental novel of the Reconstruction which had appeared in 1905, had been widely read, had been seen in dramatic form throughout the South, and whose author had dedicated it "To the memory of a Scotch-Irish leader of the South, my Uncle, Colonel Leroy McAfee, Grand Titan of the Invisible Empire Ku Klux Klan." [5] In his introduction, Dixon went on to describe his theme: "How the young South, led by the reincarnated souls of the Clansmen of Old Scotland, went forth under this cover and against overwhelming odds, daring exile, imprisonment, and a felon's death, and saved the life of a people, forms one of the most dramatic chapters in the history of the Aryan race." [6] This strong suggestion that the South's struggle is a racial epic, involving all the people of one blood in their defense against a common ancestral enemy, became, as we shall see, a major influence upon Griffith's conception of his cinematic theme. And, in addition, the novel in so many ways served as what would later be called a "treatment" from which the story would be filmed, that we must examine the book closely before we can understand the significance of the film.

The Clansman told the story of "Thaddeus Stevens' bold attempt to Africanize the ten great states of the American Union. . . ." It interpreted the history of the Reconstruction as the great Commoner's vengeance motivated partly by economics: the destruction of his Pennsylvania iron mills by Lee's army,[7] partly by religion: in his parlor there was "a picture of a nun . . . he had always given liberally to an orphanage conducted by a Roman Catholic sisterhood;" [8] but mainly by lust: his housekeeper was "a mulatto, a woman of extraordinary

---

[5] Thomas Dixon, *The Clansman* (New York: Grosset & Dunlap, 1905), Dedication, without page number.

[6] *The Clansman,* Introduction, without page number.

[7] *The Clansman,* p. 95.

[8] *The Clansman,* p. 90.

animal beauty . . ." who became, through her power over Austin Stoneman (the fictional name for Stevens) "the presiding genius of national legislation." [9] Stoneman was shown in private conference with Lincoln, whose words in his Charleston debate with Douglas were directly quoted: "I believe there is a physical difference between the white and black races which will forever forbid their living together on terms of political and social equality." [10] Stoneman's instruments in the South were all described as animals, demonstrating that the Civil War was fought to defend civilization against the barbaric and bestial. Silas Lynch, the carpetbagger, "had evidently inherited the full physical characteristics of the Aryan race, while his dark yellowish eyes beneath his heavy brows glowed with the brightness of the African jungle." [11] The Negro leader, Aleck, had a nose "broad and crushed flat against his face," and jaws "strong and angular, mouth wide, and lips thick, curling back from rows of solid teeth set obliquely. . . ." [12] The Cameron family of the Old South were the principal victims; Gus, a renegade Negro ravished Marion Cameron, the sixteen-year-old ". . . universal favorite . . ." who embodied "the grace, charm, and tender beauty of the Southern girl . . . ;" [13] Silas Lynch attempted to violate Elsie Stoneman, the betrothed of Ben Cameron. The actual rape was a climax of a series of figurative violations of the South by the North, one of which was the entry of Stoneman into the black legislature, carried by two Negroes who made "a curious symbolic frame for the chalk-white passion of the old Commoner's face. No sculptor ever dreamed a more sinister emblem of the corruption of a race of empire-builders than this group. Its black figures, wrapped in the night of four thousand years of barbarism, squatted there the 'equal' of their master, grinning at his forms of justice, the evolution of forty centuries of Aryan genius." [14] These figurative and literal ravishments provoked the formation of the Ku Klux Klan, whose like ". . . the world had not seen since the knights of the Middle Ages rode on their holy crusades." [15] The Klan saved Elsie, revenged Marion, brought dismay to the Negro, the carpetbagger, and the scallawag and, in the final words of the book, ". . . Civilization has been saved, and the South redeemed from shame." [16]

[9] The Clansman, p. 57.
[10] Paul M. Angle, Created Equal? (Chicago: University of Chicago Press, 1958), p. 235. The Clansman, p. 46 ff.
[11] The Clansman, p. 93.
[12] The Clansman, pp. 248–49.
[13] The Clansman, p. 254.
[14] The Clansman, p. 171.
[15] The Clansman, p. 316.
[16] The Clansman, p. 374.

The picture followed the book faithfully in plot, character, motivation, and theme, and became a visualization of the whole set of irrational cultural assumptions which may be termed the "Plantation Illusion." The Illusion has many elements, but it is based primarily upon a belief in a golden age of the antebellum South, an age in which feudal agrarianism provided the good life for wealthy, leisured, kindly, aristocratic owner and loyal, happy, obedient slave. The enormous disparity between this conception and the reality has been the subject of Gaines's *The Southern Plantation*[17] and Stampp's *The Peculiar Institution*.[18] But our concern is not with the reality but with what people have thought and felt about that reality; this thinking and feeling is the Illusion, and the stuff of the history of sensibility. The Illusion was embodied in Kennedy's *Swallow Barn* (1832), developed through Carruther's *The Cavaliers of Virginia* (1834) and firmly fixed in the national consciousness by Stephen Foster's "Old Folks at Home" (1851), "My Old Kentucky Home" and "Massa's in the Cold, Cold Ground" (1852), and "Old Black Joe," songs which nostalgically describe a "longing for that old plantation . . ." In 1905 Dixon summarized it in the assertion that the South before the Civil War was ruled by an "aristocracy founded on brains, culture, and blood," the "old fashioned dream of the South" which "but for the Black curse . . . could be today the garden of the world."

This was the image realized almost immediately at the beginning of *The Birth of a Nation*. A scene of Southern life before the Civil War is preceded by the title: "In the Southland, life runs in a quaintly way that is no more." A primitive cart is shown trundling up a village street, filled with laughing Negroes; there is further merriment as a few children fall from the cart and are pulled up into it; then appears a scene of a young aristocrat helping his sister into a carriage; she is in white crinoline and carries a parasol; the young Southerner helps her gallantly from the carriage, and the title reads: "Margaret Cameron, daughter of the old South, trained in manners of the old school." With the two levels of feudal society established, the scene is then of the porch of the plantation house. Dr. and Mrs. Cameron are rocking; he has a kitten in his arms, and puppies are shown playing at his feet. A pickaninny runs happily in and out among the classic columns while the Camerons look indulgently on; a very fat and very black servant claps her hands with glee.

A corollary of this aspect of the Southern Illusion, one might even say a necessary part of it, is the corresponding vision of the North as the land of coldness, harshness, mechanical inhumanity; expressed most

[17] F. P. Gaines, *The Southern Plantation* (New York: Columbia University Press, 1924), pp. 143–236.

[18] Kenneth Stampp, *The Peculiar Institution* (New York: Alfred A. Knopf, 1956).

generously, it is the description of the North as "Head" and the South as the warm human "Heart" which was Sidney Lanier's major metaphor in his Reconstruction poems. Although Lanier had called for the reunion of the heart and head, a modern Southerner, John Crowe Ransom, has scolded Lanier for preaching reconciliation when, Ransom said, what should have been preached was the "contumacious resistance" of the warm, agrarian South against the harsh industrialism and rationalism of the North.[19] *The Clansman* had emphasized the contrast between warm South and cold North by rechristening Thaddeus Stevens, "Thaddeus *Stoneman*"—the man of stone; the radical republican who is the obdurate villain of the picture. He has a clubfoot and moves angularly and mechanically; his house, his dress, are gloomy, dark, cold, as opposed to the warmth and lightness of the Southern plantation garments and scene. In the novel, Dixon had identified him as the owner of Pennsylvania iron mills, and Griffith took the hint, giving him clothes to wear and expressions to assume which, in their harshness and implacability, suggest the unyielding metal. The sense of commercialism, combined with rigidity and pious hypocrisy is identified with the North, too, by showing the presumed beginnings of slavery in America. We see a Puritan preacher sanctimoniously praying while two of the elect arrange the sale of a cringing slave; the following scene is of abolitionists demanding the end of slavery; the grouping of the two scenes, the dress and features of the characters in both, make the point strongly that these are the same people; the montage is a dramatization of Ben Cameron's assertion in the novel, that "our slaves were stolen from Africa by Yankee skippers. . . . It was not until 1836 that Massachusetts led in abolition—not until all her own slaves had been sold to us at a profit. . . ." [20]

In these opening scenes, too, we have the complete cast of characters of the plantation ideal. The Camerons are shown as they go down to the fields to mingle with the happy and trusting slaves. A title tells us that "in the two-hour interval for dinner given in their working day from six to six the slaves enjoy themselves"; then appears a view of slaves clapping hands and dancing. Ben Cameron places his hand paternally upon the shoulders of one, and shakes hands with another who bobs in a perfect frenzy of grateful loyalty: in several seconds a wonderful summary of a hundred years of romantic tradition in which "a beautiful felicity of racial contact has been presented, not as occasional but as constant; an imperious kindness on the part of the whites, matched by obsequious devotion on the part of the blacks." [21]

---

[19] John Crowe Ransom, "Hearts and Heads," *American Review*, II (March 1934), 559.

[20] *The Clansman*, pp. 124–25.

[21] Gaines, p. 210.

The plantation ideal had to explain the obvious fact that during the war and Reconstruction, many Negroes fought with the Union and greeted emancipation with joy. The illusion protected itself by explaining that the true, Southern, full-blooded Negro remained loyal throughout and after the war. It expanded the truth of individual instances of this kind into a general rule. In the Civil War sequences of *The Birth of a Nation*, the Camerons' slaves are shown cheering the parade of the Confederate soldiers as they march off to defend them against their freedom. The fat Negro cook and the others of the household staff are described as "The Faithful Souls"; they weep at Southern defeat and Northern triumph; they rescue Dr. Cameron from his arrest by Reconstruction militia.

While the illusion persistently maintained the loyalty of the true slave, it premised the disaffection of other Negroes upon several causes, all of them explicable within the framework of the plantation ideal. The major explanation was the corruption of the Negro by the North. The freed Negro, the Union soldier, is a monster of ingratitude, a renegade from the feudal code, and only evil can be expected of him. The picture shows The Faithful Soul deriding one such abomination; the title reads, "You Northern black trash, don't you try any of your airs on me." And a little later, we see her lips saying, and then read on the screen, "Those free niggers from the North sho' am crazy." The second explanation was that the mulatto, the person of mixed blood, was the archvillain in the tragedy of the South. Stoneman, the radical republican leader, is shown, as he was in the novel, under the spell of his mulatto housekeeper. A scene of Stoneman lasciviously fondling his mistress is preceded by the title: "The great leader's weakness that is to blight a nation." The mistress, in turn, has as a lover another mulatto, Silas Lynch, who is described as the principal agent in Stoneman's plans to "Africanize" the South. This dark part of the plantation illusion is further represented in the twin climaxes of the picture, both of which are attempted sexual assaults on blonde white girls, one by a Northern Negro, and the other by the mulatto, Silas Lynch.

The sexual terms into which this picture translated the violation of the Southern illusion by the North underscores the way in which the film incorporates one of the most vital of the forces underlying the illusion—the obscure, bewildering complex of sexual guilt and fear which the ideal never overtly admits, but which are, as Stampp, Cash, and Myrdal [22] have pointed out, deeply interwoven into the Southern sensibility. The mulatto, while he occasionally would be the offspring of the lowest class of white woman with Negroes, much more com-

[22] Stampp, pp. 350 ff., W. J. Cash, *The Mind of the South* (New York: Alfred A. Knopf, 1941), pp. 114–17. Gunnar Myrdal, *An American Dilemma* (New York: Harper & Bros., 1944), p. 562.

monly was the result of the debasement of the Negro woman by the
white man, and, not infrequently, by the most aristocratic of the characters in the plantation conception.[23] At the very least, then, the deep
convictions of the Protestant South about the nature of sin would cause
the Southern illusion to regard a living, visible evidence of a parent's
lust as evil in itself, and at the most, and worst, and most debilitating,
as a reminder of the burden of guilt the white must bear in the record
of sexual aggression against the Negro. *The Birth of a Nation* gives all
aspects of these sexual fears and guilts full expression. Typically, the
burden of guilt is discharged by making the mulatto the evil force in
the picture, evincing both the bestial, animal sensuality of the unrestrained Negro and the perverted intellectual powers of the white. And
the full-blooded, but renegade, black justifies any excess of the Klan,
by accomplishing that final most dreaded act of the sexual drama, the
violation of the blonde "little sister." The book had made the rape
actual: "A single tiger-spring," it narrated, "and the black claws of the
beast sank into the soft white throat." [24] The picture shows us the little
sister as she jumps off a cliff to escape dishonor; but a scene of Gus,
kneeling blackly over the white-clad, broken body, makes the sexual
point without the overt act. And this point is further reinforced by a
description of Lynch's attempts to possess Elsie Stoneman, by a portrayal of the passage of the first law of the black Reconstruction legislature legalizing miscegenation, and by a scene of Negroes who carry
signs reading "Equal rights, equal marriage."

The descriptions of Gus as "tigerlike" and of Stoneman's mistress as
a leopard, brings us to the last element of the plantation illusion—the
defense of the system on the basis of the essential nonhumanity of the
Negro. The book had been blatant in its statement of this position; the
picture projects this attitude by its shots of the eyes of mulatto and
Negro displaying animal lust and ferocity, and by its view of Gus as a
slinking animal, waiting, crouching, springing.

As the record of a cultural illusion, then, *The Birth of a Nation* is
without equal. Furthermore, it is the film to which, as the historian of
the art declares, "much of subsequent filmic progress owes its inspiration." In order to understand its significance, one has to remind one-
self of the nature of the motion-picture art. It is not an art of external
events and the people who perform them; it is an art of the camera
and the film. Before Griffith, the camera was treated as a fixed position,
much like the spectator of the drama. The interpretation was by the
actors, by their bodies, by their faces, by physical objects, and by the
settings before which these performed. Griffith made the ordering and

[23] Stampp, p. 355.
[24] *The Clansman,* p. 304.

interpretation—the art, in brief—one of the location, the angle, the movement of the camera and of the juxtaposition of the images the camera records by means of cutting and arranging these images to bring out their significance. An example of the first technique—camera position—was the famous scene of Sherman's march to the sea. The camera shows the serpentine line of Union troops in the distance, winding over the landscape. War is distant; it is simply a move of masses over territory; the camera turns slowly until it includes, in the left foreground, the figures of a weeping mother and child. Immediately a perspective is achieved; what was remote and inhuman becomes close and humanized; the human implications of such mass movements are illustrated clearly, sharply, poignantly simply by the perspective of the camera.

An example of the second aspect of the purely filmic technique was Griffith's juxtaposition of the two parallel scenes in the introduction to the plantation ideal: Negro cart and white carriage. Alone the first shot would be at worst meaningless, at best a bit of atmosphere; the second would serve merely to introduce two characters who might have been presented in an infinite variety of ways. Placed together, both scenes become significant forms because of the two elements they have in common: means of transportation, and the perfect fitness of each group of characters to that means; the juxtaposition thus serves to summarize the feudal theory—the rightness of each part of society in its place.

A second aspect of this editorial technique—the cutting and arranging of images—was also brought to its fullness of possibility in *The Birth of a Nation* after Griffith had experimented with it in earlier films. This was the intercutting of parallel scenes occurring at different locations in space, but at the same location in time, each of which has a bearing upon the other, with the meanings of both carefully interwoven, and with the tensions of either relieved only when the two are finally brought together. The famous example of this, an example which has been followed faithfully from then on, was the intercutting of shots of Lynch's attempted forced marriage to Elsie Stoneman with shots of the gathering of the Klan which will effect her rescue. A series of six shots of Lynch and Elsie is superseded by seven shots of the gathering of the Klan; then two single shots of the Klan and two of the attempted ravishment are quickly alternated; fourteen shots of Lynch and Elsie are followed by one of the Klan; a shot of long duration during which the Elsie-Lynch struggle becomes more intense is then followed by seven shots of the Klan's ride to the rescue; and so it goes until both sequences are joined in space when the Klan finally reaches Elsie. As an early critic described the meaning of this achievement: "Every little series of pictures . . . symbolizes a sentiment, a passion, or an emotion. Each successive series, similar yet different, carries the emotion to the next higher power, till at last, when both of the parallel emotions have attained the n*th* power, so to speak, they meet in the final swift shock of victory and defeat." [25] To these epoch-making achievements of camera placement, significant juxtaposition and inter-cutting, Griffith added the first uses of night photography, of soft-focus photography and moving camera shots, and the possibilities of film art were born.

And with it were born most of the problems of those of us who wish to take the art seriously. For what can we make of so awkward a com-bination of sentimental content and superb technique? We must admit, first of all, that the effect of the film's detachable content was perni-cious. It served the ugliest purposes of pseudoart—giving people a re-flection of their own prejudices, sentimental at best, vicious at worst, and a restatement of their easy explanations of the terrible complexi-ties of their history as Americans. It demonstrated how easily and how successfully the art could pander to the sentimentality of the public, how effectively and profitably it could transfer melodrama from the stage and false values from the novel. The enormous commercial suc-cess of the film at a time when men like Louis B. Mayer, later to be-come the head of the greatest studio, were starting their careers as exhibitors, cannot have but fixed the melodramatic, the cheap and obviously emotional, as the index to the potential economic success of a film.

But it showed, as well, two directions in which the film would move: one is in the direction of the epic, and the other in what may be termed "symbolic realism." Its move in the first direction, of course, was an immense and shocking perversion. Griffith apparently sensed the truth that great epics are involved with the destiny of whole races and nations, and had seized upon Dixon's hint that the South's strug-gle was part of an "Aryan" saga. The Klan was described in the book, and on the screen, as part of an "Aryan" tradition. The term is used again at a crucial point in the screen narrative, when a mob of Negro soldiers attack the embattled whites. The battle of the caucasians, the title on the screen tells us, is "in defense of their Aryan birthright." Griffith improved upon Dixon in emphasizing the "epical" quality of the story: before they ride, the Klansmen are shown partaking of a primitive barbaric rite; they dip a flag in the blood of the blonde white virgin before they go out to destroy.

The picture is no epic, but rather an epic *manqué:* partial, fragmen-tary, and therefore necessarily inartistic; in attempting to be the saga

---

[25] Henry MacMahon, "The Art of the Movies," *New York Times,* June 6, 1915, section 6, p. 8.

of a shattered fragment of a nation, in attempting to erect upon false premises a series of racial responses reputedly instinctive, it was immediately self-defeating. An epic is justified in its radical simplifications, its stereotypes, its primitive terms, by its appeal to a real national unity of belief, and by its power to reinforce that unity. The oversimplifications of *The Birth of a Nation,* however, are not the controlled and ordering images of an art based upon a set of beliefs to which an entire people subscribe, images which emotionally order and control the world of that people's experience; instead it is the projection of images of disorder, an attack upon cultural and moral unity; the images of the film are the debilitating images of a false myth, a pseudoepic.

The picture did, however, provide another cinematic genre with many of its basic situations. In 1908, with the *Bronco Billie* series, the Western setting had begun to be realized as particularly suitable to the enactment of the drama of simple primitive faiths and national aspirations. After *The Birth of a Nation,* its images of elemental struggle and black and white moral values, and its techniques for making these exciting and significant, were transferred to the Western. The epic qualities of *The Birth of a Nation* were false and vicious because they impinge upon contemporary reality, and oversimplify both actual history and contemporary social circumstance; transferred to a realm of pure mythology—the Western scene of Richard Dix, *Stagecoach,* and *High Noon,* and to the moral blackness of outlaw and moral whiteness of law, these simplifications, and the techniques for pictorializing them, have given us something much more artistically valid.

But more important, *The Birth of a Nation* pointed in the second, and the major, direction of the motion-picture art. This direction we can call "symbolic realism"—the apparent imitation of actuality which brings out the symbolic or representational meaning of that apparent reality. This "significant" or "symbolic" realism was demonstrated to be effective is the portrayal of either deep psychological or wide universal meanings. To take a rather titillating example in *The Birth of a Nation* of the first kind of surface realism arranged to illustrate unexpressed psychological truths: Lillian Gish plays an innocent love scene with the hero, returns to her room, and seats herself dreamily on the bed; the bed happens to be a four-poster each of whose posts is almost embarrassingly suggestive of masculinity; she dreamily embraces and caresses the bedpost. Some years later, Greta Garbo, as Queen Christina, after three days in bed with John Gilbert, used the bedpost in similar fashion. More significant, perhaps, is the way in which images were juxtaposed in this pioneering picture so as to bring out the universal significance of the concrete instance. The view of the army winding past the mother and child to symbolize the agony and displacements of war; the cart and the carriage as symbols of feudal

levels of society; Stoneman's clubfoot representing the maimed wrath-
ful impotence of the mechanical North; little sister adorning her coarse
postbellum dress with a bit of cotton rescued from the destroyed plantation fields—these were but a few of the large number of symbolic ex-
tensions of the surface, and they pointed the way toward the great
documentary symbolic realism of Flaherty, and the imaginative symbolic realism of *The Informer, Sous les Toits de Paris, The River,* and
the whole run of wonderful Italian neorealistic films: *Open City,
Paisan, The Bicycle Thief,* and *La Strada.*

A preliminary examination of a significant motion picture, then, has
yielded some profit as well as some disappointment. The disappointment is largely in the failure of this pioneering picture to measure up
to standards of artistic greatness: its failure to achieve that fusion of
content and technique which together make up a great work of art. Its
failure is doubly disappointing, because it involves an inversion and
debasement of epic powers in which those powers pander to popular
taste instead of attempting to reach a whole vision, sinewed with moral
responsibility. But in this very failure lies some of its profit for us as
students of American civilization; better than any other art work, it
summarizes every aspect of the plantation illusion which is so vigorous
a force in the history of American sensibility; for the student of the
art form, it will demonstrate the beginnings of techniques which both
rescue *The Birth of a Nation* from ugliness, and which, when used
to embody more aesthetically malleable content, give us the possibilities of the art of the movie.

Editing in THE BIRTH OF A NATION
by A. R. FULTON

There were more than 1,500 shots in the print of *The Birth of a Nation* at its premiere. As a result of objection to scenes of Negroes amuck in Piedmont, Griffith deleted these scenes, and the number of shots is now 1,375. However, no film before had contained even as many as 1,375 shots, nor so many different kinds. There are 28 shots in *Queen Elizabeth,* all of the same sort. The shots in *The Birth of a Nation* vary from close shots of objects—such as an eye seen through a small hole in a door, a cotton blossom, a pistol, and parched corn in a pan—to distance shots across great expanses of countryside and stills. Griffith moves his camera freely, now tilting it to take in the dogs at Dr. Cameron's feet, now panning it to encompass a battlefield, or—as in the ride-of-the-Clan sequence—mounting it on the back of an automobile to precede the riding Clansmen.

In the composition of his pictures, Griffith has a tendency to depend on masks, vignettes, split screens, and other devices rather than on the arrangement of the photographed objects, although *The Birth of a Nation* contains examples of the latter arrangement. In one of the scenes in the cotton-fields sequence, action is photographed across the rails of a fence in the foreground. Another scene is centered between tree trunks. Sherman's marchers are framed by the sides of the valley. A battle scene is revealed gradually, not by an iris-in, but by the clearing away of smoke. A particularly effective shot is that of the Clansmen lined up on horseback side-by-side, the camera aiming down the line.

Now that the making of motion pictures has become a specialized but diversified process, a director is favored if he is permitted to edit his own films. That part of the process is usually assigned to a specialist in editing. But Griffith, who, like Méliès, epitomized the industry

From Motion Pictures: The Development of an Art from Silent Films to the Age of Television, *by A. R. Fulton (Norman, Okla.: University of Oklahoma Press, 1960), pp. 89–101. Copyright 1960 by the University of Oklahoma Press. Reprinted by permission of the publisher. Title supplied.*

which the motion pictures have become, was his own editor. It is difficult to imagine how his films could have been edited otherwise, for not only did he shoot his pictures without a prepared script, but only he knew how the parts were to be fitted together. The greatness of *The Birth of a Nation* depends on the exact order in which the 1,375 shots appear on the screen, that is, on editing.

Although Porter discovered the principle of editing, it was Griffith who developed its possibilities far beyond those illustrated, for example, by *The Great Train Robbery*. Porter's editing is limited to shifts in scene and implications of parallel action. There is no editing within the scenes of *The Great Train Robbery* and, except for the single close-up of the bandit, there is no change in the position of the camera. The contents of each scene are presented as unselectively as those in *Queen Elizabeth*. But Griffith came to see that by editing he could control the spectator's attention absolutely and thus give the scenes meaning and subtleties otherwise difficult, if not impossible.

Compare, for example, the scene of the shooting of the passenger in *The Great Train Robbery* with the assassination scene in *The Birth of a Nation*. Porter photographed his scene in a single shot, the camera remaining stationary throughout. There is nothing to identify the passenger who tries to escape except his acting. Before he breaks away from the group lined up along the railroad track and is shot for doing so, he sways back and forth, but his motion is inconspicuous. Because the scene is not edited, no relationship is established, except by acting, between this man and the other passengers. Nor, except by acting, is attention drawn to the bandit who shoots him. But in *The Birth of a Nation,* Griffith edits the assassination scene to make it appear not only more real than the shooting scene in *The Great Train Robbery* but also more meaningful. According to the script prepared by Theodore Huff, Griffith edits the scene as follows:[1]

TITLE:
A gala performance to celebrate the surrender of Lee, attended by the president and staff.
THE YOUNG STONEMANS PRESENT.
An historical facsimile of Ford's Theater as on that night, exact in size and detail with the recorded incidents, after Nicolay and Hay in *Lincoln, a History.*   24 feet

---

[1] "The figure at the right of each scene is the footage; it also can be taken as the number of seconds the scene lasts. When scenes were under three feet, they were measured exactly the figure in parentheses being the number of frames. Thus 2 (4) means two feet plus four frames, or a total of thirty-six frames (sixteen frames per foot-second)"—Preface to the script.

SCENE 444
Iris-In to Circle Bottom of Screen
Elsie and her brother come to seats—speak to acquaint-
ances—
*Iris Opens to Full Screen to Long Shot of Theater (From
above One Side Showing Stage 1—Orchestra, Boxes, Gal-
lery, etc.)*   18 feet
SCENE 445
Semi-Close-Up of Phil and Elsie
She looks through her opera glasses.   3 feet

TITLE:
"The play: *Our American Cousin,* starring Laura Keene."   4 feet
SCENE 446
As 444
The painted curtain rises—maid dusting table.   7 feet
SCENE 447
Medium-Long Shot of Stage
Star enters grandly.   3 feet
SCENE 448
As 446
Star bows to audience's applause.   4½ feet
SCENE 449
As 445
Elsie with fan—applauds—smiles at brother.   6 feet
SCENE 450
As 447
Star blows kisses to audience—bows.   3½ feet
SCENE 451
As 448
Star comes forward to footlights—receives flowers—ap-
plause—   9 feet

TITLE:
"Time, 8:30
The arrival of the president, Mrs. Lincoln, and party."   4½ feet
SCENE 452
¾ Shot of Stairs Back of Box (Sides Rounded)
Stairs dark and shadowy—guard leads man, two women,
and Lincoln up stairs.   8 feet
SCENE 453
Medium Shot of Theater Box
First of party enter.   3 feet

SCENE 454
As 452
Lincoln hands hat and coat to man—enters box door
right.   5 feet
SCENE 455
As 453
Lincoln comes forward in box.   4½ feet
SCENE 456
Semi-Close-Up of Phil and Elsie
They see Lincoln—applaud—rise.   6 feet
SCENE 457
Long Shot of Theater
Audience standing up, cheering.   2½ feet
SCENE 458
As 453
Lincoln bows.   2 (6)
SCENE 459
As 457
Audience cheering.   2½ feet
SCENE 460
As 458
Lincoln and party sit down.   6½ feet

TITLE:
"Mr. Lincoln's personal bodyguard takes his post out-
side the presidential box."   6 feet
SCENE 461
¾ *Shot of Hall Back of Box (Corners Rounded)*
Guard enters—sits in chair in front of box door.   10½ feet
SCENE 462
As 459
Audience still standing—play tries to go on—   4 feet
SCENE 463
As 460
The box—President and Mrs. Lincoln bowing.   8 feet
SCENE 464
Medium-Long Shot of Audience and Box (Corners Soft)
Cheers—waving handkerchiefs.   3 feet
SCENE 465
Medium Shot of Stage
Old-style footlights—painted scenery—people leave stage
—couple alone, come forward—spotlight follows them.   9 feet

TITLE:
"To get a view of the play, the bodyguard leaves his
post."

SCENE 466
Medium Shot of Hall, Rear of Box (Edges Rounded)
Guard tries to see play.   3½ feet

SCENE 467
Medium Shot of Stage   3 feet

SCENE 468
As 466
Guard gets up—opens rear door to gallery.   6½ feet

SCENE 469
Long Shot of Theater   Iris-Up toward Boxes and Gallery
Guard comes.   3 feet

SCENE 470
Medium Shot of Gallery (Circle)
The guard seats himself at edge.   4 feet

TITLE:
"Time, 10:13
Act III, scene 2"   2 feet

SCENE 471
*Long Shot of Theater   Iris at Upper Right Corner of
Screen*
The gallery—man in shadows.   _____   4 feet

SCENE 472
Semi-Close-Up of Phil and Elsie
Watching play—Elsie laughing behind fan—points with
fan to man in balcony—asks who he is.   7 feet

TITLE:
"John Wilkes Booth."   (14)

SCENE 473
Semi-Close-Up of Booth (Circle Iris)
(Napoleon pose) in the shadows of gallery.   2 (2)

SCENE 474
As 472
Elsie is amused by his mysterious appearance—laughs
behind fan—looks at him thru opera glasses.   6 feet

SCENE 475
As 473
Booth waiting.   2 (3)

SCENE 476
Medium-Long Shot of Gallery and Audience (Sides Rounded)
Booth waiting.   5½ feet

SCENE 477
As 475
Booth waiting.   4 feet

SCENE 478
Medium Shot of Stage Play
Comedy line—man waves arms.   3½ feet

SCENE 479
Medium Shot of Lincoln's Box
They laugh—Lincoln feels draught—reaches for shawl.   6½ feet

SCENE 480
As 477
Booth watches.   3 feet

SCENE 481
As 479
The box—Lincoln drawing shawl around shoulders.   5½ feet

SCENE 482
Long Shot of Theater as 471   Iris Opens
Booth goes to box door.   5 feet

SCENE 483
Medium Shot (Circle)
Guard in gallery—Booth opens door behind him.   1 (7)

SCENE 484
Medium Shot of Hall Back of Box (Corners Softened)
Heavy shadows—Booth enters softly—closes and locks
door—peeks thru keyhole at box door—stands up ma-
jestically—pulls out pistol—tosses head back—actor-
like—   12½ feet

SCENE 485
Close-Up of Pistol (Circle Vignette)
He cocks it.   3 feet

SCENE 486
As 484
Booth comes forward—opens door to box—enters.   9 feet

SCENE 487
The Box as 479
Booth creeps in behind Lincoln.   4½ feet

SCENE 488
The Play as 478
The comic chases woman out—cheers.   4 feet

SCENE 489
Medium Shot of Box
Lincoln is shot—Booth jumps from left side of box.   4½ feet

SCENE 490
Long Shot of Theater
Booth jumps on stage—shouts.   2½ feet

TITLE:
"Sic semper tyrannis!"   2 feet

SCENE 491
Medium Shot of Booth on Stage
Holds arms out—limps back quickly.   3 feet

SCENE 492
Medium Shot of Box
Lincoln slumped down—Mrs. Lincoln calls for help.   2 (6)

SCENE 493
Semi-Close-Up of Phil and Elsie
They hardly realize what has happened—rise—   4½ feet

SCENE 494
Long Shot of Theater
Audience standing up in turmoil—Elsie in foreground
faints—Phil supports her—   4 feet

SCENE 495
As 492
Man climbs up into box to Lincoln's aid.   5 feet

SCENE 496
Medium-Long Shot of Theater and Boxes
Audience agitated.   3½ feet

SCENE 497
Long Shot of Excited Throng
Phil and Elsie leave.
Fade-Out   11½ feet

SCENE 498
Medium Shot of Box
They carry Lincoln out.
Fade-Out   10½ feet

If the scene were done like Porter's, there would be only a single
shot, or two at the most, to show parallel action in the passage outside

the president's box. However, by breaking the scene down into fifty-five shots, Griffith obtains effects that would not be possible in one or two long shots. He establishes a relationship between Lincoln and Booth—showing Lincoln's unconsciousness of danger and Booth's intention; between Lincoln and the play—showing where Lincoln's attention is directed; between the bodyguard and the play—showing why the bodyguard leaves his post; and even between Lincoln and the audience in Ford's Theater, particularly Elsie and Phil—showing that the audience too is unconscious of the terrible deed about to be committed. Griffith emphasizes Booth's murderous intention by the close shot of the pistol. He interpolates shots of the stage not only to indicate where all of the characters except Booth are centering their attention but also to create suspense. This suspense is heightened by having Elsie direct Phil's attention to the balcony at the side of the box, and then cutting to Booth—his first appearance in the film: will anything come of his thus being noticed? These and other details, such as Lincoln's premonitory gesture of drawing the shawl over his shoulders, would be ineffective if done in the manner of *The Great Train Robbery*.

Editing is effected in various other ways. In *The Birth of a Nation*, Griffith not only cuts scenes before they are ended but also juxtaposes long, medium, and close shots—thus obtaining variety in the spatial length of the shots. He also varies the temporal length—the length of time a shot remains on the screen—and the objects which the shots contain. Any sequence in *The Birth of a Nation* illustrates this variety. An excellent sequence to study is that of the climax, which involves a typical Griffith last-minute rescue—or rather two rescues. It represents simultaneous action, not just in two different places, but in several—an office, a room adjoining the office, a street, the exterior and the interior of a cabin, and various parts of the countryside. It illustrates variety in the temporal length of the shots and variety in the objects photographed. Griffith tends to begin a sequence with a temporally long shot and decrease the temporal length as the sequence progresses. This pattern, modified by a variety in the spatial length, gives the film its rhythm.

The very nature of editing admits of effects which are not artistically possible in any other medium of storytelling. One of these is cross-cutting. In the Ford Theater sequence, for example, Griffith cuts from the auditorium to the passageway behind the president's box to show simultaneous action in both places. In this sequence the places happen to be close together. But cross-cutting permits as easily the presentation of action happening simultaneously in places widely separated, as in the ride-of-the-Clan sequence. On the other hand, shots may be juxtaposed merely to show contrast, as in the cutting between scenes of battle and those of the Camerons at home. Editing is not limited, however, to the way in which the shots are arranged—each sequence beginning with a title and a fade-in (or an iris-in) and closing with a fade-out (or an iris-out).

Whereas Méliès, having discovered the dissolve, incorporated it in his films primarily as part of the trickery, Griffith adopted the dissolve as a linking device, a cinematic transition. A particularly effective dissolve in *The Birth of a Nation* is that in the Masters Hall sequence. The sequence opens with a still, an interior scene of the hall, a sub-title having identified it as the original building. Then the photograph dissolves to Griffith's replica of the hall occupied by the actors. In linking the scenes, the dissolve establishes historical authenticity.

The iris is also a linking device. The effect of an iris-in or an iris-out is now achieved in the developing room as part of the editing process. In Griffith's time, however, the shutter on the lens of the camera was manipulated to decrease the spatial limits of a scene by a contracting circle or increase the limits by an expanding one. In *The Birth of a Nation,* Griffith uses both the iris-in and the iris-out freely. The iris-in is particularly effective in the scene in which the mother and the children are huddled on the side of the valley. As the iris opens, more and more of the scene is revealed until one sees, in the valley below, the cause of the terror. The iris-in links effect with cause. It is comparable to the panning of the camera in *The Great Train Robbery* to reveal what the robbers are running toward. The iris-in has another implication: by gradually enlarging the image on the screen, it directs the attention of the observer. One does not notice everything simultaneously. If the scene opened with the marchers in the valley and the woman and children on the hillside, the connection between the two groups would not be conveyed to every spectator, or at least not to every spectator at the same time. The Masters Hall sequence is concluded by an iris-out to the upper right-hand corner of the frame to draw attention from the whole scene—the Negroes on the floor and the whites in the gallery—to only the gallery part of the scene.

The fade is used somewhat similarly, except that the fade tends to be used only to begin or end a sequence. It is comparable to a curtain which opens or closes a scene on the stage.

Griffith sometimes blacks out part of the screen for particular effect. Shots of the riding Clansmen are masked in elliptical shape to emphasize horizontal extent. A round mask frames the shot entitled "the masked batteries." This device, called a mask, or iris, is still used in the motion pictures, as, for example, in the shape of a keyhole or of field glasses to establish a particular point of view. Griffith frames some of his shots in vignette. Originally meaning a running ornament of vine leaves, a vignette (from *vigne,* vine) is a photograph which shades off gradually into the surrounding ground. Thus in the motion pictures a similarly shaded shot is also called a vignette. Griffith frames flashbacks in vignette as if thus making a distinction between present and past. He does not, however, limit the vignette to flashbacks. A vignette, for example, frames a distant shot of the besieged cabin, which is thereby made prominent by separation from its natural surroundings.

The composition of a shot may be effected by editing in another way. During the march-to-the-sea sequence, the screen appears to be cut diagonally in two, the scene of the burning of Atlanta occupying the upper triangle and that of the marchers the lower. This device, called the split screen, Griffith uses again in the epilogue.

Although titles are not inherent in the cinematic method—the first films had no titles—Griffith incorporates them variously and effectively in *The Birth of a Nation.* There are continuity titles, that is, titles to link scenes or indicate action to follow. Griffith effects irony by following the title "War's Peace" with stills of the corpse-strewn battlefield. Then there are subtitles, which indicate dialogue, but Griffith depends on these sparingly. Margaret Cameron's refusal of Phil Stoneman, as pointed out, is represented thus to obviate subtitles. The "Grim Reaping" episode, introduced by Lynch's saying, "See, my people fill the streets," and constituting sixty-six shots, contains only two other subtitles.

Whatever the purpose of editing—to emphasize a particular detail, to increase suspense, to recall the past, to symbolize, to effect irony, to represent speech, or to "photograph thought"—the result must be clear to the observer. Editing must not be obvious, but it must not be obtuse. The observer should be impressed by the result rather than by the way the result is obtained. Even though successive shots may have been photographed days apart and in widely separated places, their arrangement can merge them into a coherent effect, and it is this effect which Griffith gets in his film.

D. W. Griffith: THE BIRTH OF A NATION
by LEWIS JACOBS

The second period (1914–17) of D. W. Griffith's career saw the production of his two greatest films, *The Birth of a Nation* and *Intolerance*. High points in the history of the American movie, these two pictures far surpassed other native films in structure, imaginative power, and depth of content, and they marked Griffith's peak as a creative artist. They foreshadowed the best that was to come in cinema technique, earned for the screen its right to the status of an art, and demonstrated with finality that the movie was one of the most potent social agencies in America.

Neither *The Birth of a Nation* nor *Intolerance* was an accident— a "lucky fluke" of directorial frenzy: both were the consummation of five years of intensive moviemaking. Griffith's Biograph apprenticeship is replete with presages of these two compositions. Ingenious organizational devices, startling compositional sketches, sentimental cameos, and high-powered episodes, which time and again had appeared in his hundreds of Biograph miniatures, reappeared in these two works with superlative effects. Without his experimental years at Biograph it is doubtful whether Griffith could have made at this time two such profound and triumphant films.

After leaving Biograph, Griffith produced for his new employers, Mutual, four films in quick succession, none of which particularly interested him: *Home, Sweet Home; The Escape; The Avenging Conscience (The Telltale Heart)*; and *The Battle of the Sexes*. Griffith was getting $1,000 a week salary, and he did these minor pictures rapidly to accumulate money—this time not so he could quit filmmaking, but so he could make bigger and better films than any he had yet done. The specter of the European film successes still tormented him. He had been constantly on the lookout for a subject that would lend itself

From Lewis Jacobs, The Rise of the American Film: A Critical History *(New York: Teachers College Press, 1939), pp. 171–88. Copyright 1939. Reprinted by permission of the publisher. Title supplied.*

to a spectacular use of his talents and would put him ahead of his foreign rivals. But he did not yet have more than a vague sense of what he wanted.

Discussing his needs with Frank Woods, the former film critic who had become a leading scenario writer through Griffith's encouragement, Griffith learned of Thomas Dixon's successful dramatization of his novel *The Clansman*. Woods rhapsodized over the novel's motion-picture possibilities. He had already written a scenario of *The Clansman* for Kinemacolor Corporation, which had begun but was unable to finish the production. Griffith was naturally excited by the appeal of such a theme—the South and the Civil War—and the opportunity it offered for his particular talents. *The Clansman* seemed to fit his enlarged ambitions perfectly; so he bought the film rights.

In planning the story, Griffith added material from another Dixon book, *The Leopard's Spots*, and supplemented it with his own recollections of his father's reminiscences. The story he finally evolved was more extensive than any he had yet attempted. It covered the years immediately before the Civil War, the war itself, and part of the Reconstruction period. Griffith called it *The Clansman*.

Griffith now began production on a vast scale. Big though the undertaking was, it was still the creation of one mind. Like George Méliès before him, but with plans magnified a thousandfold, Griffith shouldered not only the responsibility of production but all the incidental business and financial obligations as well. Before he shot his first scene he put his company through six weeks of grueling rehearsals; then followed nine more weeks of painstaking shooting. An entire county is said to have been rented for the photographing of the rides and battle scenes. Unexpected difficulties developed when Griffith tried to get horses, which were urgently required in the war in Europe. Thousands of yards of cotton sheets had to be put on the Clansmen, and this material too was a war scarcity. Whole communities were combed for white goods. But one of the heaviest burdens was the feeding, paying, and management of the hundreds of extras.

The making of the picture was marked by an unceasing struggle for money, an unbroken series of desperate financial difficulties and day-to-day borrowings. Everything Griffith possessed—his reputation, his personal fortune, whatever money he could raise from his friends—was poured into his gigantic enterprise. Besieged by mounting debts, hounded by creditors, discouraged by associates, he pushed the production to completion. According to his cameraman, Bitzer, he remained calm throughout, kept his troubles to himself, and moved steadily forward, filled with a creative urge that had to run its course regardless of time, personalities, debts, and other restraints or obstacles.

To the wonder of everyone, Griffith proceeded with his costly venture without a "shooting script." He had combined, condensed, and charted the material in his mind without the use of a written continuity. Even the details for the settings, costumes, properties, and specific scene actions were not written down. Carrying the general plan in his mind, he depended largely upon the intuition of the moment for specific action, and improvised freely as he went along. Lillian Gish, who played the heroine, revealed years later how Griffith quickly took advantage of every dramatic opportunity he saw and how he shaped his material as he went. Said Miss Gish:

> At first I was not cast to play in *The Clansman*. My sister and I had been the last to join the company and we naturally supposed . . . that the main assignments would go to the older members. But one day while we were rehearsing the scene where the colored man picks up the Northern girl gorilla-fashion, my hair, which was very blond, fell far below my waist and Griffith, seeing the contrast in the two figures, assigned me to play Elsie Stoneman (who was to have been Mae Marsh).[1]

Such impulsive decisions were typical of Griffith. His method of work was in direct opposition to the careful planning of a director like Thomas Ince, who worked from minutely detailed shooting scripts. Griffith's reliance upon his instincts in shooting for continuity often explains the absurdities that sometimes crop up in his films. As Dwight Macdonald remarked, Griffith was:

> a practical genius who can make things work but who is not interested in "theory," i.e., the general laws that govern his achievements . . . his fitful talent throwing off the wretchedest as well as the most inspired productions. He grew up unaware of his own powers . . . guided only by his extraordinary flair for the cinema.[2]

Finally completed in February 1915, the production was the longest American film yet made—twelve reels—"a frightful waste and audacious monstrosity." The conservative coterie of film producers refused to handle its distribution, and Griffith was forced to form his own distribution outlets. In a letter supposed to have been written by William De Mille to Samuel Goldwyn on February 10, 1915, one can clearly sense the short-sightedness and narrow attitude of the industry generally:

[1] *Stage,* January 1937. [See also this volume, pp. 42–55.]
[2] *The Symposium,* April and July 1933.

I also heard rumors that the film cost nearly a hundred thousand dollars! This means, of course, that even though it is a hit, which it probably will be, it cannot possibly make any money. It would have to gross over a quarter of a million for Griffith to get his cost back and, as you know, that just isn't being done. Remember how sore Biograph was with Griffith when he made *Judith of Bethulia* and how much money that lost even though it was only a four-reeler? So I suppose you're right when you say there is no advantage in leading if the cost of leadership makes commercial success impossible. *The Clansman* certainly establishes Griffith as a leader and it does seem too bad that such a magnificent effort is doomed to financial failure.[3]

When we think of the great fortune the film reaped, such remarks seem ironic indeed.

The first American picture to get a two-dollar top admission, *The Birth of a Nation* enjoyed such enduring popularity that its total earnings makes it one of the greatest moneymakers in the history of the American screen.

The picture was first exhibited at Clune's Auditorium in Los Angeles on February 8, 1915, under the title of the book, *The Clansman*. On February 20 a print was run off in New York for the censors and a specially invited group. At this showing Thomas Dixon, the author of the original book, became so excited that during the applause he shouted to Griffith that the title *The Clansman* was too tame for so powerful a film: that it should be renamed *The Birth of a Nation*. This became the famous picture's title.

From the moment of its public opening on March 3, 1915, at the Liberty Theater in New York, *The Birth of a Nation* won phenomenal success. It was the first film to be honored by a showing at the White House: President Woodrow Wilson is said to have remarked, "It is like writing history with lightning." Critics, greeting the picture with boundless enthusiasm, called it "a new milestone in film artistry, astonishing even the most sanguine by its success, and inspiring the most dramatic new departure in dissipating the supremacy of the theater." [4] *Variety* excitedly headlined its front page with "Griffith's $2 Feature Film Sensation of M. P. Trade," going on to say:

Daily newspaper reviewers pronounced it the last word in picture-making. . . . Mr. Griffith has set such a pace, it will be a long time

[3] *Stage,* December 1937.
[4] *Variety,* March 12, 1915.

before one will come along that can top him in point of production, action, photography, and direction. . . .[5]

and concluding its lengthy panegyric with the pronouncement, "This picture is a great epoch in picturemaking, great for the name and fame of D. W. Griffith and great for pictures."

This great picture reviewed the Civil War, the despoiling of the South, and the revival of the South's honor through the efforts of the Ku Klux Klan. After a short introduction which showed the bringing of slaves to America and summarized the abolitionist movement, the story proper began with Phil and Tod Stoneman, of Pennsylvania, visiting their boarding-school chums, the Cameron boys, at Piedmont, South Carolina. Phil Stoneman falls in love with Margaret Cameron, while Ben Cameron becomes enamored of the daguerreotype of Phil's sister, Elsie Stoneman. Then the Civil War breaks out. Phil and Tod leave to fight for the Union, while Ben and his two brothers join the Confederate army. During the ensuing war years the two younger Cameron boys and Tod are killed; Piedmont undergoes "ruin, devastation, rapine, and pillage." Ben, the "Little Colonel," is wounded and becomes the prisoner of Captain Phil Stoneman. Nursed by Elsie Stoneman, Ben finally recovers. Elsie and his mother visit Lincoln, "the Great Heart," and win Ben's release.

The father of Elsie and Phil Stoneman is a leader in Congress; he agitates for the punishment of the South. Lincoln refuses to countenance revenge, but Stoneman persists with his plans and grooms the mulatto, Silas Lynch, to become a "leader of his people." After the surrender at Appomattox and the assassination of Abraham Lincoln, Stoneman swiftly gains power. With Elsie and Phil he goes to the South to carry out his "equality" program for the Negroes. He rents a house next door to the Camerons'. Elsie and Ben now become engaged, but Margaret cannot bring herself to accept Phil.

Meanwhile the Reconstruction period and:

> The reign of the carpetbaggers begins. The "Union League," so-called, wins the ensuing state election. Silas Lynch, the mulatto, is chosen lieutenant-governor. A legislature, with carpetbag and Negro members in overwhelming majority, loots the state. Lawlessness runs riot. Whites are elbowed off the streets, overawed at the polls, and often despoiled of their possessions.[6]

[5] Ibid.
[6] From the Special Program Notes given out at the initial Liberty Theater performance.

The organization of the "invisible empire" of Clansmen is thus inspired and justified. Ben Cameron becomes their leader, and when Stoneman learns of it he forces Elsie to break her engagement to Ben. Events rapidly arouse the ire of the Clan and fill Ben with a desire for vengeance. The Camerons' Negro servant, Gus, becomes a militia-man and joins Lynch's mob. When Gus makes advances to Flora, Ben's younger sister, she flees from him through the woods until, in despair, she hurls herself over a cliff. There Ben discovers her, dying.

Later Dr. Cameron is arrested for harboring the Clansman. Phil, desperate on seeing to what lengths the carpetbaggers are going, helps to rescue the doctor. With Mrs. Cameron, Margaret, and the faithful servants, Phil and the doctor find refuge in a log cabin. Here they attempt to fight off an attack by the Negro militia. Meanwhile Lynch, to whom Elsie Stoneman has come pleading that he save Phil and the Camerons, demands that she marry him, and he confronts her father with the proposal.

The climax comes when the Clansmen, headed by Ben, arrive in the nick of time to mow down the Negro militia, take the Lynch man-sion, free Elsie and the Stonemans, kill Gus, and save the Camerons in the cabin just as they are about to be massacred. Thus the Ku Klux Klan heroically dispenses "justice." A double honeymoon, symbolic of the reunion of North and South, concludes the story. An epilogue rejoices that peace reigns once again:

> The establishment of the South in its rightful place is the birth of a new nation. . . . The new nation, the real United States, as the years glided by, turned away forever from the blood-lust of war and anticipated with hope the world-millennium in which a brotherhood of love should bind all the nations.

The film was a passionate and persuasive avowal of the inferiority of the Negro. In viewpoint it was, surely, narrow and prejudiced. Griffith's Southern upbringing made him completely sympathetic to-ward Dixon's exaggerated ideas, and the fire of his convictions gave the film rude strength. At one point in the picture a title bluntly editorial-ized that the South must be made "safe" for the whites. The entire portrayal of the Reconstruction days showed the Negro, when freed from white domination, as arrogant, lustful, villainous. Negro congress-men were pictured drinking heavily, coarsely reclining in Congress with bare feet upon their desks, lustfully ogling the white women in the balcony. Gus, the Negro servant, is depicted as a renegade when he joins the emancipated Negroes. His advances on Flora, and Lynch's proposal to Elsie Stoneman, are overdrawn to make the Negro appear obnoxious and audacious. The Negro servants who remain with the Camerons, on the other hand, are treated with patronizing regard for their faithfulness. The necessity of the separation of Negro from white, with the white as the ruler, is passionately maintained throughout the film.

The social implications of this celebrated picture aroused a storm of protest above the Mason-and-Dixon line. Negroes and whites united in attacking the picture because of its extreme bias. In Boston and other "abolitionist" cities race riots broke out. The Boston branch of the National Association for the Advancement of Colored People issued a pamphlet against the film. President Charles E. Eliot of Harvard charged the movie "with a tendency to perversion of white ideals," [7] Oswald Garrison Villard condemned it as "a deliberate attempt to humiliate ten million American citizens," [8] and Jane Addams was "painfully exercised over the exhibition." [9] Local politicians and office-holders jumped into the arena, choosing the side that offered the most votes.

In response to widespread attacks, Griffith himself became an out-raged pamphleteer and published at his own expense *The Rise and Fall of Free Speech in America.* Its text contained extracts from editorials in various periodicals—*The Saturday Evening Post,* the *Chicago Tribune,* and the *Boston Transcript,* to mention three—upholding the right of *The Birth of a Nation* to freedom of the screen. He campaigned for "the freedom of the screen," issuing statements, making speeches, and writing letters to proclaim the "fundamental rights of expression" which he held to be self-evident. He must have realized, however, the wanton injury he had done to a race, for in a subsequent picture he attempted to atone for it by showing a white soldier kissing his wounded Negro comrade. Though heartfelt, such a sentimental concession could do little to compensate for the harm done by his prejudice in *The Birth of a Nation.*

The raging controversy awakened the nation to the social import of moving pictures. But this realization was overshadowed by the great acclaim for the picture's artistry, its rich imagery and powerful construction. So advanced was the film structurally that even today it stands as an accomplishment of great stature. All Griffith's earlier experiments are here consolidated: the use of camera to build scenes, the pacing of shots, the sensitive manipulation of camera devices for transitions, simultaneous action, movement of all kinds—all fused by brilliant cutting. The chief difference between this film and Griffith's

[7] Terry Ramsaye, *A Million and One Nights,* p. 643.
[8] Ibid.
[9] Ibid.

past efforts lies in the intensity and scale of the application of the cinematic elements. Griffith's conception had ripened; an unerring command of the medium was now his.

The Birth of a Nation pulsates; it is life itself. From the very beginning, shots are merged into a flux. Either the actions within the shots have some kind of movement or the duration of shots is so timed that the effect is one of continuous motion. This motion creates a "beat" which accents the relationships of the separate elements of the film and produces a single powerful effect.

In the Petersburg sequences, the undercurrent of movement has remarkable variety partly because of the nature of the raw material, and it is marked by extensive and resourceful uses of cinematic principles. The passages that reach a climax in the battle itself, being basically all action, are broken down by Griffith into juxtaposed scenes of long, medium, close, and detail shots, varied in duration and so contrasting in imagery that they re-create in the spectator the excitement of the battle itself. In the hand-to-hand fighting, a group of soldiers swarming across the left side of the screen are followed by a group crossing at the right, so that the feeling of conflict is intensified. Often the contrast of numbers is brought into play: shots of individual soldiers are opposed to shots of many soldiers. There is also opposition of space relationships, as in scenes in which an extreme long shot is followed by an extreme close shot. Finally there is the expressive opposition of a still shot of a dead body to the moving shot of a soldier clambering up the ramparts to place a waving flag in position. Throughout this entire section of the film Griffith ingeniously employed these structural and dramatic oppositions, giving the picture a dynamic quality that carried the spectator away by its sheer sweep.

The Reconstruction sequences, starting with the struggle between the defeated Southerners (the impoverishment of the Camerons is significantly stressed) and the emancipated Negroes (made to appear vulgar, ostentatious, and arrogant), rises to a masterly climax in the ride of the Clansmen. Here the tension is heightened by staccato cutting. The dramatic power is enhanced by night photography, acute angle shots, extreme long and close shots, sweeping pans, and moving-camera shots. The movement of the whole has a fast and uneven tempo emphasizing the excitement.

Typical of Griffith's vigorous style is the beginning of the "Grim Reaping" episode in the Reconstruction section. In the following excerpt from the script, made from the film by Theodore Huff of the Museum of Modern Art Film Library, can be seen Griffith's brilliant use of intercutting to relate simultaneous action and thus produce high tension:

Shot No.			*Footage*	
1107	*Full Shot*	Lynch has Elsie Stoneman alone in his office. Lynch turns to her, raises his two hands.	2	feet
	Title	"See! My people fill the streets. With them I will build a black empire and you as a queen shall sit by my side."	10½	feet
1108	*Full Shot*	Lynch raises his arms in the air. Elsie sinks on chair. Lynch kneels, kisses the hem of her dress. She draws away in horror —rises—staggers to door, turning about. Lynch follows—sits at left. Elsie pounds on door.	21	feet
1109	*Semi-Close-Up*	(Circle vignette) Lynch leaning back in chair—smiles—indicates his people outside.	7	feet
1110	(*As* 1108)	Elsie begs him—pleads with hands outstretched to let her go.	6½	feet
1111	(*As* 1109)	Lynch smiles at her.	2 13	feet, frames
1112	(*As* 1110)	Elsie turns away—screams.	3	feet
1113	*Long Shot*	By the barn. Two Clansmen on horses come from right.	5½	feet
1114	*Fade-In*	Open country. Another Clansman dashes back.	7½	feet
	Title	"Summoning the Clans."	3	feet
1115	*Semi-Close-Up*	Two Clansmen by the barn— one holding up the fiery cross— the other blowing a whistle.	3	feet
1116	(*As* 1113) *Long Shot*	By the barn. They ride forward.	6½	feet
1117	*Fade-In* (*As* 1114)	Open country. Clansman calling —comes forward.	7½	feet
1118	*Iris-In* (*As* 1116) *Long Shot*	By the barn. Five more Clansmen (having heard signal) come forward from barn.	8	feet
1119	¾ *Shot*	Lynch and Elsie. She rushes to window, left. Lynch after her—		

Shot No.			Footage	
		she pulls away—he shouts at her. Elsie sees it is no use—his people are outside.	9½	feet
1120	*Medium- Long Shot*	Woods. Two Clansmen with a signal dash forward.	5	feet
1121	(*As* 1119)	Lynch and Elsie. Lynch pounds his chest with fist, boastingly.	3½	feet
1122	*Fade-In Long Shot*	Stream of water. Two Clansmen dash up stream. Fade-out.	9	feet
1123	(*As* 1121)	Lynch and Elsie. Lynch arrogantly points to window.	1 12	foot, frames
1124	¾ *Shot*	Inner room. Man and woman listening, furtively.	1 12	foot, frames
1125	(*Back to* 1123)	Lynch and Elsie. Lynch calls— Elsie is horrified.	1 1	foot, frame
1126	(*As* 1124)	Inner room. Man at door hears Lynch's call.	2 13	feet, frames
1127	*Semi- Close-Up*	(Circle vignette) Doorman—he enters Lynch's office.	1 12	foot, frames
1128	¾ *Shot*	Office—different angle. Man comes to Lynch. Elsie rises.	3	feet
	Title	"Lynch, drunk with power, orders his henchman to hurry preparations for a forced marriage."	7½	feet
1129	(*As* 1128)	Office. Man goes. Lynch turns to Elsie—her hand over her mouth, shocked.	3	feet
1130	(*As* 1127)	(Circle vignette—door) Henchman rushes to carry out Lynch's order.	14	frames
1131	(*As* 1126)	Inner room. Henchman calls subordinate—sends him out, right.	10	feet
1132	(*As* 1125)	Elsie and Lynch. Elsie looks frantically about—rushes forward to door, left.	5½	feet
1133	¾ *Shot*	(Circle vignette—door) Elsie speeds to it.	5 2 1	feet, frame

Shot
No.   *Footage*

1134	(*As* 1132)	Elsie and Lynch. Lynch shouts to her to come back.	2	feet
1135	(*As* 1133)	(Circle vignette—door) Elsie tries to open door, can't, turns terrified.	1 11	foot, frames
1136	*Fade-In* *Long Shot*	Stream. A large group of Clansmen dash forward across shallow stream.	6	feet
1137	(*As* 1134)	Elsie and Lynch. Lynch calls Elsie back.	1 11	foot, frames
1138	(*As* 1135)	(Circle vignette—door) Elsie comes forward, terrified.	3½	feet
1139	(*As* 1137)	Elsie comes forward slowly.	4	feet
1140	*Long Shot*	Crossroads. Two Clansmen stop—give signal, dash on.	8	feet
1141	(*As* 1139)	Elsie and Lynch. Elsie pushes him away—rushes back to rear door—he after her—she escapes—comes forward around chairs—he chases her.	8	feet
1142	*Fade-In* *Long Shot*	Army of Clansmen lined up and forming—Ben in background.	7½	feet
1143	*Semi-* *Close-Up*	(Circle vignette) Ben on horse—surveys army (mask off).	4	feet
1144	(*As* 1140)	Crossroads. Several more Clansmen come.	5½	feet
1145	*Fade-In* *Long Shot*	Field. Joining the army, Ben salutes.	6	feet
1146	*Long Shot*	Silhouette of hill. Horsemen (tiny specks) riding along ridge.	5	feet
1147	*Medium-* *Long Shot*	Stream and cornfield. Two signal riders dash along.	3	feet
1148	*Medium* *Shot*	(Moving) Two signal riders (camera on car precedes them).	13	feet
1149	(*As* 1141)	Lynch and Elsie. Elsie rises from chair—she tries to get back.	5	feet
1150	*Medium* *Shot*	Street outside Lynch's office. Horse and wagons come, fol-		

Shot No.			Footage	
		lowed by Negroes, etc. Two men on horses enter, also.	10	feet
1151	(*As* 1141)	Lynch and Elsie. Elsie falls back in faint—Lynch supports her.	3½	feet
1152	*Medium Shot*	Entrance to Lynch's office. Horse and carriage stop before it—crowd around cheering.	7	feet
1153	(*As* 1151)	Lynch, holding Elsie, hears—	2	feet
1154	¾ *Shot*	A carriage. Stoneman steps out.	4	feet
1155	*Medium Shot*	Stoneman goes on porch through cheering crowds.	3	feet
1156	(*As* 1153)	Lynch and Elsie. Lynch draws Elsie closer to him.	2 11	feet, frames
1157	¾ *Shot*	Hall. Stoneman comes—knocks.	1 15	foot, frames
1158	(*As* 1156)	Lynch hears—turns to Elsie.	2 3	feet, frames
1159	(*As* 1157)	Stoneman is impatient—asks guard the trouble—guard doesn't know.	6	feet
1160	(*As* 1158)	Lynch wonders what to do.	2 12	feet, frames
1161	(*As* 1159)	Hall. Stoneman impatient—paces—pounds cane—asks reason for delay.	12½	feet
1162	(*As* 1160)	Lynch and Elsie. Lynch carries Elsie forward.	6	feet
1163	¾ *Shot*	Inner dining room. Lynch brings her forward (unconscious, hair streaming)—sets her in chair, left. Orderlies instructed to guard her.	10	feet
1164	(*As* 1151)	Stoneman starts away.	2 10	feet, frames
1165	(*As* 1163)	Inner dining room. Lynch leaves —crosses room.	4	feet
1166	¾ *Shot*	Office. Lynch goes to outside door—unlocks it.	3½	feet

Shot No.			*Footage*	
1167	(*As* 1161)	Hall. Stoneman hears—turns back—is admitted.	5½	feet
1168	(*As* 1166)	Office. Lynch and Stoneman come forward—Lynch apologizes—Stoneman gives him paper.	4	feet
1169	*Long Shot*	Clansmen forming in field. More going—Ben waves.	7½	feet
1170	(*As* 1168)	Office. Stoneman starts back. Lynch stops him.	5	feet
	Title	"I want to marry a white woman."	5	feet
1171	(*As* 1170)	Stoneman pats him on shoulder —"Sure, go right ahead"— shakes hands—smiles.	5	feet
	Title	"The Clans, being assembled in full strength, ride off on their appointed mission."	8	feet
1172	*Fade-In Long Shot*	Field. Several hundred Clansmen come forward (horses rearing) to Ben, who salutes them. He rides off—motions to others —they follow with banners and fiery crosses in clouds of dust.	28	feet
	Title	"And meanwhile other fates—"	4	feet

The conception in 1915 of such a remarkable cutting sequence, marked by significantly few titles, demonstrated an unusual mastery of the movie medium. As can be seen from the footage of the shots, they are trimmed down so that only one essential fact is given each time. The effect builds up shot by shot, and the suspense increases, in a manner which the great Russian directors were later to develop with amazing skill. There is, furthermore, an extraordinary audacity displayed in the cutting from one scene to another without allowing either to terminate and from one episode to another so that the threads of meaning are cunningly interwoven. The tension that develops in the spectator is not relieved until Griffith resolves both episodes. This "constant shifting of scenes" is the essence of filmic technique. Henry MacMahon was one of the first to realize Griffith's accomplishment and succinctly pointed out in the *New York Times*, June 6, 1915:

Every little series of pictures, continuing from four to fifteen seconds, symbolizes a sentiment, a passion, or an emotion. Each successive series, similar yet different, carries the emotion to the next higher power, till at last, when both of the parallel emotions have attained the *nth* power, so to speak, they meet in the final swift shock of victory and defeat.

Many other episodes could be cited to prove the excellence of the film's structure. Of the rioting of the Negroes in the streets, for example, Vachel Lindsay in 1915 said, "Splendidly handled, tossing wildly and rhythmically like the sea." [10] A typically striking use of the "switchback" occurs in the episode of Phil's proposal to Margaret. We see a medium shot of Margaret considering the offer; then the film flashes back to scenes of her brothers being killed by Northerners. The following close shot of Margaret refusing her suitor is thus made forceful to the spectator without use of words, titles, or pantomime. Again, the three-cornered chase involving Flora, Gus, and Ben in the woods is filled with fearful suspense through cumulative editing: the contrast of extreme long and close shots and Flora's zigzagging course convey to the audience the desperation of Flora in her wild, headlong run.

These impressive devices are supplemented by another celebrated one: the iris, strikingly used in the sequence of Sherman's march to the sea and the burning of Atlanta. In the upper left-hand corner of a black screen, a small iris discloses the pitiful detail of a mother and three children huddled together. Gradually the iris opens to reveal more of the scene, and when it is fully opened we see the reason for the misery of these figures: in the valley below an army of Northern invaders is marching through the town the woman has just fled. The scene is startling in its implications; the dramatic effect is far more gripping than it would have been if, through mere cutting, the shot of the army had been placed to follow the shot of the mother and children. The iris functioned not only as a dramatic means of presenting an action and its cause, but as a transitional device to frame the sequence. A daring and masterly use of the camera for a psychological effect, it shows Griffith's precise sensitivity to the dramatic possibilities of the medium.

Besides having such prime technical devices, *The Birth of a Nation* was one of the first films to make much use of symbolism. Suitable objects and animals were introduced to heighten a mood, sharpen an inference, or delineate a character. In an ecstasy of emotion, Elsie (Lillian Gish) embraces a mahogany bedpost. (Years later Greta Garbo as Queen Christina, after being closeted with her lover for three days,

[10] *The Art of the Moving Picture*, p. 49.

plays the scene similarly.) Lynch, the villainous mulatto, is shown mistreating an animal. The "Little Colonel" is shown fondling small birds (a symbol taken over notably by von Stroheim in *Greed,* and since used so often that today it is a cliché).

The Birth of a Nation also introduced the practice of accompanying movies with a specially arranged orchestral score. Although this was not actually the first time music had been so used—as early as 1908 several imported French pictures had carried musical-score sheets—Griffith had exploited the possibilities of music far beyond the ordinary practice of the day.

The cultural world rapturously hailed *The Birth of a Nation,* and Griffith was enthroned as the film's first master. The acclaim was sweet to his ears, more than compensating for the public's temporary neglect of him during the preceding year, when the sensational European films had held America's admiration. He now stood at the peak of his career, the summit of his six years of struggle to make the movie an eloquent, vital, and respectable medium for art.

The Birth of a Nation was produced less than a decade and a half after motion pictures had learned to narrate. But its technique was incomparably superior to that of its primitive progenitors. If *The Great Train Robbery* was the giant of American pictures in 1903, *The Birth of a Nation* made it seem a pigmy in 1915.

The Birth of a Nation propelled the film into a new artistic level. A high point in the American movie tradition, it brought to maturity the editing principle begun with Méliès and furthered by Porter. So rich and profound in organization was this picture that for years thereafter it directly and indirectly influenced filmmakers everywhere and much of the subsequent filmic progress owes its inspiration to this master achievement.

Plot Synopsis

The prologue to *The Birth of a Nation* presents the view that Reconstruction actually started with the importation of slaves by seventeenth-century New England traders, the ancestors of nineteenth-century abolitionists.

In 1860 Austin Stoneman, a power in the House of Representatives, learns from his daughter Elsie that his sons plan to visit the Cameron family in Piedmont, South Carolina. There, amid idyllic scenes of black and white plantation contentment, Phil Stoneman falls in love with Margaret Cameron and Ben Cameron discovers his ideal in a picture of Elsie Stoneman.

Responding to Lincoln's call for volunteers, the Stoneman and the Cameron boys next meet on the battlefield. The two youngest sons die in each other's arms. In the South, the Camerons lose everything, Atlanta suffers bombardment, and Petersburg falls. In a Washington, D.C., hospital, Ben Cameron, wounded but nursed by Elsie Stoneman, faces a mysterious death warrant. After Elsie and Mrs. Cameron save Ben by interceding with President Lincoln, the mother returns to Piedmont. Soon rejoined by a recuperated Ben, the Cameron family begins to rebuild a battered homeland.

After Lincoln's assassination, Austin Stoneman implements his program of Negro equality by sending his mulatto protégé, Silas Lynch, to Piedmont to organize the Southern blacks. Later an ill Austin Stoneman arrives in Piedmont with Elsie and with Phil, who tries unsuccessfully to rekindle Margaret's love.

Soon the newly franchised Negroes repress the white population and elect Silas Lynch lieutenant-governor and an ill-prepared and uncouth, largely Negro legislature. Ben Cameron, distraught over emerging black supremacy, sees some white children in bedsheets frighten some Negro children and forms the idea of the Ku Klux Klan. When Elsie learns of Ben's involvement in the Klan, loyal to her father, she ends their relationship.

Flora, carelessly leaving her home, jumps to her death to save her honor from the renegade Negro Gus. After a brief trial, the Klan executes Gus and deposits his body on Silas Lynch's doorstep. Lynch sends the Negro militia out into Piedmont's streets during Stoneman's temporary absence and also arrests Dr. Cameron for aiding the Klansmen. While Elsie intercedes with Lynch for Cameron, his friends help him escape to a cabin, soon surrounded by the Negro militia. Lynch proposes that Elsie become his queen of the Black Empire. When she refuses, he locks her in a room and prepares for a forced marriage. The gathering Klans ride out to quell the marauding Negroes, rescue Dr. Cameron, and free Elsie, who now realizes Ben's true value. Controlled by the Klan, fearful blacks do not vote at the next election. The Black Empire collapses and the two Cameron-Stoneman marriages occur.

The epilogue shows the god of war dissolve into the Prince of Peace.

Content Outline

I. Pre-Civil War

A. Slaves brought to America; abolition movement begins.

B. Austin Stoneman house—Elsie says goodbye to the boys as they depart for Piedmont.

C. The Piedmont visit—lovely domestic scenes; love starts between Margaret and Phil; Ben idealizes Elsie's picture; group watches happy slaves dance; war news ends visit and Stonemans prepare to return home.

D. Stoneman meets with Secretary Charles Sumner; Lydia Brown, Stoneman's mulatto mistress, appears.

E. Stoneman and Cameron brothers part in Piedmont.

F. Lincoln signs call for volunteers (facsimile).

G. Elsie says goodbye to war-bound brothers.

H. Piedmont stages an elaborate farewell dance and parade; Camerons leave saddened family.

I. Elsie and Austin Stoneman embrace sorrowfully.

II. Civil War

A. Ben reads Flora's letter about her grown-up condition.

B. Negro marauders ransack the Cameron house.

C. Ben kisses Elsie's picture.

D. Ted Stoneman and Duke Cameron die together.

E. Camerons and Stonemans respond to deaths.

F. Camerons give away last belongings.

G. Elsie nurses at military hospital.

H. Sherman marches to the sea as battle rages at Petersburg, where Ben receives serious wound.

I. Ben and Elsie meet in hospital.

J. Mrs. Cameron rushes in and learns of Ben's scheduled execution.

K. Mrs. Cameron successfully intercedes with Lincoln.
L. Appomattox surrender (facsimile).
M. Ben leaves hospital to return home.
N. Lincoln and Stoneman meet to discuss Reconstruction angrily.
O. Camerons start to rebuild their shattered homeland.
P. Phil and Elsie witness Lincoln's assassination.
Q. Thunderstruck, the Camerons ask: "What is to become of us now?"

III. RECONSTRUCTION

A. Stoneman sends his mulatto protégé Silas Lynch to Piedmont.
B. Lynch and others induce Negroes to misuse funds and refuse work.
C. Stonemans arrive in Piedmont.
D. Election rally shows raucous, vulgar Negroes trying to use democratic process.
E. Ben-Elsie and Ted-Margaret loves develop.
F. Negroes vote, win, and parade.
G. Ben relates series of Negro outrages to friends.
H. Uncouth Negro legislature passes intermarriage bill.
I. Gus and Lynch behave too familiarly with Flora and Margaret.
J. Ben conceives of KKK.
K. First KKK terrorist attack.
L. Lynch and friend shoot three Klansmen.
M. Elsie rejects Ben because he is a Klansman.
N. Flora, chased by Gus, leaps to death.
O. Gus found, tried, executed, and dumped on Lynch's porch.
P. Stoneman leaves temporarily; Silas orders Negro militia out.
Q. Ben consecrates Flora's blood and calls Klans from surrounding communities.
R. Dr. Cameron arrested and then rescued by friends.
S. Elsie asks Lynch to aid Cameron, but instead he proposes to her; when rejected, he ties her up and plans forced marriage.
T. Negro militia attack the cabin where the Camerons have been hiding.
U. Rampaging Negroes fill Piedmont streets.
V. Klan arrives to clear streets, free Elsie, rescue the embattled Cameron party, and parade in streets.

IV. THE BIRTH OF A NATION

A. New election—white-dominated—restores old order.
B. Camerons and Stonemans marry.
C. God of war dissolves into Prince of Peace.

Filmography

THE BIOGRAPH FILMS (1908–13)

D. W. Griffith averaged 120 one-reel pictures a year during his Biograph years. While the majority were indeed the "sausages" Billy Bitzer later recalled, many indicate the range of Griffith's subjects as well as the growth of his control over his medium. The following very partial list contains the more representative of Griffith's output during this period. The subject categories appear in Robert M. Henderson, *D. W. Griffith: The Years at Biograph* (New York, Farrar, Straus & Giroux, 1970). A complete list of Griffith's Biograph years will probably never be compiled. Additional information regarding this period can be found in: Iris Barry, *D. W. Griffith: American Film Master*, with an annotated list of films by Eileen Bowser (New York, 1965); Russell Merritt, *The Impact of D. W. Griffith's Motion Pictures from 1908 to 1914 on Contemporary American Culture* (unpublished Ph.D. dissertation, Harvard University, 1970); Seymour Stern, *An Index to the Creative Work of D. W. Griffith*, Index Series, nos. 2, 4, 7, 8, 10c (London: British Film Institute, 1944).

1908

The Adventures of Dolly (contemporary action—gypsy)
The Taming of the Shrew (Elizabethan farce)
The Guerrilla (Civil War melodrama)

1909

The Jones Have Amateur Theatricals (situation comedy)
Edgar Allan Poe (mid-nineteenth-century melodrama)
The Drunkard's Reformation (temperance melodrama)
What Drink Did (temperance drama)
The Lonely Villa (contemporary melodrama)
1776, or The Hessian Renegades (American Revolution melodrama)
In Old Kentucky (Civil War melodrama)
Pippa Passes (nineteenth-century romance-fantasy)

A Corner in Wheat (contemporary social melodrama)
The Honor of His Family (Civil War melodrama)

1910

In the Border States (Civil War melodrama)
The House with Closed Shutters (Civil War melodrama)
The Usurer (contemporary melodrama)
Rose O' Salem Town (Puritan witchcraft melodrama)
The Fugitive (Civil War melodrama)
His Trust (Civil War drama)
His Trust Fulfilled (Civil War drama)

1911

Fisher Folks (seaside melodrama)
The Lonedale Operator (contemporary railroad melodrama)
Enoch Arden (seaside melodrama)
Bobby the Coward (slum melodrama)
A Country Cupid (pastoral romance)
Swords and Hearts (Civil War drama)
The Battle (Civil War drama)
The Miser's Heart (slum melodrama, child centered)

1912

Man's Genesis (primitive-man melodrama)
Man's Lust for Gold (desert miner's melodrama)
The Musketeers of Pig Alley (gangster melodrama)
The New York Hat (contemporary romance)
The Informer (Civil War melodrama)
The Massacre (melodrama of Custer's Last Stand)

1913

The Mothering Heart (domestic tragedy)
The Battle at Elderbush Gulch (Western action melodrama)
In Prehistoric Days (primitive-man melodrama)
Judith of Bethulia (Biblical melodrama)

THE MAJOR FILMS AND DECLINE (1914–31)

For the interested reader, a complete list of Griffith's post-Biograph films, compiled and annotated by Eileen Bowser, appears in the revised edition of his Barry, *D. W. Griffith: American Film Master* (New

York: The Museum of Modern Art, 1965). I am indebted to Mrs. Bowser for her divisions into production groups. Griffith wasted so much of his later life in financial wrangles that such categories seem appropriate. The full story of these entanglements remains to be told. The dates indicate New York City openings.

The Mutual Films (1914–15)

The Battle of the Sexes (April 12, 1914)
Home, Sweet Home (May 17, 1914)
The Escape (June 1, 1914)
The Avenging Conscience (August 2, 1914)
The Birth of a Nation (March 3, 1915)
Intolerance (September 5, 1916)

The Artcraft Films (1918–19)

Hearts of the World (April 4, 1918)
The Great Love (August 11, 1918)
The Greatest Thing in Life (December 22, 1918)
A Romance of Happy Valley (January 26, 1919)
The Girl Who Stayed Home (March 23, 1919)
True Heart Susie (June 1, 1919)
Scarlet Days (November 10, 1919)

The First National Pictures (1919–20)

The Greatest Question (December 28, 1919)
The Idol Danced (March 21, 1920)
The Love Flower (August 22, 1920)

The United Artists Films (1919–24)

Broken Blossoms (May 13, 1919)
Way Down East (September 3, 1920)
Dream Street (April 12, 1921)
Orphans of the Storm (December 28, 1921)
One Exciting Night (September 12, 1922)
The White Rose (May 21, 1923)
America (February 21, 1924)
Isn't Life Wonderful (December 5, 1924)

The Paramount Films (1925–26)

Sally of the Sawdust (August 2, 1925)
That Royle Girl (January 10, 1926)
The Sorrows of Satan (October 12, 1926)

The Art Cinema Corporation Films (1928–30)
Drums of Love (January 24, 1928)
The Battle of the Sexes (October 12, 1928)
Lady of the Pavements (January 22, 1929)
Abraham Lincoln (October 25, 1930)
The Struggle (December 10, 1931)

Bibliography

I. CONTEMPORARY RESPONSE

Reviews, news stories, editorials, letters, and reams of publicity about *The Birth of a Nation* flooded American newspapers in 1915. Clippings of these items fill thousands of pages in almost a dozen scrapbooks, which Griffith gave to The Museum of Modern Art Film Study Center. Since most of this material is no longer available elsewhere, anyone interested in the state of American culture in 1915 should consult this invaluable source. The following list, representing a tiny fraction of what appeared, includes material printed in this volume.

Reviews

"The Birth of a Nation," *New York Times,* March 4, 1915.

"A Stirring Film Drama Shown," New York *Tribune,* March 4, 1915.

"The Birth of a Nation: Summit of Picture Art," New York *Dramatic Mirror,* LXX (March 10, 1915), 28.

Controversy

The Boston, Massachusetts, newspapers recorded the most extended and intense activity for and against *The Birth of a Nation* in 1915. The Boston *Evening Transcript,* the Boston *Herald,* and the *Christian Science Monitor* covered the unfolding story from the first public demonstration to the resolution of censorship debates: April 18–June 15, 1915.

The following items record the fledgling NAACP's attempts to prevent showing of *The Birth of a Nation* in various locations.

"*The Clansman*: An Editorial," *The Crisis,* X (May 1915), 33.

"Fighting Race Calumny," *The Crisis,* X (May–June 1915), 40–42, 87–88.

"Fighting a Vicious Film: Protest against *Birth of a Nation*," Boston NAACP, 1915.

Publicity

The following items and others, part of the first major promotion of a film, appeared in the newspapers of every city where *The Birth of a Nation* played:

Anonymous, "Staging a Play on a Stage Five Miles Long."

D. W. Griffith, "Two-Dollar Motion Picture Spectacle Only a Start."

———, "The Motion Picture and Witch Burners."

II. LATER STUDIES AND RECOLLECTIONS

When one considers the cinematic importance of *The Birth of a Nation*, the relative scarcity of good material about the film becomes a scandal. Much of what has appeared combines inaccurate facts with even shakier judgments. The following bibliography, which preserves what seems valuable as well as pieces representing particular attitudes, does not include material reprinted in the text of this book. *The Film Index: A Bibliography*, vol. 1, *The Film as Art* (New York: The Museum of Modern Art and the H. W. Wilson Company, 1941; reprint ed., New York: Arno Press, 1966) provides listings for material prior to the late 1930s; Robert M. Henderson, *D. W. Griffith: The Years at Biograph* (New York: Farrar, Straus & Giroux, 1970) supplements that volume to some extent.

Aitken, Roy E., as told to Al P. Nelson. *The Birth of a Nation Story*. Middleburg, Va.: William A. Denlinger, 1965. A chatty, warm recollection by one of the founders of Mutual-Reliance. Provides a sense of film financing in the early days, as well as details about Griffith's personal manner.

Barry, Iris. *D. W. Griffith: American Film Master* (with an annotated list of films by Eileen Bowser). New York: The Museum of Modern Art, 1965. A still valuable pioneer monograph written when Griffith had passed into temporary eclipse. Mrs. Bowser's annotated list supplements the Barry work and provides an excellent introduction to the films.

Bravermann, Barnet. "David Wark Griffith: Creator of Film Form." *Theater Arts* 29 (April 1945): 240–50. A balanced short appraisal of Griffith's contribution to film art.

Brownlow, Kevin. *The Parade's Gone By*. New York: Alfred A. Knopf, Inc., 1968, pp. 47–51. Contains Joseph Henabery's recollection of how he got to play Lincoln in *The Birth of a Nation*.

Cook, Raymond A. "The Man Behind *The Birth of a Nation*." *The North Carolina Historical Review* 29 (1962): 519–40. Solidly researched essay on Thomas Dixon, Jr., particularly his career related to Griffith and *The Birth of a Nation*. Cook has also written Dixon's biography, *Fire from the Flint* (Charlotte, N.C.: University of North Carolina Press, 1968).

Crowther, Bosley. The Great Films: Fifty Golden Years of Motion Pictures. New York: G. P. Putnam's Sons, 1967, pp. 12–16. Crowther presents a sound appreciation of *The Birth of a Nation*.

Croy, Homer. *Star Maker: The Story of D. W. Griffith*. New York: Duell, Sloan, and Pearce, 1949. An inaccurate example of how never to write a biography, critical or otherwise, but, surprisingly, the only biography to date.

Everson, William K. "The Films of D. W. Griffith, 1907–1939." *Screen Facts* 3 (May–June 1963): 1–27. A knowledgeable overview of Griffith's work and of the silent-film period with useful commentary on print availability.

"The Film Art of D. W. Griffith and Billy Bitzer." *American Cinematography* 50 (January 1969): 86–91, 148–53, 172–73. A valuable, fairly detailed analysis of the development of Billy Bitzer, particularly in his work with Griffith. An important essay on a seldom explored relationship.

Geduld, Harry M., ed. *Focus on D. W. Griffith*. Englewood Cliffs, N.J.: Prentice-Hall, Inc., 1971. An extremely useful introduction to Griffith; contains major statements about his life and work, his own essays and comments, plus a solid bibliography of primary and secondary sources.

Griffith, D. W. *The Rise and Fall of Free Speech in America*. 1916. A pamphlet Griffith published at his own expense, without requesting copyright, to defend the right of the artist to free expression.

Griffith, Linda Arvidson. *When the Movies Were Young* (with an introduction by Edward Wagenknecht). New York: E. P. Dutton, 1925; reprint ed., New York: Dover Publications, 1969). The first Mrs. Griffith's highly anecdotal and charming account of Griffith's years up to 1915 furnishes important insight into both the man and that period. Newly reissued with index and additional stills.

Henderson, Robert M. *D. W. Griffith: The Years at Biograph*. New York: Farrar, Straus & Giroux, 1970. A more scholarly than usual presentation of the 1908–13 Griffith years. See also the work by Russell Merritt, below.

Huff, Theodore. *A Shot Analysis of D. W. Griffith's "The Birth of a Nation."* New York: The Museum of Modern Art, 1961. Now out of print, this monograph represents the best noncelluloid breakdown of the film.

Hutchins, Charles L. "A Critical Evaluation of the Controversies Engendered by D. W. Griffith's *The Birth of a Nation*." Master's thesis, University of Iowa, 1961. A solid discussion of the Reconstruction racial controversy.

Lawson, John Howard. *Film: The Creative Process*. 2d ed. New York: Hill & Wang, Inc., 1967. The chapter "Film as History—D. W. Griffith" describes Griffith's view of history as pessimistic.

Lennig, Arthur. *The Silent Voice: A Text*. Troy, N.Y.: Walter Snyder, 1969, pp. 32–49. In the chapter dealing with *The Birth of a Nation* Lennig offers some astute insights into the film, but at times defends needlessly the Dixon-Griffith view of Reconstruction.

Leyda, Jay. "The Art and Death of D. W. Griffith." *Sewanee Review* 57 career written when the director died.
(April 1949): 350–56. A very moving but shrewd assessment of Griffith's

Lindsay, Vachel. *The Art of the Moving Picture*. New York: The Macmillan Company, 1915; reprint ed., New York: Liveright, 1970, pp. 67–78. Contains a suggestive essay on *The Birth of a Nation* entitled "The Picture of Crowd Splendour."

Long, Robert E. *David Wark Griffith*. New York: D. W. Griffith Service, 1920. Produced by Griffith's press service, the tone of the material on *The Birth of a Nation* anticipates that of later film souvenir pamphlets.

Merritt, Russell. "The Impact of D. W. Griffith's Motion Pictures from 1908 to 1914 on Contemporary American Culture." Ph.D. dissertation, Harvard University, 1970. Particularly valuable analysis of dominant themes in

Griffith's Biograph films; provides good background for the Southernness of *The Birth of a Nation*.

Messell, Rudolph. "D. W. Griffith." In *This Film Business*. London: Ernest Benn, Ltd., 1928, pp. 86–121. Contains a somewhat cranky but generally fair British assessment of Griffith's work, including *The Birth of a Nation*.

Meyer, Richard J. "The Films of David Wark Griffith: The Development of Themes and Techniques in Forty-two of His Films." *Film Comment* 4 (Fall–Winter 1967): 92–104. A thoughtful introduction to the major Griffith films based on the 1965 Museum of Modern Art Griffith retrospective.

Platt, David D. "The Negro in Hollywood." *Daily Worker*, February 19–28, 1940. An example of what has been dismissed as leftist nonsense. Platt's series and his article on *The Birth of a Nation* turn out to be accurate and balanced.

Stern, Seymour. "Griffith: I. *The Birth of a Nation*." *Film Culture* 36, Special Griffith Issue (Spring–Summer 1965). Many have called this monograph long-winded and eccentric, but it remains (outside of the Museum of Modern Art D. W. Griffith Collection) the best single source for many details, anecdotes, and reactions to *The Birth of a Nation*.

Vardac, A. Nicholas. *Stage to Screen: Theatrical Method from Garrick to Griffith*. Cambridge, Mass.: Harvard University Press, 1949. Invaluable critical study of American melodramatic theater in which both America and Griffith prepared for the advent of films.

Wagenknecht, Edward. *The Movies in the Age of Innocence*. Norman, Okla.: University of Oklahoma Press, 1962, pp. 99–109. This thoroughly delightful commentary on early film history includes a thoughtful comparison between *The Birth of a Nation* and its Dixon sources.

Index